CASE STUDIES IN

CULTURAL ANTHROPOLOGY

GENERAL EDITORS

George and Louise Spindler

STANFORD UNIVERSITY

————————————

YĄNOMAMÖ

The Fierce People

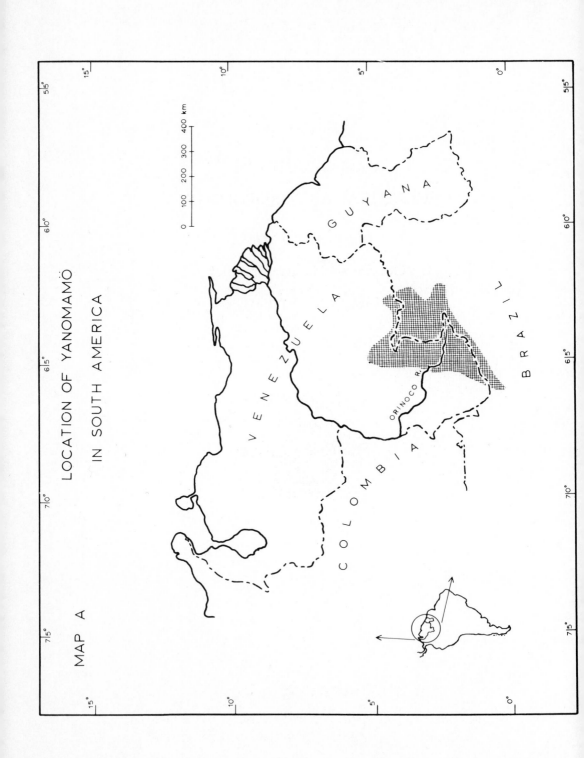

MAP A

LOCATION OF YANOMAMÖ
IN SOUTH AMERICA

YĄNOMAMÖ

The Fierce People

Third Edition

By

NAPOLEON A. CHAGNON

Northwestern University

HOLT, RINEHART AND WINSTON, INC.

FORT WORTH   CHICAGO   SAN FRANCISCO   PHILADELPHIA
MONTREAL   TORONTO   LONDON   SYDNEY   TOKYO

To Kąobawä, Rerebawä, and Dedeheiwä, valiant and cherished friends who taught me much about being human.

Cover: Yąnomamö archer on a hunting trip.

Library of Congress Cataloging in Publication Data

Chagnon, Napoleon A., 1938–
    Yąnomamö: the fierce people.

    (Case studies in cultural anthropology)
    Bibliography: p. 217
    Includes index.
    1. Yąnomamö Indians.   I. Title.   II. Series.
    F2520.1.Y3C5 1983   306'.08998   83-313

    ISBN 0-03-062328-6

Requests for permission to make copies of any part of the work should be mailed to: Copyrights and Permissions Department, Holt, Rinehart and Winston, Inc., Orlando, Florida 32887.
Printed in the United States of America
1 2 3 4 016 20 19 18 17 16 15 14 13

Holt, Rinehart and Winston, Inc.
The Dryden Press
Saunders College Publishing

Foreword

ABOUT THE SERIES

These case studies in cultural anthropology are designed to bring to students, in beginning and intermediate courses in the social sciences, insights into the richness and complexity of human life as it is lived in different ways and in different places. They are written by men and women who have lived in the societies they write about and who are professionally trained as observers and interpreters of human behavior. The authors are also teachers, and in writing their books they have kept the students who will read them foremost in their minds. It is our belief that when an understanding of ways of life very different from one's own is gained, abstractions and generalizations about social structure, cultural values, subsistence techniques, and the other universal categories of human social behavior become meaningful.

ABOUT THE AUTHOR

Napoleon A. Chagnon was born the second of twelve children in Port Austin, Michigan, in 1938. He is married and has two children. He began his academic training at the Michigan College of Mining and Technology at Sault Ste. Marie, Michigan (now called Lake Superior State College), in the physics curriculum. After one year there, he transferred to the University of Michigan, changed his major to anthropology, and received his B.A. (1961), M.A. (1963), and Ph.D. (1966) degrees in anthropology at the University of Michigan. He then joined the faculty of the Department of Human Genetics at the University of Michigan Medical School from which position he participated in an extensive multidisciplinary study of the Yąnomamö Indians of Venezuela and Brazil. During that time he also held a joint appointment in the Department of Anthropology at the University of Michigan, where he taught anthropology courses.

In 1972 he moved to the Pennsylvania State University to continue his data analysis and field research among the Yąnomamö, developing a long-term project funded by the U.S. National Science Foundation, the U.S. National Institute of Mental Health, and the Harry Frank Guggenheim Foundation. This project brought him and several of his graduate students into the field between 1974 and 1976 on several trips. To date, Chagnon has made ten field trips among the Yąnomamö and has spent 42 months in their villages, mostly in Venezuela.

In 1968 and 1971 Chagnon was joined in the field by his film colleague Timothy Asch, during which time they shot documentary film that has led to the production of 21 educational films, distributed on a nonprofit basis for use in anthropology classes. These are listed on page 221.

v

In 1980 Chagnon was an invited participant in the King's College Research Centre, Cambridge University, and a Visiting Scholar in the Department of Social Anthropology, Cambridge University.

Chagnon joined the faculty of Northwestern University in 1981 and was appointed Chairman of the Anthropology Department in 1983. He is a Fellow of the American Association for the Advancement of Science, the American Anthropological Association, and Current Anthropology. He presently serves as Editor for the Psychological Cinema Register, the Pennsylvania State University's nonprofit film distribution unit, and is on the Editorial Board of the journal *Ethology and Sociobiology* and the series Ediciones Venezolano de Antropologia.

Chagnon has published numerous articles and book chapters on various aspects of his work among the Yąnomamö, and a methods study (1974) detailing the procedures he used in the field to collect the information on which most of his ethnographic publications are based. Since 1975 his interests have shifted more toward the strategies used by individuals in their kinship and marriage behavior; some of this work can be found in his 1979 book, co-edited with William Irons. He plans to return to the Yąnomamö to continue his research on kinship, demography, and reproduction.

ABOUT THE THIRD EDITION

When *Yąnomamö: The Fierce People* first appeared in 1968, it immediately became the most widely used study in the series of which it is a part. The second edition appeared in 1977. Its popularity has continued. Instructors of anthropology and students alike are intrigued with the character of the Yąnomamö, their conflicts and how they resolve them, and the fact that they yet retain their tribal sovereignty. Though no single people can be held to be representative of tribal life everywhere, before serious inroads have been made by the outside world, the Yąnomamö are indisputably sovereign, indisputably tribal, and indisputably themselves. Their sovereignty is now seriously threatened. Some of their villages are now permanently contacted by missionaries and, more recently, they are being increasingly impacted by tourists, developers, and adventurers, whose visits can only lead to misfortune to the Yąnomamö way of life. In Brazil, their lands are coveted by others and they may be soon confined to "reservations" that are totally inadequate in size for Yąnomamö traditional economic needs. When or if this happens, their fate may be sealed. The situation in Venezuela is more hopeful, but could rapidly change.

But the way of life Chagnon describes in this case study is still intact over a significant fraction of Yąnomamö territory where most of his research was conducted. In the last chapter he tells us something of the nature of cultural change and the inroads on the integrity of Yąnomamö culture as it developed during his field studies. But this is not the focus of the study. The focus is on the Yąnomamö culture and sociopolitical organization as it exists in its own sovereign environment, a product of long-term sociocultural evolution without intervention from outside alien populations and life ways.

Yąnomamö: The Fierce People is a particularly useful aid to instruction in anthropology because it is about a tribal people celebrating their own sovereign existence. Its value is enhanced by the availability of films shot in Yąnomamö villages by Chagnon and Timothy Asch of a wide variety of events and behaviors, ranging from everyday domestic activities to elaborate feasts and gripping duels and fights. In our extended experience as instructors of introductory anthropology at Stanford University, the combination of a challenging, exciting case study and well-executed ethnographic films is unbeatable. The behaviors and norms of people who are very different from us become, though shocking and disturbing at times, real and comprehensible when placed into anthropological perspective. An annotated list of available Yąnomamö films is included at the end of the study.

This case study is also valuable as an aid to teaching anthropology because it deals with processes that are found in some form in all of human social life. Violence, for example, is explicitly represented in some form in nearly all human societies, and implicitly represented in the rest. Violence among the Yąnomamö in its several graded forms from chest pounding, side slapping, club fighting, ax fighting to all-out warfare and treacherous massacres is described and explained in this case study: far from being random and senseless, it is well regulated and an integral component of both internal social organization of villages and political dealings between villages. An important feature of this edition is a more extensive analysis of fissioning of Yąnomamö villages, a phenomenon noted in prehistoric archaeological materials and in many areas of the tribal world outside Amazonia. Chagnon provides exceptionally rich data on the kinship, demographic, and ecological dimensions of this important process and relates it to the important political variables characterizing all tribal societies of the kind that the Yąnomamö represent.

This new edition is marked by major additions and changes that enhance the utility of *Yąnomamö* as a Case Study in Cultural Anthropology, many of them stemming from the fact that Chagnon spent many more months among the Yąnomamö after the first and second editions were written. He also has acceded to requests from readers and from the editors to include more on his own field experiences. Opportunities to learn about fieldwork among sovereign tribal peoples soon will be nonexistent. Chagnon's experiences are entertaining. They are adventurous at times. They also tell us something about the Yąnomamö, about anthropology, and about Chagnon. Their inclusion in the first chapter is, we think, an excellent introduction to the case study.

The author also has completely rewritten the chapter on social organization. He has provided enhanced descriptions of daily routine, the roles of men and women, and the experience of children. He has added significantly more material on myth and ideology. His treatment of social organization in this edition is more streamlined and contrasts the more formal approach of structuralism with the more quantitative approach of statistical models, focusing largely on the process of village fissioning as an outcome of the interactions among several variables, especially relationships among kin and marriage allies. His analysis is not a standard textbook treatment: it introduces new kinds of data and new ideas, and applies them to standard anthropological problems in a refreshing way.

Chagnon has not avoided discussing controversies, some of which have been provoked by earlier editions of this case study and his other publications. His response to critics who accuse him of overemphasizing violence or failing to consider the politics of protein maximization are all too brief but interesting. Readers who are familiar with past editions will see that Chagnon's thinking as well as his knowledge of the Yąnomamö have expanded.

We recommend *Yąnomamö: The Fierce People* as one of the most instructive and compelling writings available in anthropology. The first two editions of this case study have made the Yąnomamö one of the most important examples of tribal culture in the ethnographic literature; this edition will enhance our understanding of a truly remarkable and exciting people.

GEORGE AND LOUISE SPINDLER
General Editors

Preface to the Third Edition

I have visited some sixty Yąnomamö villages since I began my initial field research in 1964 when I was a doctoral candidate at the University of Michigan. I have been back to the Yąnomamö ten times thus far and have spent a total of 42 months living among them in various villages. Most of that time was spent in several clusters of villages near the headwaters of the Orinoco River in Venezuela, and this case study is largely based on my many experiences in that region, especially in the village of Bisaasi-teri where my first work began. The general pattern of my long-term field research has been to travel further and further into uncontacted regions attempting to document political histories of specific villages as the Yąnomamö know them from memory, to document the process of village (population) growth and dispersal by collecting meticulous data on demographic variables (births, deaths, marriage, 'divorce'), to identify and verify all genealogical ties between all individuals, and to collect data on conflicts both within and between villages. In addition, I have investigated Yąnomamö religious and mythical beliefs and a host of other anthropological topics commonly studied by fieldworkers. While most of my field effort in collecting these kind of data has been concentrated in some dozen villages, I also collected a good deal of similar information in the fifty or so other villages I visited in other regions. I am very much aware of the variations that occur from region to region and the similarities that can be found as well. I would like it to be clearly understood by both the students who read this book and my colleagues who have done field research in other regions of the Yąnomamö tribe that this case study does *not* purport to describe all Yąnomamö villages everywhere or suggest that there is no variation among villages and regions. A significant fraction of my published work in fact emphasizes and draws attention to some of the differences between both villages and whole clusters of villages, particularly for village size, composition, intensity of warfare, mortality, alliance patterns, marriage patterns, demographic properties of villages and village clusters, reproductive variation, styles of headmanship, and other cultural attributes (see Chagnon, 1968b; 1974; 1975b; 1979a for examples).

This edition of *Yąnomamö: The Fierce People* differs from the two previous editions in several significant regards. The first edition (published in 1968) was based on my initial 15 months of work. The present edition takes account of some of the additional data and understandings that resulted from two more years of continued field research in Yąnomamö villages. The second edition (1977) differed from the first only by the inclusion of a new chapter that focused on the kinds of changes that were then beginning to be significant in Yąnomamö culture as missionary activity and government presence in the tribal area began to accelerate. The final chapter of this edition is substantially the same as it was in the second edition, but it must be assumed that in 1983 much more change has taken place and at a faster pace, and is no longer confined to the mission posts where it began.

This edition also provides a more simplified description and treatment of Yąnomamö kinship and marriage. Students and teachers alike have indicated that the original chapter on Yąnomamö social organization was too detailed and complex for a case study intended for new students in anthropology. Hopefully the revised treatment, which is more "behavioral" and "empirical" than "structural," will be easier to read and follow. It does, however, focus on an important set of anthropological issues and theory—"ideal" versus "actual" social organization/structure.

Several additional changes and modifications should be noted. I have substantially extended my discussion of Yąnomamö myth, attempting to provide material that, when supplemented with the films on myth, will give those teachers and students interested in this dimension of culture more to work with. I have also added a large amount of information on Yąnomamö settlement pattern and village histories to underscore the tremendous importance of past history on contemporary social relationships within and between villages, to provide a larger cultural ecological framework for the data on social organization, and to make it more possible for archaeology teachers and students to develop "ethnographic models" that might be used to interpret ancient settlement patterns that are revealed partially through archaeological field studies.

As in the first two editions, I have presented much of the description in a historical context, particularly the intervillage conflicts and wars. In this fashion, the reader can more easily appreciate and understand how specific events in particular villages set the course for many subsequent events and influence the quality of political ties between groups—and understand more fully how conflicts, once begun, endure for many years.

Finally, I have extended my discussion of what it is like to do field research as a member of North American culture. Students have responded very enthusiastically to this material in the first two editions and have indicated an interest in having more of it. In this edition I have added a section on what it is like to make first contact with a remote, previously uncontacted village and the dangers, risks, mishaps, frustrations, fun, excitement, and satisfaction that goes along with it. The possibility of having this sort of experience is rapidly vanishing. I dearly hope that the bigger picture of a shrinking world and the disappearance of whole types of human societies is clear to the reader. There are very few places left on earth where "first contact" with an unknown tribe can still happen, and it is rapidly disappearing even in Yąnomamö land. When such societies are gone forever, we will be left only with the recollections of old informants who might be able to recite important events and facts, but who can never communicate the quality of life that exists in a sovereign, primitive culture whose members firmly believe that they are the only people on earth or, if there are others, they are degenerate, inferior copies of themselves. These beliefs and convictions invest their daily behavior with a quality that cannot ever be obtained second hand or simulated in even the most sophisticated computer. When it disappears, it is gone forever, a page torn from human history.

It has been a distinct privilege and onerous responsibility to have been able to read that historical page when it was still in the book, a book that still has a few chapters left yet to be read, but what must be gleaned from them depends very heavily on the skill of the reader.

N. A. C.

May 1983

Acknowledgments

The research on which this case study is based has been supported by a number of public and private foundations. My initial field research for the doctorate degree at the University of Michigan was supported by a Predoctoral Fellowship from the National Institute of Mental Health (1964–1966). During the six years I was on the faculty of the Department of Human Genetics at the University of Michigan Medical School (1966–1972), I made a series of field trips as a participant in a multidisciplinary study of the Yąnomamö. Funds for that work were initially provided by the U.S. Atomic Energy Commission (see footnote 1, Chapter 7) and, later, by the National Science Foundation. The Wenner-Gren Foundation for Anthropological Research supported one of my field trips (1968). Support for the film work I conducted with Timothy Asch was provided by the National Science Foundation, resulting, to date, in 21 documentary films distributed on a nonprofit basis (see p. 221). Between 1974 and 1978 my field research and data-analysis efforts were supported by grants from the National Institute of Mental Health, the National Science Foundation, and the Harry Frank Guggenheim Foundation. Additional support from the Harry Frank Guggenheim Foundation after 1978 has enabled me to continue my data analysis and develop new methodology and theoretical approaches to human kinship behavior, conflict resolution, genealogical relatedness, demography, and the reproductive attributes of individuals.

I am greatly indebted to many friends, colleagues, teachers, students, missionaries, government officials, and others who have helped me in many ways during my long study of the Yąnomamö. These are legion and the kinds and amounts of support they provided are too varied and numerous to list here. I do want to thank my life-long friend William Irons for the many stimulating discussions we have had about anthropology as a science, discussions that have caused both of us to pursue new directions and tackle old problems in new ways (see Irons' publications in the bibliography).

As the pages that follow will indicate, I am deeply indebted to a large number of Yąnomamö who generously took me under their protection and into their confidence and shared the many secrets of genealogy, political history, and kinship relationships on which most of this case study is based. Hopefully their descendants will be pleased with what it was that we did, and that I will continue to enjoy the esteem of the Yąnomamö in the future.

Finally, I owe the greatest debt to my wife, Carlene, who patiently and selflessly encouraged me in my work during the many years I have been studying the Yąnomamö and the many months I was away, in some unnamed, unmapped, unexplored jungle "doing fieldwork." Few will be able to appreciate how difficult this is or can be for family life when the children have to be told that "dad is living with the Indians again." Our children are neat people, and many of their desirable, admirable qualities are in large measure due to my wife's indefatiguable extra efforts brought about by often having had to be a double parent. For years the children thought that everyone's father, if out of town, was living somewhere with "the Indians." Now that they are young adults, they understand and appreciate what it was that compelled me to be away from them so often and so long when they were children, and I am grateful for their understanding.

Contents

Prologue

There is a large tribe of Tropical Forest Indians on the border between Venezuela and Brazil. They number approximately 12,000 people and are distributed in some 125 widely scattered villages. They are gardeners and they have lived until very recent time in isolation from our kind of culture. The authorities in Venezuela and Brazil knew very little about their existence until anthropologists began going there. The remarkable thing about the tribe, known as the Yąnomamö, is the fact that they have managed, due to their isolation in a remote corner of Amazonia, to retain their native patterns of warfare and political integrity without interference from the outside world. They have remained sovereign and in complete control of their own destiny up until a few years ago. The remotest, uncontacted villages are still living under those conditions.

This case study is about the Yąnomamö and about their sovereignty. It is based on 41 months of residence in many of their villages, on fieldwork that began in 1964—before the major vectors of change began to impinge on some of their villages. My initial 15 months of field research, between 1964 and 1966, was conducted when very little accurate information existed about their culture, geographical distribution, tribal size, and cultural history.

I want to begin with a story, a description of an event that happened 15 years before I went to live with the Yąnomamö, an event I had to reconstruct from bits and pieces of information given to me by many Yąnomamö informants after I learned their language, for they spoke no other language when I first went there and I did not know their language then. The event that I describe below led to the development of political relationships, alliances, and wars between many Yąnomamö villages and dominated their social activities while I was there, but I had to proceed in ignorance because I knew nothing about the event. The story contains a message about anthropological fieldwork on the one hand, and the nature of Yąnomamö political organization on the other. As to fieldwork, the lesson is that it is in some cases impossible to understand a society's 'social organization' by studying only one village or community of that society, for each community is bound up in and responds to the political ties to neighboring groups and the obligations and pressures these ties impose on them. Regarding Yąnomamö political organization, the lesson is that past events and history must be understood to comprehend the current observable patterns. As the Roman poet Lucretius mused, nothing yet from nothing ever came.

The Killing of Ruwähiwä

The members of the village of Bisaasi-teri lived several days' walk from their southernmost neighbors, the Konabuma-teri. The Bisaasi-teri were a splinter village of a much larger village: Patanowä-teri. They were themselves at odds with the larger 'mother' village and beginning to fission away from them, forging their own new identity and seeking new allies. They saw in their southern neighbors, the Konabuma-teri, an opportunity to strengthen their political image by cultivating friendship with them.

The recent history of both groups (Patanowä-teri/Bisaasi-teri and Konabuma-teri) entailed a gradual, general migration from the northeast to the southwest as past wars and current alliances caused their villages to periodically relocate in new, virgin areas of the Tropical Forest. They spoke slightly different dialects of Yąnomamö, but no different from what obtains between North Carolina and Upstate New York. Hunters from each group began running into each other in the lands between their villages and eventually, in the late 1940s, they decided to begin visiting and trading with each other.

Apparently the trading visits increased in regularity and frequency, and members of the two groups got to know each other well. They got to know each other's personal names, a task that is not easy in view of the stringent taboos on using a person's real name.

In Yąnomamö politics, members of allied villages often need each other's support, but often they cannot and do not trust each other much—especially if the allies are not historically and therefore genealogically related to each other, as was the case here.

All deaths other than those obviously caused by human or animal intervention—killings with arrows or being attacked by jaguars for example—are attributed to harmful magic. The Yąnomamö, and all tribal populations, suffer a high infant mortality rate: babies do not have a good chance of survival, but die frequently for a host of reasons that we, with our technical medical knowledge, could diagnose and describe in precise, mechanical biomedical terms. But the Yąnomamö do not have such knowledge, and to them, babies die because someone sent harmful spirits—*hekura*—to steal their souls, or someone blew magical charms at them from a great distance, charms that caused them to sicken and die. Thus, in every village, the shamans spend many hours attempting to cure sick children and sick adults, driving out the malevolent forces that have caused their illness, and in turn, sending their own spirits and charms against the children in distant villages for revenge.

Several children died in the village of Bisaasi-teri as the alliance with the people of Konabuma-teri was developing and maturing. Shamans in Bisaasi-teri began suspecting that men in Konabuma-teri were secretly sending harmful charms and magic against them and their children and ultimately convinced themselves that their new allies were truly enemies. Unaware of this, one of the prominent men from Konabuma-teri arrived at Bisaasi-teri to visit and trade. His name was Ruwähiwä, and he came alone. He entered the clearing in his pose of the visitor: erect, proud, motionless, and showing no fear. He was greeted by the host men, who came out with their weapons, cheering, hooting, and growling symbolic threats and intimidations as they inspected him. After a few minutes, he was invited to take up a hammock until food was prepared for him. Presently, a gourd of plantain soup was ready and he was invited out to drink of it before the house of the local headman. He squatted on his haunches, picked up the gourd, and began drinking, oblivious to his surroundings, happy to be welcomed in this customary way.

A man approached him silently from behind, a man named Mamikininiwä, a mature man of 40 years whose decisions few would challenge. He carried the battered, worn remains of a steel ax, hafted clumsily to a short, stout handle. Ruwähiwä paid him no attention and kept drinking the plantain soup. Mamikininiwä raised his ax high above his head and then smashed it down violently, sharp edge forward, into Ruwähiwä's skull. He lurched forward, trying to stand, but was mortally wounded. He fell to the ground and died in a pool of his own blood. Later that day, several old women carried his body out and off to his village.

Thus began the war between the village of Bisaasi-teri and Konabuma-teri, a war that was going on 15 years later when I went to the Yạnomamö, but a war I was ignorant of when I went there.

Ruwähiwä's group then set about to avenge this killing. They enlisted the support of a third village that was on friendly terms with the Bisaasi-teri and managed to get them to host a feast at which the Bisaasi-teri would be the guests of honor. They invited men from a fourth village to join them in hiding outside the village. The unsuspecting Bisaasi-teri had come en masse for the occasion: men, women, and children. Shortly after the feast began, and while the Bisaasi-teri men were lying motionless and helpless in their hosts' hammocks, someone gave the signal: the hosts suddenly set upon them with clubs, bowstaves, and arrows, attacking them in their hammocks. Many died instantly, but some managed to escape outside. There, they ran into showers of arrows from the hidden archers. More died and more were wounded, some badly enough that they later died. Between a dozen and fifteen adult men were killed that afternoon. A number of women and pubescent girls were taken captive, never to be seen by their families again. The survivors retreated deep into the jungle, to the north, and hid for many days while the wounded recovered enough to move on. The survivors, depressed and anguished, sought refuge in a village to the north, Mahekodo-teri. They arrived early in the year 1951, a date recorded by Mr. James P. Barker, the first missionary to make a sustained contact with the Yạnomamö a few months prior to this. He saw the Bisaasi-teri arrive at Mahekodo-teri, the village he had chosen for his mission station.

The Bisaasi-teri moved away from the Mahekodo-teri about a year later and settled further down the Orinoco River. They were the people I came to live with when I first went to the Yạnomamö, but I knew nothing of this tragic event in their recent history when I joined them to begin my field research. But the significance of that event slowly unraveled over the months as I learned more of their language and set about to discover something about their history and recent settlement pattern. Only then did much of what I initially witnessed begin to make sense, and only then did their raids and political dealings with neighbors become comprehensible.

Much of what follows in this book is about the Bisaasi-teri and the people who live in that village.

1/Doing Fieldwork among the Yąnomamö[1]

Vignette

The Yąnomamö are thinly scattered over a vast and verdant Tropical Forest, living in small villages that are separated by many miles of unoccupied land. They have no writing, but they have a rich and complex language. Their clothing is more decorative than protective: well-dressed men sport nothing more than a few cotton strings around their wrists, ankles, and waists. They tie the foreskin of their penises to the waiststring. Women dress about the same. Much of their daily life revolves around gardening, hunting, collecting wild foods, collecting firewood, fetching water, visiting with each other, gossiping, and making the few material possessions they own: baskets, hammocks, bows, arrows, and colorful pigments with which they paint their bodies. Life is relatively easy in the sense that they can 'earn a living' with about three hours' work per day. Most of what they eat they cultivate in their gardens, and most of that is plantains—a kind of cooking banana that is usually eaten green, either roasted on the coals or boiled in pots (Fig. 1–1). Their meat comes from a large variety of game animals, hunted daily by the men. It is usually roasted on coals or smoked, and is always well done. Their villages are round and open—and very public. One can hear, see, and smell almost everything that goes on anywhere in the village. Privacy is rare, but sexual discreetness is possible in the garden or at night while others sleep. The villages can be as small as 40 to 50 people or as large as 300 people, but in all cases there are many more children and babies than there are adults. This is true of most primitive populations and of our own demographic past. Life expectancy is short.

The Yąnomamö fall into the category of Tropical Forest Indians called 'foot

---

[1]The word Yąnomamö is nasalized through its entire length, indicated by the diacritical mark ' ' When this mark appears on any Yąnomamö word, the whole word is nasalized. The vowel 'ö' represents a sound that does not occur in the English language. It is similar to the umlaut 'o' in the German language or the 'oe' equivalent in German, as in the poet Goethe's name. Unfortunately, many presses and typesetters simply eliminate diacritical marks, and this leads to multiple spellings of the word Yąnomamö and multiple mispronunciations. Some anthropologists have chosen to introduce a slightly different spelling of the word Yąnomamö since my work began appearing in print, such as Yąnomami, leading to additional misspellings as diacritics are eliminated by some presses, and to the *incorrect* pronunciation "Yanomameee." Words with a vowel indicated as 'ä' are pronounced as the 'uh' sound in the word 'duck'. Thus, the name Kąobawä would be pronounced "cow-ba-wuh," but entirely nasalized.

*Fig. 1–1. Bahimi, wife of Bisaasi-teri head-
man, harvesting plantains, a cooking banana that comprises a large fraction of Yąnomamö diet.*

people'. They avoid large rivers and live in interfluvial plains of the major
rivers. They have neighbors to the north, Carib-speaking Ye'kwana, who are
true 'river people': they make elegant, large dugout canoes and travel
extensively along the major waterways. For the Yąnomamö, a large stream is
an obstacle and can only be crossed in the dry season. Thus, they have
traditionally avoided larger rivers and, because of this, contact with outsiders
who usually come by river.

They enjoy taking trips when the jungle abounds with seasonally ripe wild
fruits and vegetables. Then, the large village—the *shabono*—is abandoned for a
few weeks and everyone camps out a day or so away from the village and
garden. On these trips, they make temporary huts from poles, vines, and
leaves, each family making a separate hut.

Two major seasons dominate their annual cycle: the wet season, which
inundates the low-lying jungle making travel difficult, and the dry season—the
time of visiting other villages to feast, trade, and politic with allies. The dry
season is also the time when raiders can travel and strike silently at their
unsuspecting enemies. The Yąnomamö are still conducting intervillage warfare, a phenomenon that affects all aspects of their social organization,
settlement pattern, and daily routines. It is not simply 'ritualistic' war: at least
one-fourth of all adult males die violently.

Fig. 1–2. Kąobawä, headman of Upper Bi-saasi-teri, trading with his Shamatari allies for arrows, baskets, hammocks, and dogs.

Social life is organized around those same principles utilized by all tribes-men: kinship relationships, descent from ancestors, marriage exchanges between kinship/descent groups, and the transient charisma of distinguished headmen who attempt to keep order in the village and whose responsibility it is to determine the village's relationships with those in other villages. Their positions are largely the result of kinship and marriage patterns—they come from the largest kinship groups within the village. They can, by their personal wit, wisdom, and charisma, become autocrats but most of them are largely "greaters" among equals. They, too, must clear gardens, plant crops, collect wild foods, and hunt. They are simultaneously peacemakers and valiant warriors. Peacemaking often requires the threat or actual use of force, and most headmen have an acquired reputation for being *waiteri*: fierce.

The social dynamics within villages are involved with giving and receiving marriageable girls. Marriages are arranged by older kin, usually men, who are brothers, uncles, and the father. It is a political process, for girls are promised in marriage while they are young, and the men who do this attempt to create alliances with other men via marriage exchanges. There is a shortage of women due in part to a sex-ratio imbalance in the younger age categories, but also complicated by the fact that some men have multiple wives. Most fighting within the village stems from sexual affairs or failure to deliver a promised woman—or out-and-out seizure of a married woman by some other man. This can lead to internal fighting and conflict of such an intensity that villages split up and fission, each group then becoming a new village and, often, enemies to each other.

But their conflicts are not blind, uncontrolled violence. They have a series of graded forms of violence that ranges from chest-pounding and club-fighting duels to out-and-out shooting to kill. This gives them a good deal of flexibility in settling disputes without immediate resort to killing. In addition, they have developed patterns of alliance and friendship that serve to limit violence— trading and feasting with others in order to become friends (Fig. 1–2). These alliances can, and often do, result in intervillage exchanges of marriageable women, which leads to additional amity between villages. No good thing lasts forever, and most alliances crumble. Old friends become hostile and, occasionally, treacherous. Each village must therefore be keenly aware that its neighbors are fickle and must behave accordingly. The thin line between friendship and animosity must be traversed by the village leaders, whose political acumen and strategies are both admirable and complex.

Each village, then, is a replica of all others in a broad sense. But each village is part of a larger political, demographic, and ecological process and it is difficult to attempt to understand the village without knowing something of the larger forces that affect it.

Collecting the Data in the Field

I spent 41 months with the Yąnomamö, during which time I acquired some proficiency in their language and, up to a point, submerged myself in their culture and way of life.[2] The thing that impressed me most was the importance of aggression in their culture. I had the opportunity to witness a good many incidents that expressed individual vindictiveness on the one hand and collective bellicosity on the other hand. These ranged in seriousness from the ordinary incidents of wife beating and chest pounding to dueling and organized raids by parties that set out with the intention of ambushing and killing men from enemy villages. One of the villages discussed in the chapters that follow was raided approximately twenty-five times during my first 15 months of fieldwork—six times by the group among whom I was living.

The fact that the Yąnomamö live in a chronic state of warfare is reflected in their mythology, ceremonies, settlement pattern, political behavior, and

[2]I spent a total of 41 months among the Yąnomamö between 1964 and 1983. The first edition of this case study was based on the first 15 months I spent among them in Venezuela. By the time the first edition had gotten to press, I had made another field trip of four months' duration and the first edition indicated that the work was based, as it technically was, on 19 months of field research. I have, at the time of this writing, made 10 field trips to the Yąnomamö and plan to return regularly to continue my long-term study.

Fig. 1–3. Visitors dancing as a group around the shabono *during a formal feast.*

marriage practices. Accordingly, I have organized this case study in such a way that students can appreciate the effects of warfare on Yąnomamö culture in general and on their social organization and political relationships in particular (Fig. 1–3).

I collected the data under somewhat trying circumstances, some of which I will describe to give the student a rough idea of what is generally meant when anthropologists speak of "culture shock" and "fieldwork." It should be borne in mind, however, that each field situation is in many respects unique, so that the problems I encountered do not necessarily exhaust the range of possible problems other anthropologists have confronted in other areas. There are a few problems, however, that seem to be nearly universal among anthropological fieldworkers, particularly those having to do with eating, bathing, sleeping, lack of privacy, loneliness, or discovering that primitive man is not always as noble as you originally thought—or you yourself not as culturally or emotionally 'flexible' as you assumed.

This is not to state that primitive man everywhere is unpleasant. By way of contrast, I have also done limited fieldwork among the Yąnomamö's northern neighbors, the Carib-speaking Ye'kwana Indians. This group was very pleasant and charming, all of them anxious to help me and honor bound to show any visitor the numerous courtesies of their system of etiquette. In short, they approached the image of primitive man that I had conjured up, and it was sheer pleasure to work with them. Other anthropologists have also noted sharp contrasts in the people they study from one field situation to another. One of the most startling examples of this is in the work of Colin Turnbull, who first studied the Ituri Pygmies (1965, 1983) and found them delightful but then studied the Ik (1972) of the desolate outcroppings of the Kenya/ Uganda/Sudan border region, a people he had difficulty coping with intellectually, emotionally, and physically. While it is possible that the anthropologist's reactions to a particular people are personal and idiosyncratic, it nevertheless remains that there *are* enormous differences between whole peoples, differences that affect the anthropologist in often dramatic ways.

Hence, what I say about some of my experiences is probably equally true of the experiences of many other fieldworkers. I think I could have profited by reading about the pitfalls and field problems of my teachers; at least I might have been able to avoid some of the more stupid errors I made. In this regard there is a growing body of excellent descriptive work on field research. Students who plan to make a career in anthropology should consult these works, which cover a wide range of field situations in the ethnographic present.[3]

The First Day: The Longest One   My first day in the field illustrated to me what my teachers meant when they spoke of "culture shock." I had traveled in a small, aluminum rowboat propelled by a large outboard motor for two and a half days. This took me from the territorial capital, a small town on the Orinoco River, deep into Yąnomamö country. On the morning of the third day we reached a small mission settlement, the field "headquarters" of a group of Americans who were working in two Yąnomamö villages. The missionaries had come out of these villages to hold their annual conference on the progress of their mission work and were conducting their meetings when I arrived. We picked up a passenger at the mission station, James P. Barker, the first non-Yąnomamö to make a sustained, permanent contact with the tribe (in 1950). He had just returned from a year's furlough in the United States, where I had earlier visited him before leaving for Venezuela. He agreed to accompany me to the village I had selected for my base of operations to introduce me to the Indians. This village was also his own home base, but he had not been there for over a year and did not plan to join me for another three months. Mr. Barker had been living with this particular group about five years.

We arrived at the village, Bisaasi-teri, about 2:00 P.M. and docked the boat along the muddy bank at the terminus of the path used by the Indians to fetch their drinking water. It was hot and muggy, and my clothing was soaked with perspiration. It clung uncomfortably to my body, as it did thereafter for the remainder of the work. The small biting gnats were out in astronomical

[3]See Spindler (1970) for a detailed discussion of field research by anthropologists who have worked in other cultures.

numbers, for it was the beginning of the dry season. My face and hands were swollen from the venom of their numerous stings. In just a few moments I was to meet my first Yąnomamö, my first primitive man. What would he be like? I had visions of entering the village and seeing 125 social facts running about calling each other kinship terms and sharing food, each waiting and anxious to have me collect his genealogy. I would wear them out in turn. Would they like me? This was important to me; I wanted them to be so fond of me that they would adopt me into their kinship system and way of life. I had heard that successful anthropologists always get adopted by their people. I had learned during my seven years of anthropological training at the University of Michigan that kinship was equivalent to society in primitive tribes and that it was a moral way of life, "moral" being something "good" and "desirable." I was determined to work my way into their moral system of kinship and become a member of their society—to be 'accepted' by them.

How Did They Accept You?   My heart began to pound as we approached the village and heard the buzz of activity within the circular compound. Mr. Barker commented that he was anxious to see if any changes had taken place while he was away and wondered how many of them had died during his absence. I felt into my back pocket to make sure that my notebook was still there and felt personally more secure when I touched it.

The entrance to the village was covered over with brush and dry palm leaves. We pushed them aside to expose the low opening to the village. The excitement of meeting my first Yąnomamö was almost unbearable as I duck-waddled through the low passage into the village clearing.

I looked up and gasped when I saw a dozen burly, naked, sweaty, hideous men staring at us down the shafts of their drawn arrows! Immense wads of green tobacco were stuck between their lower teeth and lips making them look even more hideous, and strands of dark-green slime dripped or hung from their nostrils—strands so long that they clung to their pectoral muscles or drizzled down their chins. We arrived at the village while the men were blowing a hallucinogenic drug up their noses. One of the side effects of the drug is a runny nose. The mucus is always saturated with the green powder and they usually let it run freely from their nostrils (Fig. 1–4). My next discovery was that there were a dozen or so vicious, underfed dogs snapping at my legs, circling me as if I were to be their next meal. I just stood there holding my notebook, helpless and pathetic. Then the stench of the decaying vegetation and filth hit me and I almost got sick. I was horrified. What kind of welcome was this for the person who came here to live with you and learn your way of life, to become friends with you? They put their weapons down when they recognized Barker and returned to their chanting, keeping a nervous eye on the village entrances.

We had arrived just after a serious fight. Seven women had been abducted the day before by a neighboring group, and the local men and their guests had just that morning recovered five of them in a brutal club fight that nearly ended in a shooting war. The abductors, angry because they had lost five of their seven new captives, vowed to raid the Bisaasi-teri. When we arrived and

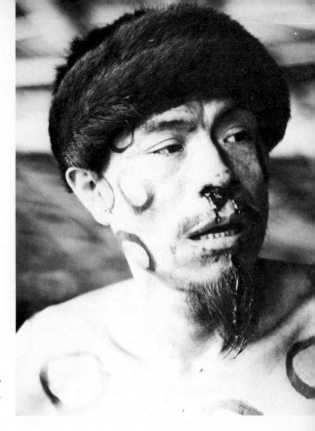

Fig. 1–4. Yąnomamö man with monkey-tail headband and ebene—*an hallucinogenic snuff powder—drizzling from his nostrils.*

entered the village unexpectedly, the Indians feared that we were the raiders. On several occasions during the next two hours the men in the village jumped to their feet, armed themselves, and waited nervously for the noise outside the village to be identified. My enthusiasm for collecting ethnographic facts diminished in proportion to the number of times such an alarm was raised. In fact, I was relieved when Barker suggested that we sleep across the river for the evening. It would be safer over there.

As we walked down the path to the boat, I pondered the wisdom of having decided to spend a year and a half with this tribe before I had even seen what they were like. I am not ashamed to admit that had there been a diplomatic way out, I would have ended my fieldwork then and there. I did not look forward to the next day—and months—when I would be left alone with the Indians; I did not speak a word of their language, and they were decidedly different from what I had imagined them to be. The whole situation was depressing, and I wondered why I ever decided to switch from physics and engineering in the first place. I had not eaten all day, I was soaking wet from perspiration, the gnats were biting me, and I was covered with red pigment, the result of a dozen or so complete examinations I had been given by as many pushy Yąnomamö men. These examinations capped an otherwise grim day. The men would blow their noses into their hands, flick as much of the mucus off that would separate in a snap of the wrist, wipe the residue into their hair, and then carefully examine my face, arms, legs, hair, and the contents of my pockets. I asked Barker how to say, "Your hands are dirty"; my comments were met by the Indians in the following way: They would 'clean' their hands by spitting a quantity of slimy tobacco juice into them, rub them together, grin, and then proceed with the examination.

Mr. Barker and I crossed the river and slung our hammocks. When he pulled his hammock out of a rubber bag, a heavy, disagreeable odor of mildewed cotton came with it. "Even the missionaries are filthy," I thought to myself. Within two weeks, everything I owned smelled the same way, and I lived with that odor for the remainder of the fieldwork. My own habits of personal cleanliness declined to such levels that I didn't even mind being examined by the Yąnomamö, as I was not much cleaner than they were after I had adjusted to the circumstances. It is difficult to blow your nose gracefully when you are stark naked and the invention of handkerchiefs is millenia away.

Life in the Jungle: Oatmeal, Peanut Butter, and Bugs   It isn't easy to plop down in the Amazon Basin for a year and get immediately into the anthropological swing of things. You have been told about horrible diseases, snakes, jaguars, quicksand, and getting lost. Some of the dangers are real, but your imagination makes them more real and threatening than many of them really are. What my teachers never bothered to tell me about, however, was the mundane, nonexciting and trivial stuff—like eating, defecating, sleeping, or keeping clean. These turned out to be the bane of my existence during the first several months of field research. I set up my household in Barker's abandoned mud hut, a few yards from the village of Bisaasi-teri, and immediately set to work building my own mud/thatch hut with the help of the Yąnomamö. Meanwhile, I had to eat and try to do my 'field research'. I soon discovered that it was an enormously time-consuming task to maintain my own body in the manner to which it had grown accustomed in the relatively antiseptic environment of the northern United States. Either I would be relatively well fed and relatively comfortable in a fresh change of clothes and do very little fieldwork, or I could do considerably more fieldwork and be less well fed and less comfortable.

It is appalling how complicated it can be to make oatmeal in the jungle. First, I had to make two trips to the river to haul the water. Next, I had to prime my kerosene stove with alcohol to get it burning, a tricky procedure when you are trying to mix powdered milk and fill a coffee pot at the same time: the alcohol prime always burned out before I could turn the kerosene on, and I would have to start all over. Or, I would turn the kerosene on, optimistically hoping that the element was still hot enough to vaporize the fuel, and start a small fire in my palm-thatched hut as the liquid kerosene squirted all over the table and walls and then ignited. Many amused Yąnomamö onlookers quickly learned the English phrase "Oh, Shit!". . . and, once they discovered that the phrase offended and irritated the missionaries, they used it as often as they could in their presence. I usually had to start over with the alcohol. Then I had to boil the oatmeal and pick the bugs out of it. All my supplies, of course, were carefully stored in rat-proof, moisture-proof, and insect-proof containers, not one of which ever served its purpose adequately.

Just taking things out of the multiplicity of containers and repacking them afterward was a minor project in itself. By the time I had hauled the water to cook with, unpacked my food, prepared the oatmeal, milk, and coffee, heated water for dishes, washed and dried the dishes, repacked the food in the containers, stored the containers in locked trunks, and cleaned up my mess, the ceremony of preparing breakfast had brought me almost up to lunch time!

Eating three meals a day was simply out of the question. I solved the problem by eating a single meal that could be prepared in a single container, or, at most, in two containers, washed my dishes only when there were no clean ones left, using cold river water, and wore each change of clothing at least a week—to cut down on my laundry problem—a courageous undertaking in the tropics. I reeked like a jockstrap that had been left to mildew in the bottom of some dark gym locker. I also became less concerned about sharing my provisions with the rats, insects, Yąnomamö, and the elements, thereby eliminating the need for my complicated storage process. I was able to last most of the day on *café con leche*, heavily sugared espresso coffee diluted about five to one with hot milk. I would prepare this in the evening and store it in a large thermos. Frequently, my single meal was no more complicated than a can of sardines and a package of soggy crackers. But at least two or three times a week I would do something 'special' and sophisticated, like make a batch of oatmeal or boil rice and add a can of tuna fish or tomato paste to it. I even saved time by devising a water system that obviated the trips to the river. I had a few sheets of tin roofing brought in and made a rain water trap; I caught the water on the tin surface, funneled it into an empty gasoline drum, and then ran a plastic hose from the drum to my hut. When the drum was exhausted in the dry season, I would get a few Yąnomamö boys to fill it with buckets of water from the river, 'paying' them with crackers, of which they grew all too fond all too soon.

I ate much less when I traveled with the Yąnomamö to visit other villages. Most of the time my travel diet consisted of roasted or boiled green plantains (cooking bananas) that I obtained from the Yąnomamö, but I always carried a few cans of sardines with me in case I got lost or stayed away longer than I had planned. I found peanut butter and crackers a very nourishing 'trail' meal, and a simple one to prepare. It was nutritious and portable, and only one tool was required to make the meal: a hunting knife that could be cleaned by wiping the blade on a convenient leaf. More importantly, it was one of the few foods the Yąnomamö would let me eat in relative peace. It looked suspiciously like animal feces to them, an impression I encouraged.

I referred to the peanut butter as the feces of babies or 'cattle'. They found this disgusting and repugnant. They did not know what 'cattle' were, but were increasingly aware that I ate several canned products of such an animal. Tin cans were thought of as containers made of 'machete skins', but how the cows got inside was always a mystery to them. I went out of my way to describe my foods in such a way as to make them sound unpalatable to them, for it gave me some peace of mind while I ate: they wouldn't beg for a share of something that was too horrible to contemplate. Fieldworkers develop strange defense mechanisms and strategies, and this was one of my own forms of adaptation to the fieldwork. On another occasion I was eating a can of frankfurters and growing very weary of the demands from one of the onlookers for a share in my meal. When he finally asked what I was eating, I replied: "Beef." He then asked: "Shąki!⁴ What part of the animal are you eating?" To which I replied, "Guess." He muttered a contemptuous epithet, but stopped asking for a share. He got back at me later, as we shall see.

Meals were a problem in a way that had nothing to do with the inconvenience of preparing them. Food sharing is important to the Yąnomamö in the context of displaying friendship. "I am hungry!" is almost a form of greeting with them. I could not possibly have brought enough food with me to feed the entire village, yet they seemed to overlook this logistic fact as they begged for my food. What became fixed in their minds was the fact that I did not share my food with whomsoever was present—usually a small crowd—at each and every meal. Nor could I easily enter their system of reciprocity with respect to food: every time one of them 'gave' me something 'freely', he would dog me for months to 'pay him back', not necessarily with food but with knives, fishhooks, axes, and so on. Thus, if I accepted a plantain from someone in a different village while I was on a visit, he would most likely visit me in the future and demand a machete as payment for the time that he 'fed' me. I usually reacted to these kinds of demands by giving a banana, the customary reciprocity in their culture—food for food—but this would be a disappointment for the individual who had nursed visions of that single plantain growing into a machete over time. Many years after beginning my fieldwork I was approached by one of the prominent men who demanded a machete for a piece of meat he claimed he had given me five or six years earlier.

Despite the fact that most of them knew I would not share my food with them at their request, some of them always showed up at my hut during mealtime. I gradually resigned myself to this and learned to ignore their persistent demands while I ate. Some of them would get angry because I failed to give in, but most of them accepted it as just a peculiarity of the subhuman foreigner who had come to live among them. If or when I did accede to a request for a share of my food, my hut quickly filled with Yąnomamö, each demanding their share of the food that I had just given to one of them. Their begging for food was not provoked by hunger, but by a desire to try something new and to attempt to establish a coercive relationship in which I would accede to a demand. If one received something, all others would immediately have to test the system to see if they, too, could coerce me.

A few of them went out of their way to make my meals downright unpleasant—to spite me for not sharing, especially if it was a food that they had tried before and liked, or a food that was part of their own cuisine. For example, I was eating a cracker with peanut butter and honey one day. The Yąnomamö will do almost anything for honey, one of the most prized

---

⁴They could not pronounce "Chagnon." It sounded to them like their name for a pesky bee, *shąki*, and that is what they called me: pesky, noisome bee.

delicacies in their own diet. One of my cynical onlookers—the fellow who had earlier watched me eating frankfurters—immediately recognized the honey and knew that I would not share the tiny precious bottle. It would be futile to even ask. Instead, he glared at me and queried icily, "Shąki! What kind of animal semen are you pouring onto your food and eating?" His question had the desired effect and my meal ended.

Finally, there was the problem of being lonely and separated from your own kind, especially your family. I tried to overcome this by seeking personal friendships among the Yąnomamö. This usually complicated the matter because all my 'friends' simply used my confidence to gain privileged access to my hut and my cache of steel tools and trade goods—and looted me when I wasn't looking. I would be bitterly disappointed that my erstwhile friend thought no more of me than to finesse our personal relationship exclusively with the intention of getting at my locked up possessions, and my depression would hit new lows every time I discovered this. The loss of the possessions bothered me much less than the shock that I was, as far as most of them were concerned, nothing more than a source of desirable items. No holds were barred in relieving me of these, since I was considered something subhuman, a non-Yąnomamö.

The hardest thing to learn to live with was the incessant, passioned, and often aggressive demands they would make. It would become so unbearable at times that I would have to lock myself in my hut periodically just to escape from it. Privacy is one of our culture's most satisfying achievements, one you never think about until you suddenly have none. It is like not appreciating how good your left thumb feels until someone hits it with a hammer. But I did not want privacy for its own sake; rather, I simply had to get away from the begging. Day and night for the entire time I lived with the Yąnomamö I was plagued by such demands as: "Give me a knife, I am poor!"; "If you don't take me with you on your next trip to Widokaiya-teri, I'll chop a hole in your canoe!"; "Take us hunting up the Mavaca River with your shotgun or we won't help you!"; "Give me some matches so I can trade with the Reyaboböwei-teri, and be quick about it or I'll hit you!"; "Share your food with me, or I'll burn your hut!"; "Give me a flashlight so I can hunt at night!"; "Give me all your medicine, I itch all over!"; "Give me an ax or I'll break into your hut when you are away and steal all of them!" And so I was bombarded by such demands day after day, month after month, until I could not bear to see a Yąnomamö at times.

It was not as difficult to become calloused to the incessant begging as it was to ignore the sense of urgency, the impassioned tone of voice and whining, or the intimidation and aggression with which many of the demands were made. It was likewise difficult to adjust to the fact that the Yąnomamö refused to accept "No" for an answer until or unless it seethed with passion and intimidation—which it did after a few months. So persistent and characteristic is the begging that the early 'semi-official' maps made by the Venezuelan Malaria Control Service (*Malarialogia*) designated the site of their first permanent field station, next to the village of Bisaasi-teri, as *Yababuhii*:

"Gimme." I had to become like the Yąnomamö to be able to get along with them on their terms: somewhat sly, aggressive, intimidating, and pushy.

It became indelibly clear to me shortly after I arrived there that had I failed to adjust in this fashion I would have lost six months of supplies to them in a single day or would have spent most of my time ferrying them around in my canoe or taking them on long hunting trips. As it was, I did spend a considerable amount of time doing these things and did succumb often to their outrageous demands for axes and machetes, at least at first, for things changed as I became more fluent in their language and learned how to defend myself socially as well as verbally: I was learning the Yąnomamö equivalent of a left jab to the jawbone. More importantly, had I failed to demonstrate that I could not be pushed around beyond a certain point, I would have been the subject of far more ridicule, theft, and practical jokes than was the actual case. In short, I had to acquire a certain proficiency in their style of interpersonal politics and to learn how to imply subtly that certain potentially undesirable, but unspecified, consequences might follow if they did such and such to me. They do this to each other incessantly in order to establish precisely the point at which they cannot goad or intimidate an individual any further without precipitating some kind of retaliation. As soon as I realized this and gradually acquired the self-confidence to adopt this strategy, it became clear that much of the intimidation was calculated to determine my flash point or my 'last ditch' position—and I got along much better with them. Indeed, I even regained some lost ground. It was sort of like a political, interpersonal game that everyone had to play, but one in which each individual sooner or later had to give evidence that his bluffs and implied threats could be backed up with a sanction. I suspect that the frequency of wife beating is a component in this syndrome, since men can display their *waiteri* (ferocity) and 'show' others that they are capable of great violence. Beating a wife with a club is one way of displaying ferocity, one that does not expose the man to much danger—unless the wife has concerned, aggressive brothers in the village who will come to her aid. Apparently the important thing in wife beating is that the man has displayed his presumed potential for violence and the intended message is that other men ought to treat him with circumspection, caution, and even deference.

After six months, the level of Yąnomamö demand was tolerable in the village I used for my base of operations. We had adjusted somewhat to each other and knew what to expect with regard to demands for food, trade goods and favors. Had I elected to remain in just one Yąnomamö village for the entire duration of my first 15 months of fieldwork the experience would have been far more enjoyable than it actually was. However, as I began to understand the social and political dynamics of this village, it became patently obvious that I would have to travel to many other villages to determine the demographic bases and political histories that lay behind what I could understand in the village of Bisaasi-teri. I began making regular trips to some dozen neighboring Yąnomamö villages as my language fluency improved. I collected local genealogies there, or rechecked and cross-checked those I had collected elsewhere. Hence, the intensity of begging was relatively constant and relatively high for the duration of my fieldwork, for I had to establish my personal flashpoint position in each village I visited and revisited.

For the most part, my own 'fierceness' took the form of shouting back at the Yąnomamö as loudly and as passionately as they shouted at me, especially at first, when I did not know much of the language. As I became more fluent and learned more about their political tactics, I became more sophisticated in the art of bluffing and brinksmanship. For example, I paid one young man a machete (then worth about $2.50) to cut a palm tree and help me make boards from the wood. I used these to fashion a flooring in the bottom of my dugout canoe to keep my possessions out of the water that always seeped into the canoe and sloshed around. That afternoon I was working with one of my informants in the village. The long-awaited mission supply boat arrived and most of the Yąnomamö ran out of the village to see the supplies and try to beg items from the crew. I continued to work in the village for another hour or so and went down to the river to visit with the men on the supply boat. When I reached the river I noticed, with anger and frustration, that the Yąnomamö had chopped up all my new floor boards to use them as crude paddles to get their own canoes across the river to the supply boat.[5] I knew that if I ignored this abuse I would have invited the Yąnomamö to take even greater liberties with my possessions in the future. I got into my canoe, crossed the river, and docked amidst their flimsy, leaky craft. I shouted loudly to them, attracting their attention: they were somewhat sheep-faced, but all had mischievous grins on their impish faces. A few of them came down to the canoe, where I proceeded with a spirited lecture that revealed my anger at their audacity and license: I explained that I had just that morning paid one of them a machete for bringing me the palmwood, how hard I had worked to shape each board and place it in the canoe, how carefully and painstakingly I had tied each one in with vines, how much I perspired, how many gnat bites I had suffered, and so on. Then, with exaggerated drama and finality, I withdrew my hunting knife as their grins disappeared and cut each one of their canoes loose and set it into the strong current of the Orinoco River where it was immediately swept up and carried downstream. I left without looking back and huffed over to the other side of the river to resume my work.

They managed to borrow another canoe and, after some effort, recovered their dugouts. Later, the headman of the village told me, with an approving chuckle, that I had done the correct thing. Everyone in the village, except, of course, the culprits, supported and defended my actions—and my status increased as a consequence.

Whenever I defended myself in such ways I got along much better with the Yąnomamö and gradually acquired the respect of many of them. A good deal

---

[5]The Yąnomamö in this region acquired canoes very recently. The missionaries would purchase them from the Ye'kwana Indians to the north for money, and then trade them to the Yąnomamö in exchange for labor, produce, or 'informant' work in translating. It should be emphasized that those Yąnomamö who lived on navigable portions of the Upper Orinoco River moved there from the deep forest in order to have contact with the missionaries and acquire the trade goods the missionaries (and their supply system) brought.

of their demeanor toward me was directed with the forethought of establishing the point at which I would draw the line and react defensively. Many of them, years later, reminisced about the early days of my fieldwork when I was timid and *mohode* ("stupid") and a little afraid of them, those golden days when it was easy to bully me into giving my goods away for almost nothing.

Theft was the most persistent situation that required some sort of defensive action. I simply could not keep everything I owned locked in trunks, and the Yąnomamö came into my hut and left at will. I eventually developed a very effective strategy for recovering almost all the stolen items: I would simply ask a child who took the item and then I would confiscate that person's hammock when he was not around, giving a spirited lecture to all who could hear on the antisociality of thievery as I stalked off in a faked rage with the thief's hammock slung over my shoulder. Nobody ever attempted to stop me from doing this, and almost all of them told me that my technique for recovering my possessions was ingenious. By nightfall the thief would appear at my hut with the stolen item or send it over with someone else to make an exchange to recover his hammock. He would be heckled by his covillagers for having got caught and for being embarrassed into returning my item for his hammock. The explanation was usually, "I just borrowed your ax! I wouldn't think of stealing it!"

Collecting Yąnomamö Genealogies and Reproductive Histories   My purpose for living among the Yąnomamö was to systematically collect certain kinds of information on genealogy, reproduction, marriage practices, kinship, settlement pattern, migrations, and politics. Much of the fundamental data was genealogical—who was the parent of whom, tracing these connections as far back in time as Yąnomamö knowledge and memory permitted. Since 'primitive' society is largely organized by kinship relationships, figuring out the social organization of the Yąnomamö essentially meant collecting extensive data on genealogies, marriage, and reproduction. This turned out to be a staggering and very frustrating problem. I could not have deliberately picked a more difficult tribe to work with in this regard. They have very stringent name taboos and eschew mentioning the names of prominent living people as well as all deceased friends and relatives. They attempt to name people in such a way that when the person dies and they can no longer use his or her name, the loss of the word in their language is not inconvenient. Hence, they name people for specific and minute parts of things, such as "toenail of sloth," "whisker of howler monkey," and so on, thereby being able to retain the words "toenail" or "whisker" but somewhat handicapped in referring to these anatomical parts of sloths and monkeys respectively. The taboo is maintained even for the living, for one mark of prestige is the courtesy others show you by not using your name publicly. This is particularly true for men, who are much more competitive for status than women in this culture, and it is fascinating to watch boys grow into young men, demanding to be called either by a kinship term in public, or by a teknonymous reference such as 'brother of Himotoma' (see Glossary). The more effective they are at getting others to avoid using their names, the more public acknowledgement there is that they are of high esteem. Helena Valero, a Brazilian woman who was captured as a child by a

Yąnomamö raiding party, was married for many years to a Yąnomamö headman before she discovered what his name was (Biocca, 1970). The sanctions behind the taboo are more complex than just this, for they involve a combination of fear, respect, admiration, political deference, and honor.

I tried to use kinship terms alone to collect genealogies at first, but Yąnomamö kinship terms, like the kinship terms in all systems, are ambiguous at some point because they include so many possible relatives (as the term "uncle" does in our own kinship system). Again, their system of kin classification merges many relatives that we 'separate' by using different terms: they call both their actual father and their father's brother by a single term, whereas we call one "father" and the other "uncle." I was forced, therefore, to resort to personal names to collect unambiguous genealogies or 'pedigrees'. They quickly grasped what I was up to and that I was determined to learn everyone's 'true name', which amounted to an invasion of their system of prestige and etiquette, if not a flagrant violation of it. They reacted to this in a brilliant but devastating manner: They invented false names for everybody in the village and systematically learned them, freely revealing to me the 'true' identities of everyone. I smugly thought I had cracked the system and enthusiastically constructed elaborate genealogies over a period of some five months. They enjoyed watching me learn their names and kinship relationships. I naively assumed that I would get the 'truth' to each question and the best information by working in public. This set the stage for converting my serious project into an amusing hoax of the grandest proportions. Each 'informant' would try to outdo his peers by inventing a name even more preposterous or ridiculous than what I had been given by someone earlier, the explanations for discrepancies being "Well, he has two names and this is the other one." They even fabricated devilishly improbable genealogical relationships, such as someone being married to his grandmother, or worse yet, to his mother-in-law, a grotesque and horrifying prospect to the Yąnomamö. I would collect the desired names and relationships by having my informant whisper the name of the person softly into my ear, noting that he or she was the parent of such and such or the child of such and such, and so on. Everyone who was observing my work would then insist that I repeat the name aloud, roaring in hysterical laughter as I clumsily pronounced the name, sometimes laughing until tears streamed down their faces. The 'named' person would usually react with annoyance and hiss some untranslatable epithet at me, which served to reassure me that I had the 'true' name. I conscientiously checked and rechecked the names and relationships with multiple informants, pleased to see the inconsistencies disappear as my genealogy sheets filled with those desirable little triangles and circles, thousands of them.

My anthropological bubble was burst when I visited a village about 12 hours' walk to the southwest of Bisaasi-teri some five months after I had begun collecting genealogies on the Bisaasi-teri. I was chatting with the local headman of this village and happened to casually drop the name of the wife of the Bisaasi-teri headman. A stunned silence followed, and then a villagewide roar of uncontrollable laughter, choking, gasping, and howling followed. It seems that the Bisaasi-teri headman was married to a woman named "hairy cunt." It also seems that the Bisaasi-teri headman was called "long dong" and his brother "eagle shit." The Bisaasi-teri headman had a son called "asshole" and a daughter called "fart breath." And so on. Blood welled up to my temples as I realized that I had nothing but nonsense to show for my five months' of dedicated genealogical effort, and I had to throw away almost all the information I had collected on this the most basic set of data I had come there to get. I understood at that point why the Bisaasi-teri laughed so hard when they made me repeat the names of their covillagers, and why the 'named' person would react with anger and annoyance as I pronounced his 'name' aloud.

I was forced to change research strategy—to make an understatement of a serious situation. The first thing I did was to begin working in private with my informants to eliminate the horseplay and distraction that attended public sessions. Once I did this, my informants, who did not know what others were telling me, began to agree with each other and I managed to begin learning the 'real' names, starting first with children and gradually moving to adult women and then, cautiously, adult men, a sequence that reflected the relative degree of intransigence at revealing names of people. As I built up a core of accurate genealogies and relationships—a core that all independent informants had verified repetitiously—I could 'test' any new informant by soliciting his or her opinion and knowledge about these 'core' people whose names and relationships I was confident were accurate. I was, in this fashion, able to immediately weed out the mischievous informants who persisted in trying to deceive me. Still, I had great difficulty getting the names of dead kinsmen, the only accurate way to extend genealogies back in time. Even my best informants continued to falsify names of the deceased, especially closely related deceased. The falsifications at this point were not serious and turned out to be readily corrected as my interviewing methods improved (see below). Most of the deceptions were of the sort where the informant would give me the name of a living man as the father of some child whose actual father was dead, a response that enabled the informant to avoid using the name of a deceased kinsman or friend.

The quality of a genealogy depends in part on the number of generations it embraces, and the name taboo prevented me from making any substantial progress in learning about the deceased ancestors of the present population. Without this information, I could not, for example, document marriage patterns and interfamilial alliances through time. I had to rely on older informants for this information, but these were the most reluctant informants of all for this data. As I became more proficient in the language and more skilled at detecting fabrications, my informants became better at deception. One of them was particularly cunning and persuasive, following a sort of Mark Twain policy that the most effective lie is a sincere lie. He specialized in making a ceremony out of false names for dead ancestors. He would look around nervously to make sure nobody was listening outside my hut, enjoin me never to mention the name again, become very anxious and spooky, and grab me by the head to whisper a secret name into my ear. I was always elated after a session with him, because I managed to add several generations of ancestors for particular members of the village. Others steadfastly refused to give me such information. To show my gratitude, I paid him quadruple the rate that I had been paying the others. When word got around that I had increased the pay for genealogical and demographic information, volunteers began pouring into my hut to 'work' for me, assuring me of their changed ways and keen desire to divest themselves of the 'truth'.

Enter Rerebawä: Inmarried Tough Guy   I discovered that the old man was lying quite by accident. A club fight broke out in the village one day, the result of a dispute over the possession of a woman. She had been promised to a young man in the village, a man named Rerebawä, who was particularly aggressive. He had married into Bisaasi-teri and was doing his 'bride service'— a period of several years during which he had to provide game for his wife's father and mother, provide them with wild foods he might collect, help them in certain gardening and other tasks. Rerebawä had already been given one of the daughters in marriage and was promised her younger sister as his second wife. He was enraged when the younger sister, then about 16 years old, began having an affair with another young man in the village, Bäkotawä, making no attempt to conceal it. Rerebawä challenged Bäkotawä to a club fight. He swaggered boisterously out to the duel with his 10-foot-long club, a roof-pole he had cut from the house on the spur of the moment, as is the usual procedure. He hurled insult after insult at both Bäkotawä and his father, trying to goad them into a fight. His insults were bitter and nasty. They tolerated them for a few moments but grew enraged. They came out of their hammocks and ripped out roof-poles, now returning the insults verbally, and rushed to the village clearing. Rerebawä continued to insult them, goading them into striking him on the head with their equally long clubs. Had either of them struck his head—which he held out conspicuously for them to swing at—he would then have the right to take his turn on their heads with his club. His opponents were intimidated by his fury, and simply backed down, refusing to strike him, and the fight ended. He had outbluffed them. All three retired pompously to their respective hammocks, exchanging nasty insults as they departed. But Rerebawä had won the showdown and thereafter swaggered around the village, insulting the two men behind their backs at every opportunity. He was genuinely angry with them, to the point of calling the older man by the name of his long-deceased father. I quickly seized on this incident as an opportunity to collect an accurate genealogy and pumped Rerebawä about his adversary's ancestors. Rerebawä had been particularly 'pushy' with me up to this point, but we soon became warm friends and staunch allies: we were both 'outsiders' in Bisaasi-teri and, although he was a Yąnomamö, he nevertheless had to put up with some considerable amount of pointed teasing and scorn from the locals, as all inmarried "sons-in-law" must (Fig. 1–5). He gave me the information I requested of his adversary's deceased ancestors, almost with devilish glee. I asked about dead ancestors of other people in the village and got prompt, unequivocal answers: he was angry with everyone in the village. When I compared his answers to those of the old man,

Fig. 1–5. Rerebawä, one of my closest friends and constant companion on long trips into remote villages.

it was obvious that one of them was lying. I then challenged his answers. He explained, in a sort of "you damned fool, don't you know better?" tone of voice that everyone in the village knew the old man was lying to me and gloating over it when I was out of earshot. The names the old man had given to me were names of dead ancestors of the members of a village so far away that he thought I would never have occasion to check them out authoritatively. As it turned out, Rerebawä knew most of the people in that distant village and recognized the names given by the old man.

I then went over the complete genealogical records with Rerebawä, genealogies I had presumed to be close to their final form. I had to revise them all because of the numerous lies and falsifications they contained, much of it provided by the sly old man. Once again, after months of work, I had to recheck everything with Rerebawä's aid. Only the living members of the nuclear families turned out to be accurate; the deceased ancestors were mostly fabrications.

Discouraging as it was to have to recheck everything all over again, it was a major turning point in my fieldwork. Thereafter, I began taking advantage of local arguments and animosities in selecting my informants, and used more extensively informants who had married into the village in the recent past. I also began traveling more regularly to other villages at this time to check on genealogies, seeking out villages whose members were on strained terms with the people about whom I wanted information. I would then return to my base in the village of Bisaasi-teri and check with local informants the accuracy of the new information. If the informants displayed annoyance when I mentioned the new names that I had acquired from informants in distant villages, I was almost certain that the information was accurate. I had to be careful, though, and scrupulously select my local informants in such a way that I would not be inquiring about *their* closely related kin. Thus, for each of my local informants, I had to make lists of names of certain deceased people that I dared not mention in their presence. But despite this precaution, I would occasionally hit a new name that would put my informant into a rage, or into a surly mood, such as that of a dead brother or sister whose existence had not been indicated to me by other informants. This usually terminated my day's work with that informant, for he or she would be too touchy or upset to continue any further, and I would be reluctant to take a chance on accidentally discovering another dead close kinsman soon after discovering the first.

These were always unpleasant experiences, and occasionally dangerous as well, depending on the temperament of my informant. On one occasion I was planning to visit a village that had been raided recently by one of their enemies. A woman, whose name I had on my census list for that village, had been killed by the raiders. Killing women is considered to be bad form in Yąnomamö warfare, but this woman was deliberately killed for revenge. The raiders were unable to bushwhack someone who stepped out of the village at dawn to urinate, so they shot a volley of arrows over the roof into the village and beat a hasty retreat. Unfortunately, one of the arrows struck and killed a woman, an accident. For that reason, her village's raiders *deliberately* sought out and killed a woman in retaliation—whose name was on my list. My reason for going to the village was to update my census data on a name-by-name basis and estimate the ages of all the residents. I knew I had the name of the dead woman in my list, but nobody would dare to utter her name so I could remove it. I knew that I would be in very serious trouble if I got to the village and said her name aloud, and I desperately wanted to remove it from my list. I called on one of my regular and usually cooperative informants and asked him to tell me the woman's name. He refused adamantly, explaining that she was a close relative—and was angry that I even raised the topic with him. I then asked him if he would let me whisper the names of *all* the women of that village in his ear, and he would simply have to nod when I hit the right name. We had been 'friends' for some time, and I thought I was able to predict his reaction, and thought that our friendship was good enough to use this procedure. He agreed to the procedure, and I began whispering the names of the women, one by one. We were alone in my hut so that nobody would know what we were doing and nobody could hear us. I read the names softly, continuing to the next when his response was a negative. When I ultimately hit the dead woman's name, he flew out of his chair, enraged and trembling violently, his arm raised to strike me: "You son-of-a-bitch!" he screamed. "If you say her name in my presence again, I'll kill you in an instant!" I sat there, bewildered, shocked, and confused. And frightened, as much because of his reaction, but also because I could imagine what might happen to me should I unknowingly visit a village to check genealogy accuracy without knowing that someone had just died there or had been shot by raiders since my last visit. I reflected on the several articles

I had read as a graduate student that explained the "genealogical method," but could not recall anything about its being a potentially hazardous technique. My furious informant left my hut, never again to be invited back to be an informant. I had other similar experiences in different villages, but I was always fortunate in that the dead person had been dead for some time, or was not very closely related to the individual into whose ear I whispered the forbidden name. I was cautioned to desist from saying any more names lest I get people 'angry'.

Kąobawä: The Bisaasi-teri Headman Volunteers to Help Me   I had been working on the genealogies for nearly a year when another individual came to my aid. It was Kąobawä, the headman of Upper Bisaasi-teri. The village of Bisaasi-teri was split into two components, each with its own garden and own circular house. Both were in sight of each other. However, the intensity and frequency of internal bickering and argumentation was so high that they decided to split into two separate groups, but would remain close to each other for protection in case they were raided. One group was downstream from the other; I refer to that group as the "Lower" Bisaasi-teri and call Kąobawä's group "Upper" (upstream) Bisaasi-teri, a convenience they themselves adopted after separating from each other. I spent most of my time with the members of Kąobawä's group, some 200 people when I first arrived there. I did not have much contact with Kąobawä during the early months of my work—he was a somewhat retiring, quiet man, and among the Yąnomamö, the outsider has little time to notice the rare quiet ones when most everyone else is in the front row, pushing and demanding attention. He showed up at my hut one day after all the others had left. He had come to volunteer to help me with the genealogies. He was "poor," he explained, and needed a machete. He would work only on the condition that I did not ask him about his own parents and other very close kinsmen who had died. He also added that he would not lie to me as the others had done in the past.

This was perhaps the single most important event in my first year and a half of field research, for out of this incidental meeting evolved a very warm friendship, and what followed from it was a wealth of accurate information on the political history of Kąobawä's village and related villages, highly detailed genealogical information, and hundreds of valuable insights into the Yąnomamö way of life. Kąobawä's familiarity with his group's history and his candidness were remarkable (Fig. 1–6). His knowledge of details was almost encyclopedic, his memory almost photographic. More than that, he was enthusiastic about making sure I learned the truth, and he encouraged me, indeed, demanded that I learn all details I might otherwise have ignored. If there were subtle details he could not recite on the spot, he would advise me to wait until he could check things out with someone else in the village. He would often do this clandestinely, giving me a report the next day, telling me who revealed the new information and whether or not he thought they were in a position to know it. Between Kąobawä and Rerebawä, I made enormous gains in information and understanding toward the end of my first field trip and became lifelong friends with both. And both men knew that I had to get

Fig. 1–6. Kąobawä, the headman, alert for any telltale sign from the forest.

his genealogy from the other one. It was one of those understandings we all had and none of us could mention.

Once again I went over the genealogies with Kąobawä to recheck them, a considerable task by this time: they included about two thousand names, representing several generations of individuals from four different villages. Rerebawä's information was very accurate, and Kąobawä's contribution enabled me to trace the genealogies further back in time. Thus, after nearly a year of intensive effort on genealogies, Yąnomamö demographic patterns and social organization began to make a good deal of sense to me. Only at this point did the patterns through time begin to emerge in the data, and I could begin to understand how kinship groups took form, exchanged women in marriage over several generations, and only then did the fissioning of larger villages into smaller ones emerge as a chronic and important feature of Yąnomamö social, political, demographic, economic, and ecological adaptation. At this point I was able to begin formulating more sophisticated questions, for there was now a pattern to work from and one to flesh out. Without the help of Rerebawä and Kąobawä it would have taken much longer to make sense of the plethora of details I had collected from not only them, but dozens of other informants as well.

I spent a good deal of time with these two men and their families, and got to know them much better than I knew most Yąnomamö. They frequently gave their information in a way which related themselves to the topic under discussion. We became warm friends as time passed, and the formal "informant/anthropologist" relationship faded into the background. Eventually, we simply stopped 'keeping track' of work and pay. They would both spend hours talking with me, leaving without asking for anything. When they wanted something, they would ask for it no matter what the relative balance of reciprocity between us might have been at that point. I will speak of both of them—and their respective families—frequently in the following chapters, using them as 'examples' of life in Yąnomamö culture. For many of the customary things that anthropologists try to communicate about another culture, these two men and their families might be considered to be 'exemplary' or 'typical'. For other things, they are exceptional in many regards, but the reader will, even knowing some of the exceptions, understand Yąnomamö culture more intimately by being familiar with a few examples.

Kąobawä was about 40 years old when I first came to his village in 1964. I say "about 40" because the Yąnomamö numeration system has only three numbers: one, two, and more-than-two. It is hard to give accurate ages or dates for events when the informants have no means in their language to reveal such detail. Kąobawä is the headman of his village, meaning that he has somewhat more responsibility in political dealings with other Yąnomamö groups, and very little control over those who live in his group except when the village is being raided by enemies. We will learn more about political leadership and warfare in a later chapter, but most of the time men like Kąobawä are like the North American Indian 'chief' whose authority was characterized in the following fashion: "One word from the chief, and each man does as he pleases." There are different 'styles' of political leadership among the Yąno-mamö. Some leaders are mild, quiet, inconspicuous most of the time, but intensely competent. They act parsimoniously, but when they do, people listen and conform. Other men are more tyrannical, despotic, pushy, flamboy-ant, and unpleasant to all around them. They shout orders frequently, are prone to beat their wives, or pick on weaker men. Some are very violent. I have met headmen who run the entire spectrum between these polar types, for I have visited some 60 Yąnomamö villages. Kąobawä stands at the mild, quietly competent end of the spectrum. He has had six wives thus far—and temporary affairs with as many more, at least one of which resulted in a child that is publicly acknowledged as his child. When I first met him he had just two wives: Bahimi and Koamashima. Bahimi (Fig. 1–1) had two living children when I first met her; many others had died. She was the older and enduring wife, as much a friend to him as a mate. Their relationship was as close to what we think of as 'love' in our culture as I have seen among the Yąnomamö (Fig. 1–7). His second wife was a girl of about 20 years, Koamashima. She had a new baby boy when I first met her, her first child (Fig. 1–8). There was speculation that Kąobawä was planning to give Koamashima to one of his younger brothers who had no wife; he occasionally allows his younger brother to have sex with Koamashima, but only if he asks in advance. Kąobawä gave another wife to one of his other brothers because she was *beshi* ("horny"). In fact, this earlier wife had been married to two other men, both of whom discarded her because of her infidelity. Kąobawä had one daughter by her. However, the girl is being raised by Kąobawä's brother, but acknowledged to be Kąobawä's child.

Bahimi, his oldest wife, is about five years younger than he. She is his cross-cousin (see Glossary)—his mother's brother's daughter. Ideally, all Yąno-mamö men should marry a cross-cousin, as we shall discuss in a later chapter. Bahimi was pregnant when I began my fieldwork, but she destroyed the infant when it was born—a boy in this case—explaining tearfully that she had no choice. The new baby would have competed for milk with Ariwari, her youngest child, who was still nursing. Rather than expose Ariwari to the dangers and uncertainty of an early weaning, she chose to terminate the newborn instead. By Yąnomamö standards, this has been a very warm, enduring marriage. Kąobawä claims he only beats Bahimi 'once in a while, and only lightly' and she, for her part, never has affairs with other men.

Kąobawä is a quiet, intense, wise, and unobtrusive man. It came as something of a surprise to me when I learned that he was the headman of his village, for he stayed at the sidelines while others would surround me and press their demands on me. He leads more by example than by coercion. He can afford to be this way at his age, for he established his reputation for being forthright and as fierce as the situation required when he was younger, and the other men respect him. He also has five mature brothers or half-brothers in his village, men he can count on for support. He also has several other mature 'brothers' (parallel cousins, whom he must refer to as 'brothers' in his kinship system) in the village who frequently come to his aid, but not as often as his

Fig. 1–7. Kąobawä and his oldest wife, Bahimi. She is his mother's brother's daughter, and favorite wife.

Fig. 1–8. *Koamashima and her first child. She is one of Kaobawä's younger wives and because of her youth enjoys his favor more regularly.*

'real' brothers do. Kaobawä has also given a number of his sisters to other men in the village and has promised his young (8-year-old) daughter in marriage to a young man who, for that reason, is obliged to help him. In short, his 'natural' or 'kinship' following is large, and with this support, he does not have to display his aggressiveness to remind his peers of his position.

Rerebawä is a very different kind of person. He is much younger—perhaps in his early twenties (Fig. 1–5). He has just one wife, but they have already had three children. He is from a village called Karohi-teri, located about five hours' walk up the Orinoco, slightly inland off to the east of the river itself. Kaobawä's village enjoys amicable relationships with Rerebawä's, and it is for this reason that marriage alliances of the kind represented by Rerebawä's marriage into Kaobawä's village occur between the two groups. Rerebawä told me that he came to Bisaasi-teri because there were no eligible women for him to marry in his own village, a fact that I later was able to document when I did a census of his village and a preliminary analysis of its social organization.[6]

Rerebawä is perhaps more typical than Kaobawä in the sense that he is chronically concerned about his personal reputation for aggressiveness and goes out of his way to be noticed, even if he has to act tough. He gave me a hard time during my early months of fieldwork, intimidating, teasing, and

[6]In 1980 word reached me from a friend who was doing medical work among the Yanomamö that Kaobawä's village attacked a village that was a splinter group of Rerebawä's and killed a large number of men. This was confirmed for me in 1982 by an ecologist who was working near that area. What this will do to the relationships between Kaobawä's village and Rerebawä's village in the future is problematic, but their groups are probably on very strained terms now.

insulting me frequently. He is, however, much braver than the other men his age and is quite prepared to back up his threats with immediate action—as in the club fight incident just described above. Moreover, he is fascinated with political relationships and knows the details of intervillage relationships over a large area of the tribe. In this respect he shows all the attributes of being a headman, although he has too many competent brothers in his own village to expect to easily move into the leadership position there.

He does not intend to stay in Kąobawä's group and refuses to make his own garden—a commitment that would reveal something of an intended long-term residence. He feels that he has adequately discharged his obligations to his wife's parents by providing them with fresh game for several years. They should let him take his wife and return to his own village with her, but they refuse and try to entice him to remain permanently in Bisaasi-teri to continue to provide them with game when they are old. It is for this reason that they promised to give him their second daughter, their only other child, in marriage. Unfortunately, the girl was opposed to the marriage and ultimately married another man.

Although Rerebawä has displayed his ferocity in many ways, one incident in particular illustrates what his character can be like. Before he left his own village to take his new wife in Bisaasi-teri, he had an affair with the wife of an older brother. When it was discovered, his brother attacked him with a club. Rerebawä responded furiously: he grabbed an ax and drove his brother out of the village after soundly beating him with the blunt side of the single-bit ax. His brother was so intimidated by the thrashing and promise of more to come that he he did not return to the village for several days. I visited this village with Kąobawä shortly after this event had taken place; Rerebawä was with me as my guide. He made it a point to introduce me to this man. He approached his hammock, grabbed him by the wrist, and dragged him out on the ground: "This is the brother whose wife I screwed when he wasn't around!" A deadly insult, one that would usually provoke a bloody club fight among more valiant Yąnomamö. The man did nothing. He slunk sheepishly back into his hammock, shamed, but relieved to have Rerebawä release his grip.

Even though Rerebawä is fierce and capable of considerable nastiness, he has a charming, witty side as well. He has a biting sense of humor and can entertain the group for hours with jokes and clever manipulations of his language. And, he is one of few Yąnomamö that I feel I can trust. I recall indelibly my return to Bisaasi-teri after being away a year—the occasion of my second field trip to the Yąnomamö. When I reached Bisaasi-teri, Rerebawä was in his own village visiting his kinsmen. Word reached him that I had returned, and he paddled downstream immediately to see me. He greeted me with an immense bear hug and exclaimed, with tears welling up in his eyes, "Shąki! Why did you stay away so long? Did you not know that my will was so cold while you were gone that I could not at times eat for want of seeing you again?" I, too, felt the same way about him—then, and now.

Of all the Yąnomamö I know, he is the most genuine and the most devoted to his culture's ways and values. I admire him for that, although I cannot say that I subscribe to or endorse some of these values. By contrast, Kąobawä is older and wiser, a polished diplomat. He sees his own culture in a slightly different light and seems to even question aspects of it. Thus, while many of his peers enthusiastically accept the 'explanations' of things given in myths, he occasionally reflects on them—even laughing at some of the more preposterous of them. Probably more of the Yąnomamö are like Rerebawä than like Kąobawä, or at least try to be.

Beyond the Bisaasi-teri and into the Remote Villages

As my work progressed with Kąobawä, Rerebawä, and many other informants, a very important scientific problem began to emerge, one that could only be solved by going to visit many distant Yąnomamö villages to collect genealogies, demographic data, and local histories from the people there. But the fieldwork required to solve the scientific question led to some exciting and even dangerous adventures, for it meant contacting totally unknown Yąnomamö—people who had never before seen foreigners. The 'first contact' with a primitive society is a phenomenon that is less and less likely to happen, for the world is shrinking and 'unknown' tribes or villages are now very rare. In fact, our generation is probably the last that will have the opportunity to know what it is like to make first contact. For this reason, I include a description of what one such situation was like, put into the context of the scientific reasons for going into the unknown Yąnomamö area.

The Scientific Problem That Emerged   It became increasingly clear that each Yąnomamö village was a 'recent' colony or splinter group of some larger village, and a fascinating set of patterns—and problems—began to emerge. I could see that there were cause/effect relationships among a number of variables. These included village size, genealogical composition of villages, age and sex distributions, and marriage ties or 'alliances' between 'families'. Moreover, it became abundantly clear that intervillage warfare was an indelible force that affected village size and village distribution—how large villages got to be before they would 'fission' and divide into two groups, and where the newly created groups would move as they avoided their old enemies, attempted to get away from those they had just separated from, or sought new allies in distant places. I will discuss the details of this problem in a later chapter, but the simple discovery of the pattern had a marked influence on my fieldwork: it meant that I would have to travel to many villages in order to document the genealogical aspects of the pattern, take detailed censuses, collect local versions of 'historical truth' from all parties concerned, and map as best I could the locations of existing villages and locations of sites that they had abandoned in the recent past, sometimes penetrating new, virgin, unknown forest as pioneers on the expanding front of their population. What was exciting about this was the formal and ecological similarity that it suggested during the early centuries of the discovery of agriculture, and how our own ancestors in Eurasia and Africa spread agriculture into new lands, lands formerly inhabited by hunters and gatherers, or lands that had never been occupied.

Getting to some of these new villages turned out to be a staggering problem for a number of reasons. First, I was living in Bisaasi-teri, and old wars and current animosities prevented me from easily recruiting trustworthy guides who were politically able to visit some of the distant villages, or if able, willing to. Second, I had to deal with the political presures put on any of my guides by the older men in the village, who would have much preferred to have me dispense all my goods and gifts in *their* village and not take them inland to other Yąnomamö. Some of the older men went to great lengths to sabotage my plans to visit other villages, putting pressure on my guides to back out or to cause me to turn back once started. Third, some of the villages were at a great distance away and their precise locations to my guides unknown: they were uncontacted villages many days by trail away, and usually bitter, mortal enemies of the Bisaasi-teri among whom I lived—and with whom I was somewhat identified by Yąnomamö in all surrounding villages. My first year's research, which unraveled many details of previous wars, killings and treachery, convinced me that the Bisaasi-teri were justified in holding very caustic, hostile attitudes toward some of their distant neighbors, particularly members of villages that they collectively referred to as "the Shamatari." The Shamatari turned out to be a congeries of many interrelated villages to the south, some of which had a long history of bitter warfare with the Bisaasi-teri. All the Shamatari villages were related to each other and had come into existence as larger villages fissioned into smaller ones, grew, fissioned again, and occupied new lands, moving in a general direction from northeast to southwest (see maps in Chapter 2). Two of the closest villages lay immediately to the south of the Bisaasi-teri, and I visited both of them on foot my first year in the field—a 10-hour walk to the closest one, a two-day walk to the more distant one. These two groups were on somewhat friendly terms with the Bisaasi-teri, and a number of intermarriages had recently taken place between them. They were allies. But a good deal of mutual suspicion and occasional expressions of contempt also marked their relationships.

Far to the south of these two Shamatari villages lay other Shamatari villages, enemies to the Bisaasi-teri. It became clear to me, as my genealogical, demographic, and settlement pattern histories accumulated, that I would have to visit them: they had never before seen outsiders and the Bisaasi-teri chronically advised me about their treachery and viciousness, particularly Kąobawä and Rerebawä, who gradually became intimate friends with me and genuinely had my personal safety at heart.

The group of Shamatari I wanted to reach on my initial foray into this region was known to the Bisaasi-teri as "Sibarariwä's" village, Sibarariwä being the headman of the village and a man who was hated by all Bisaasi-teri for engineering a treachery that led to the deaths of many Bisaasi-teri, including Kąobawä's father (see Prologue). Sibarariwä was *waiteri* and had a reputation for aggressiveness in many villages, even in villages whose members had never met him or members of his village.

The first attempt I made to contact Sibarariwä's village was in 1966, near the end of my first field trip. It was unsuccessful primarily because my young guides, three in number, forced me to turn back. Two were from Bisaasi-teri and the third was from one of the friendly Shamatari villages, Mǫmaribӧwei-teri, a 10-hour walk away. We ascended the Mavaca River for about two days, chopping our way through large trees and tons of brush that clogged the river and made canoe passage very difficult. The river had not been ascended that far up in many years, perhaps 100 years if the historical sources reveal any clues (Rice, 1921). The last adventurers ran into hostile Yąnomamö and some died at their hands (Rice, 1921). Apparently my young guides banked on the assumption that the hardships would discourage me and I would give up. Much to their consternation, I refused to turn back and, on the third day's travel, we began running into fresh signs that Shamatari hunters or travelers had recently crossed the Mavaca: we found their flimsy foot bridges made of poles and vines. These signs began to worry my guides as we ran into more and more of them. By that night they were adamantly opposed to going any further and even refused to sleep at the place where I had pulled in the canoe: it turned out to be right on a recently traveled trail, a trail that my young guides concluded was used only by raiders. Angered, I had no choice but to go back downstream to a location more suitable to them. We left for Bisaasi-teri the next morning, and on reaching it, I was pressed for the payment my guides had been promised. I was reluctant to pay them because they forced me to turn back, and when I asked them why they went in the first place, they responded: "For the machetes you promised to us! We *never* thought we would get to the Shamatari!" Foiled again.

It was too late that year to make another attempt, but I did so on my next field season in Kąobawä's region. This time I chose my guides more carefully—or at least that was my plan. I picked an older man whose name translates into "Piranha." He was from a village far to the north, and had married into Kąobawä's village recently. Thus, he had no personal reasons to either fear the Shamatari or be despised by them, but he *was* from Kąobawä's village at this point and that might be taken with hostility by the Shamatari. The other guide I picked was just a kid, a boy named Karina. I had met him briefly the year before, when he and his mother straggled into the village of Mǫmaribӧwei-teri—the Shamatari village 10 hours' walk south of Kąobawä's. He and his mother had been abducted by Sibarariwä's group some 10 years earlier, so Karina had grown up, to the extent he was grown at all, in Sibarariwä's village and knew all the current residents. He was terrified at my sight—his first glimpse of a non-Yąnomamö—the year before (Fig. 1–9), but several visits to Kąobawä's village exposed him to the missionaries there and he gradually lost his fear of foreigners. Still, he was only about 12 or 13 years old. This actually was an advantage in one respect—he was still innocent enough to give me the accurate names and shallow genealogies of all the residents of Sibarariwä's village before I had even reached it.

The first attempt in 1968 ended when I discovered that all my 'gasoline' had been stolen and replaced with water, a common problem in the Upper

Fig. 1–9. Karina, my young guide when I first met him—a year before he led me into Shamatari country.

Orinoco where gasoline is scarce, has to be hauled in by an eight-day river trip, and filched by all who come in contact with it at every step of the way, including the very people you paid to bring it to you. We had gotten far up the Mavaca when I switched to my reserve gasoline stores and the motor died—it was plain water. We thus had to return to Bisaasi-teri where I had other gasoline and where I could dismantle my motor and spend the night cleaning it.

We set off again the next morning with fresh gasoline supplies and again were high up the Mavaca when I switched to my reserve supplies. This time it wasn't water, but it wasn't gasoline either. It was kerosene. Back down the Mavaca again, clean the engine again, and set off again. By this time— four or five days after starting the first trip—my guides were growing impatient and weary. My older guide failed to show up at dawn as agreed, and Karina, the 12-year-old, was running a high fever and didn't want to go. I pursuaded Karina that his fever would break and he would be 'cured' in a single day, but I still had to carry him physically to the canoe to pander his whims.

He was my only guide at this point. I sat in my canoe, tired and depressed, wondering if I should try to make it with just a 12-year-old guide. It was a murky, dismal dawn. I hadn't slept more than a few hours each night, for I had to dismantle and reassemble my outboard motor each time we floated back

home, a task I had to do at night to save time to assure my waning guides that
we would make progress. As I sat there, half ready to throw in the towel, a
young man—Bäkotawä—appeared at the river to take an early bath. He was
the one that Rerebawä had challenged to the club fight over the possession of
Rerebawä's wife's younger sister. He knew that my other guide had backed
out and that I was down to just one. I asked him if he were willing to go with
me to Sibarariwä's village. He thought about it for a moment. "I'm a Bisaasi-
teri and they might kill me," he said, adding ". . .but I could tell them that I'm
really a Patanowä-teri and they wouldn't know the difference." I turned to
Karina, who lay wimpering in the canoe in the most comfortable 'bed' I could
arrange, using my pack and gasoline tanks as props. "Would you vouch for him
if he said he was a Patanowä-teri?" I asked. He grunted, painfully, that he'd go
along with the deception and agreed that it was better than being a Bisaasi-teri.
At that, we agreed that Bäkotawä would be my second guide. He rushed off to
the shabono to collect his hammock and a few items to trade, and returned a
few minutes later, ready for the great adventure into unknown lands where his
older kin feared to tread. I brought along a second shotgun that I said he could
'use' (he didn't know which end to put the cartridges in), and this pleased him
immensely, not to mention bolstering his confidence. We thus set off for the
upper Mavaca in my large wooden dugout canoe, on top of which I carried a
smaller, lighter aluminum canoe for negotiating the high Mavaca where the big
boat could not get through. My plan was to go as far in the bigger, heavier boat
as we could, dropping off gasoline and other stores along the way for the trip
back.

The dry season was at its peak and the rivers were very low, so low that we
only made it about a day and a half upstream in the larger canoe before
reaching an insurmountable obstacle: two very large trees had fallen across the
river and were half submerged. They were too thick to chop through with
axes, and too much of the trunks was above the water to permit the three of us
to horse the heavy dugout over. We thus had to leave the big canoe at that
point, transfer everything to the smaller aluminum canoe, and set off, badly
overloaded, for the headwaters of the Mavaca.

Karina's fever broke and he returned to the healthy land of the living
adventurers. He began goading Bäkotawä, asking rhetorically, "What would
they do if they knew you were really a Bisaasi-teri?" "Maybe I might slip and
tell them that you are Bisaasi-teri." Bäkotawä grew silent, then moody, then
visibly shaken. On the third day, Karina rose up to his knees, began looking
intently at the river banks on both sides, and then exclaimed: "I know this
place! We're getting close to Sibarariwä's village! Their trail to Iwähikoroba-
teri is just a short way off the river, over there!" as he pointed to the east bank
of the tangled, narrow river, a stream so small at this point that it would have
been difficult to turn the canoe around without lifting it most of the way. We
proceeded a few hours further upstream, slowly, because the river was both
shallow and narrow, but mostly because it was now choked with deadfalls and
branches through which we had to regularly chop our way.

We pulled over about midday and dragged the canoe up a bank after
unloading the supplies. We would walk inland from this point, for the river

was now too narrow to proceed any further with the canoe. We were in a hilly region and could catch glimpses of relatively high peaks, all covered with dense vegetation and punctuated with scraggy outcroppings of rocks. We were in the headwaters of the Mavaca, and beyond the stark ridge ahead of us lay the almost legendary Shukumöna kä u, the River of Parakeets and homeland of the Shamatari—and lair of the legendary Sibarariwä and his warriors.

I divided the supplies into those we would take inland with us and those we would leave behind for the return trip. As I did, I was alarmed at the relatively small amount of food we had at that point. In my concern over gasoline and sputtering motors, I had failed to restock the food after each aborted trip. There was enough for several days, but if we failed to contact the Shamatari, we would have to ration ourselves carefully.

Karina said the village was to the southeast, indicating the distance as Yanomamö always do, by pointing to where the sun would be if we left now and where it would be when we reached the village. It was about a 4- or 5-hour walk by his description, and it meant that we would reach the village just before dark—not a good thing to do on a first contact. Even the Yanomamö like to have as much daylight as they can get when they visit a strange village. That way, you have time to make friends and assess the situation. We set off with our back packs about 2:00 P.M., and soon began running into fresh signs of human activity—footprints made a day before, husks of palm fruits, discarded items of no value, broken twigs where someone cleared the trail as he proceeded along it, and so on. My heart began to pound, for clearly we were close to Sibarariwä's village.

A ferocious rain hit us about an hour after we began walking, and we had to huddle together under a small nylon tarp I always carried for such occasions. We lost about an hour because of the rain, and decided that we should camp for the night: we would reach the village too late in the day to 'make friends'. We ate some boiled rice and strung our hammocks as dusk settled. Karina began teasing Bäkotawä about the nastiness of Sibarariwä's group, reminding him mischievously that he was really a Bisaasi-teri, not a Patanowä-teri. Bäkotawä lay sullenly and unhappily in his hammock, and I had to scold Karina for his ill-natured humor. At dawn we got up and began packing. Bäkotawä quietly informed me that he was going no further and intended to return to the canoe: he honestly and frankly admitted, "Ya kirii." I am frightened.

I gave him a share of the food and a quick lesson in how to load and fire the shotgun, providing him with a box of 25 or so cartridges. I told him we would be gone about "three days" (indicating the duration by three fingers) before we would rejoin him at the canoe. He assured me that whereas he was frightened here, he would be safe at the canoe and make his camp there, waiting for our return. Karina and I set off to to the southeast. Bäkotawä disappeared silently into the shadowy forest heading north toward the canoe.

Karina and I walked for several hours, continuing to run into fresh signs of Yanomamö travelers. We found footprints that had been made just that morning, last night's rainwater still oozing into the depressions. A banana peeling here, a discarded bunch of palm fruits there. We were now very close.

Karina grabbed my arm and whispered excitedly: "The village is just beyond the top of this hill!" We crept to the ridge and looked down into the valley below, where a gigantic, well-kept banana plantation surrounded a large, circular village. We were there. Karina peered intently and then urged me to follow. In a few minutes we were in the garden, and shortly after we could see the back side of the shabono, the village structure and clearing. But something was wrong: no noise. No babies crying, no men chanting to the *hekura* spirits, no smoke, no dogs barking, and no buzzing of voices. The shabono was *broke*— empty.

Deserted, but only recently deserted. Karina went to investigate the garden, returning with a pile of ripe plantains a few minutes later, and with the information that someone had been in the garden that very morning to harvest plantains. He guessed that Sibarariwä's group was camped out, but camped close enough to the garden that they could return easily to harvest food. He guessed that they would be further upstream, at a place they often camped at this time of the year because certain wild fruits were in season there. We decided to leave our packs behind, in the abandoned village, and strike off to find them. The sun was high, and we would have all afternoon to look for them.

By this point I was down to my sneakers, my shotgun, and a red loincloth I had borrowed from one of the Bisaasi-teri men. Karina brought only his bow, several arrows, and a large wad of now-aging tobacco tucked behind his lower lip—and his own loincloth. As we walked, we ran into fresher and more abundant signs of Sibarariwä's group, and I knew that we would soon run into them. As dusk began to settle we smelled smoke and, a few minutes later, saw a lazy cloud of bluish smoke drifting through the grey forest and rising slowly to the tree tops. Then we heard the chatter of many voices and babies crying. We had found their camp at last.

We approached quietly and cautiously, stopping at a small stream just short of the campsite to 'beautify' ourselves. Karina scolded me and urged me to clean up—my legs were all muddy and my loincloth dangled haphazardly between by scratched knees. I made myself as 'presentable' as I could, washing the mud and perspiration off, straightening my loincloth, and tying my sneakers. We had no feathers or red *nara* paint to add final touches. Karina handed me his bow and arrows and took up my shotgun, commenting, as he headed for the camp: "They might be frightened of your shotgun, so I'll take it. You carry my bow and arrows and wait for me to tell you to come in. They'll really be scared to see a foreigner!" He disappeared into the jungle ahead, whistled a signal that a visitor was coming in. A chorus of cheers, whistles, and welcoming hoots rebounded through the darkening jungle as they welcomed him in.

I suddenly became aware of my situation and the magnitude of what I was doing. Here I stood, in the middle of an unexplored, unmapped jungle, a few hundred feet from an uncontacted group of Yąnomamö who had a reputation of enormous ferocity and treachery, led there by a 12-year-old kid. My only marks of being human were my red loincloth, my muddy and torn sneakers, and a bow with three skinny arrows.

An ominous hush fell over the forest ahead: Karina had obviously told them that I was waiting outside, and they were now pondering what to do. Uncomfortable recollections flashed through my head and I recalled some of the tales that Kąobawä had recited to me about the Shamatari. I reflected on his intensely serious warnings that it would be hazardous to try to find them. They would pretend to be friendly, he explained, but when my guard was down they would fall on me with bowstaves and clubs and kill me. Perhaps they would do it on the spot, but they might wait until I had taken up a hammock, as visitors are supposed to do, and lay there defenseless. Perhaps they would do it at night, as I slept.

Silence. Anxiety. My temples pounded. I wanted to run. I could hear the hushed buzzing of voices and people moving around in the jungle, spreading out: some of them were leaving the camp. Were they surrounding me? Could I trust Karina? Was someone now staring at me down the long shaft of his war arrow?

Karina suddenly appeared on the trail and motioned for me to come—to present myself. I tried to give the expected visitor's announcement, but I had trouble puckering my dry lips and only a pathetic hiss of meaningless air came forth as I tried to whistle. I walked by Karina and noticed his curious look. I could not decide if it were the same look he had when he told Bäkotawä he would vouch that he was a Patanowä-teri, but it was too late now to consider weighty implications and too late to do anything about them.

I was greeted by a host of growling, screaming men, naked and undecorated, who pranced nervously around me, menacingly pointing their long, bamboo-tipped war arrows at my face, nocked in the strings of their powerful bows. I stood my ground, motionless and as poised as I could be, trying desperately to keep my legs from trembling, trying to look dignified, defiant, and fearless. After what seemed like an eternity, one of them gruffly told me to follow him to one of the temporary huts. As we walked toward it, I could see young men scrambling to clear off the ground and straighten a nara-stained cotton hammock—intended for my temporary use. They worked quickly and nervously, and scattered as I approached. Karina placed my shotgun at the backpost and I reclined in the hammock, striking the visitor's pose—one hand over my mouth, staring at the space above me and swaying gently, pretending I was on display in Macy's front window with a noontime crowd peering in.

Eventually a few of the bolder men came closer, hissing commands to the others to "get some food prepared, quickly!" They began whispering excitedly to each other, describing my most minute and most private visible parts. "Look at how hairy his legs are! Look at all that ugly hair on his chest! Look how pale he looks! Isn't his hair an unbelievable color—*frarefrare*, like a ripe banana! Isn't he strange looking, and did you see how long he was when he was standing there? I wonder if he has a regular penis? What are those skins he has tied to his feet?" Their curiosity gradually became overwhelming. The bolder ones came in closer, duck-waddling right at me. A hand came forward and cautiously and ever so delicately touched my leg. The hand retracted quickly with a hiss of amazement from its owner—"Aaahhh!" A chorus of admiring tongue clicks followed from the less bold, and then more touches and hisses, and soon many hands were touching me all over, pulling on my hairs, and they smelled my spoor repeatedly in their red-stained cupped hands, clicking their tongues and marveling that someone so different was so similar. Just a bit longer, hairier, and lighter than they were. Then I spoke to them, and again they marveled: I spoke a 'crooked' version of Yąnomamö, like the Bisaasi-teri do, but they understood me.

Soon we were jabbering and visiting like long-lost friends. They scolded me for not having come sooner, for they had known about me for years and had wanted to meet me. The Reyaboböwei-teri had told them about me and had passed on what they themselves had known directly from meeting me personally, and what they had learned from the Mömariböwei-teri or the Bisaasi-teri second-hand. The Yąnomamö language is very precise about what is known firsthand and what has come from second, hearsay, sources. I was flabbergasted at the detail and accuracy of what they knew about me.[7] They knew I had a wife and two children, and the sexes and approximate ages of my children. They could repeat with incredible accuracy conversations I had had with Yąnomamö in many different villages. One of them even wanted to see a scar on my left elbow. When I asked what he meant, he described in intimate detail a bad fall I had taken several years earlier on a trip to Reyaboböwei-teri when I slipped on a wet rock and landed on my elbow, which bled profusely. He even quite accurately repeated the string of vulgarities I uttered at the time, and my complaint to my guides that their goddamned trails foolishly went up and down steep hills when they could more efficiently go around them! For people who had never before seen a non-Yąnomamö, they certainly knew a great deal about at least one of them![8]

I stayed with them for several days, but Karina had revealed that I had a small treasure of trade goods at my canoe and they were anxious to go there to examine them. They were also disappointed that Bäkotawä did not come to the village, for "they wouldn't have harmed a hair on his head." After systematically checking the genealogical data that Karina had given me about the current families and visiting with them at length, I reluctantly decided to take them to my canoe and the cache of gifts I left there.

It had taken Karina and me at least six hours of walking to get from the canoe to this place, but since they were anxious to see the canoe and the trade goods, they made very rapid time guiding me back to where I had left the river: we ran most of the way. They carried only their weapons. No food and no hammocks. I didn't know what they planned to do for sleeping or eating,

---

[7]A more detailed version of this account can be found in my 1974 case study in methodolgy (Chagnon, 1974).

[8]In 1972 several of my colleagues from the University of Michigan Medical School made a trip to the Brazilian Yąnomamö to continue the biomedical research we had jointly pursued between 1966 and 1972. One of them casually mentioned my Yąnomamö name, Shąki, in front of a Yąnomamö. The Yąnomamö immediately and excitedly demanded to know where I was and if I were going to visit them. This Yąnomamö village was many miles away from any Yąnomamö village I had ever visited.

since we left for the canoe near midday. I guess I assumed that they planned to spend the night in their abandoned shabono, which they could probably have reached by dark even if they spent an hour at the canoe with me.

We came upon the spot where we had separated from Bäkotawä. Soon after we came upon two expended shotgun shells, then soon after that, two more, then two more, and so on. It appeared as though Bäkotawä had fired the gun every few minutes as he retreated to the canoe, and it was obvious that he was out of ammunition by the time he reached it.

We crossed the last rise before reaching the spot where I had left the canoe and supplies and, much to my horror, I discovered that the canoe, gasoline, food, tarps, and trade goods were all gone. Bäkotawä had panicked and had taken off, leaving me stranded with people he was sure would kill all of us.

I was in a considerable pickle at that point, for nobody except a few Yąnomamö knew where I was. I couldn't walk out, for that would have taken at least two weeks in the best of conditions, and it had been raining regularly since I arrived. The river was now swelling, and that meant that the land between me and Bisaasi-teri was beginning to flood. We spent a miserable wet night huddling under my small tarp thinking about the problem. I decided that the only way to get out would be by river.

My first scheme was to build a raft, similar to the log palisades the Yąnomamö make around their villages. I had a machete and we set about cutting numerous trees and vines for the raft. At the end of the day we assembled it in the river and, when I stepped onto it, it promptly sank.

The next day we went into Plan II—building a 'trough' of the sort that the Yąnomamö characteristically use when they have ceremonial feasts. They make a bark trough and fill it full of plantain soup, but the same trough is occasionally used by them, when reinforced with a few ribs, as a temporary canoe that is suitable only for floating downstream (Fig. 1–10). It is a kind of 'throw-away' canoe, useful in the kind of circumstance I was presently in. No suitable trees could be found in the immediate area to make such a trough, or at least that is what they told me. They suggested that since I was a foreigner and since foreigners make canoes, why didn't I just make myself a canoe? I explained that it wasn't quite that simple. Canoe making is a complex enterprise, and I was from one of those foreign villages where we had to 'trade' with others for our canoes—we had 'forgotten' how to make them, as they had 'forgotten' how to make clay pots in some villages. They insisted that it was easy to remember lost arts. I said that it took axes to make canoes. They said they had axes at the village. They would not take "No" for an answer, and sent young men running off to the village to fetch the axes. They returned in record time, after dark, with two of the most miserable 'axes' I have ever seen. They had been worn down by years—perhaps decades—of heavy use and were about one third the size they had been when they were first manufactured. But their confidence inspired me, so we set about looking for the largest, pithiest tree we could find—one that could be easily hollowed out for a single voyage. We found one, cut it, and began hollowing it out. It took all day. It looked like a long, fat cigar with a square notch cut into it. We dragged it to the river. I

Fig. 1–10. Woman in a bark canoe. These canoes are occasionally made by the Yąnomamö for a single trip downstream or for fording rivers. After a few days they sag, leak, and deteriorate beyond use.

knew it would roll over as soon as any weight were put into it, so I designed an outrigger system that served also as a pair of seats where the two poles were lashed to the gunwales. I then lashed a pithy long pole parallel to the axis of the canoe (Fig. 1–11). We spent much of another day whittling canoe paddles—three of them. One for Karina, one for me, and one for a spare. They had given me a large number of bows and arrows in exchange for the knives that I had carried in my pack. We loaded these into the outrigger and then climbed in, very gently. We sank. As the water rose to my neck, my last pack of cigarettes popped out of my shirt pocket and floated off in the current. We unloaded the bows and arrows and all nonnecessary items from my pack. I kept only my notes, hammock, food, camera, and a small transistor radio for monitoring Mission broadcasts. With our burden thus reduced, we climbed in again, and to my delight, the water rose only to about half an inch from the gunwales: we could float and stay afloat if we kept perfectly balanced. But the Yąnomamö are 'foot' Indians, not 'river' Indians, and Karina was perhaps the classic example of what that meant. If the Yąnomamö had decided to be river Indians, they would be extinct. We probably swamped and sank 30 or 40 times in the first two days, despite my passionate explanations that it was hazardous to lean too far to the right or the left when paddling.

It still amazes me that we managed to make it all the way back down to the spot where we had earlier left the large canoe, and amazes me even more that Bäkotawä had left the large canoe there as he passed by, for he had stopped at every place and collected my stores of gasoline in his voyage downstream.

Eventually, we made it back to Bisaasi-teri, much to the genuine relief of Kąobawä and Rerebawä, who had assumed the worst. Bäkotawä had gotten back several days before we did, and there was much anxiety in the village about our safety. I knew it would have been disastrous to hunt Bäkotawä down when I returned, for my mind was full of very hideous and vindictive plans for his future. In anthropological jargon, I wasn't in a very relativistic mood. We eventually had our predicted confrontation, the details of which I have discussed elsewhere (Chagnon, 1974). He is alive and well yet today, as far as I know, but he doesn't go on trips with me anymore.

That is what it is sometimes like to meet an uncontacted tribe of South American Indians. Other experiences I have had were much less fun and far more dangerous, for my hosts very nearly succeeded in killing me as I slept (Chagnon, 1974: Chapter V). While I was prompted to go into uncontacted Yąnomamö villages by scientific questions, the larger human drama ultimately became the more significant dimension of the ventures. It is now, after all is done, very satisfying to reflect on what I did, even though at the time it was risky. It is also very sad that this frontier is disappearing and, when it does, we will forever after be unable to ask certain kinds of important questions or, worse yet, will have that hollow feeling that an epoch in our species' history has ended.

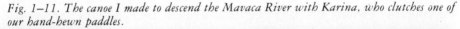

Fig. 1–11. The canoe I made to descend the Mavaca River with Karina, who clutches one of our hand-hewn paddles.

2/Cultural Ecology

People everywhere must come to grips with the physical environments within which they live in order to survive and reproduce offspring who carry on their traditions. The physical environment, however, contains not only lands, forests, resources, and foods, it contains many other things as well. Perhaps one of the most compelling ingredients in the environment is other people: from the vantage of members of a particular community—a village, for example—the world beyond has both a physical and a sociopolitical dimension, and one must come to grips with both. Anthropologists usually discuss this process as cultural adaptation: the social, technical, and ideological means by which people adjust to the world that impinges on them. Much of that world is ontologically 'real' in the sense that an outsider from a different culture can 'see' and document it in a fashion that can be verified by other observers. But much of it lies hidden in the minds of the observed natives, whose cultural traditions, meanings, and assumptions infuse it with spirits, project into it meanings, and view it in a way that the outsider can only discover by learning the language and, through language, the intellectual dimensions of culture. This chapter explores Yąnomamö adaptations to the natural dimensions of the environment and how people 'make a living' in that environment. More important, it explores the relationship between ecology, culture, and village dispersion over the landscape, describing how the Yąnomamö settlements fission and relocate in new areas. This process clearly must have been of enormous significance in our own culture's history when agriculture was developed and led to the rapid growth of populations, an event that we now call the "agricultural revolution." What we can learn from studying the Yąnomamö settlement pattern process can shed light on our own population's early history, a history we know now only through archaeology.

The next chapter will consider the 'intellectual' dimensions of how the Yąnomamö cope with their world through myths and ideology.

The Physical Environment

Kąobawä's village is located at the confluence of the Mavaca and Orinoco Rivers, the Mavaca being a relatively large tributary of the latter. His village lies at an elevation of about 450 feet above sea level on a generally flat, jungle-covered plain that is interrupted occasionally by low hills. None of the hills qualify as mountains, but in some areas the terrain is very rugged and hilly and difficult to traverse on foot. Most of the rivers and streams begin in the hills as

42

tiny trickles that are dry at some times of the year but dangerous torrents at other times. A sudden heavy rain can have a dramatic effect on even larger streams, and the Yąnomamö therefore avoid larger streams when they select garden and village sites. The Yąnomamö are 'foot' Indians as distinct from 'river' Indians, a basic cultural division in the Amazon Basin.

While the hills do not qualify as mountains, they do reach heights of 3000 feet in some places. Almost all of them are covered with jungle, but to the east of Kąobawä's village, in the Parima 'mountains', relatively large natural savannas occur at higher elevations, and one finds Yąnomamö villages there as well. Much of the lowland area is inundated during the wet season, making it either impossible to travel there or unwise to locate a village and garden there.

The jungle is relatively dense and contains a large variety of palm and hardwood trees. The canopy keeps the sunlight from reaching the ground, and on overcast days it can be very dark and gloomy in the jungle. Scrub brush and vines grow in most areas, making travel by foot difficult. Along the rivers and streams where the sunlight can penetrate to the ground, luxuriant vegetation grows, a haven for many kinds of birds and animals.

Trails and Travel   Yąnomamö villages are scattered irregularly, but usually thinly, over this vast tropical landscape. Distances between the villages can be as short as a few hours' walk to as much as a week or 10 days' walk, depending on the political relationships between the groups. Warfare between villages generally keeps them widely separated, while alliances of various sorts (see below) and descent from common ancestors tend to reduce the distance, but there are exceptions.

All villages have trails leading out into the jungle and to various villages beyond. Many trails simply go to the gardens that surround the village and terminate there. A Yąnomamö trail is not an easy thing to see, let alone follow, particularly a trail that is used only sporadically. Most of them wind through brush, swamps, rivers, and hills, but tend to be quite direct. Annoyingly so at times, as when they go straight up a steep hill to the peak, and then straight down the other side—instead of following more convenient terrain that the anthropologist might have chosen.

It takes experience to recognize a Yąnomamö trail. The most certain spores are the numerous broken twigs at about knee height, for the Yąnomamö constantly snap off twigs with their fingers as they walk along. Another frequent sign is a footworn log across a stream or ravine, usually so slippery that at first I had to shimmy across them on hands and knees while my traveling companions roared with laughter. Most Yąnomamö trails cross streams and rivers, often going for several hundred feet in the river itself. It is easy to get lost on these trails, for it is never obvious when the trail leaves the stream and continues across land.

Friendly neighbors visit regularly, and the most commonly used trail from Kąobawä's village went south, to the two friendly Shamatari villages: Reya-boböwei-teri and Mömariböwei-teri. Hardly a week went by during the dry season without someone, usually small groups of young men, going from one of the Shamatari villages to Bisaasi-teri or vice versa. Young men can make the trip easily in one day, for they travel swiftly and carry nothing but their bows and arrows. A family might also make it in one day if it kept on the move, but it would be a dawn-to-dusk trip if the women had to carry their babies or items they or their men planned to trade. Should the whole village decide to visit, it might be a two- or three-day trip, depending on how anxious they were to reach the village. On one occasion, Kąobawä invited me to accompany his entire village on a trip to Mǫmaribȫwei-teri. I packed my supplies carefully and left with them. We walked about 20 minutes inland, to the south, and stopped to let the women and children rest. Much to my surprise and chagrin, that is where we made our first night's camp! We were barely outside their garden! It would have taken them at least a week to reach their destination at that pace, so I simply went on with a young man to guide me, spent a day and a night visiting, and returned home before the Bisaasi-teri even reached the village.

On this trail, and many others like it, there are numerous temporary 'camping places' along the route, a collection of dilapidated pole huts in various stages of decay where earlier visitors spent a night. These huts can be put back into repair in a few minutes by simply replacing the dry, leaky roof leaves, but the whole structure can be built from scratch in about 15 minutes.

Walking entails certain kinds of risks. The Yąnomamö have no shoes or clothing, so thorns are always a problem. A party of 10 men can rarely go more than an hour without someone stopping suddenly, cursing, and sitting down to dig a thorn out of his foot with the tip of his arrow point. While their feet are hardened and thickly calloused, walking in streams and through muddy terrain softens the callouses and then the thorns can get deeply imbedded.

Snakebite is another hazard. A surprisingly large number of Yąnomamö die from snakebites, and almost everyone, if he lives long enough, eventually gets bitten by a snake.[1] Most bites are not fatal, although all are painful. I treated several nonfatal bites with antivenom during my work, but no case was very serious. A few bites can be severe enough to cause the loss either of the limb or its use. One of my Yąnomamö friends lost his leg some 15 years prior to my fieldwork—it just rotted away and fell off. He hopped around rather effectively on his remaining leg. Snakebites are almost as frequent in the garden or near the village as they are on the remote trails, and one must always be careful when picking up firewood from the pile or wandering around in the garden. The Yąnomamö try to keep the garden and paths weeded with this in mind.

In Kąobawä's area, most travel between villages is done from September through April, the dry season. During the wet season, substantial portions of the trail are under water and small 'lakes' replace the swampy lowlands. Communication between villages nearly ceases at the peak of the rainy season and most villages are isolated from most outside visits at that time. Streams that were mere trickles in March become raging torrents in May and June. If the group must travel in the wet season, it will make simple pole-and-vine

[1] I eventually compiled statistics on causes of death of adult Yąnomamö (see Chagnon, 1974:160, for statistics).

Fig. 2–1. Clay pots were common when I began my fieldwork, but these have been almost completely replaced by aluminum ware that is traded from village to village.

bridges over the smaller streams, but will have to avoid large streams altogether and make wide detours around them. These bridges are essentially a series of "X" frames linked together with long poles (where the legs of the X cross) and vine railings. Generally a gap of 10 to 15 feet separates each X until the stream is bridged. Bridges are usually washed out within a few weeks, but occasionally a few of the poles will last into the dry season. In any case, they are not expected to last very long.

Technology Much of Yąnomamö technology is like the pole-and-vine bridge just described: crude, easy to fashion from immediately available materials, effective enough to solve the current problem but not destined to last forever. Perhaps the only durable artifact that an archaeologist would readily find in ancient, abandoned sites is the crude, poorly fired clay pot traditionally used by the Yąnomamö (Fig. 2–1). It is nearly an inch thick at the bottom and tapers to almost nothing at the rim. It is undecorated, very fragile, and pointed at the bottom. Women, who are considered clumsy by the men, are rarely allowed to use them. The pots are often used to prepare food for a feast—and men do all the food preparation for that. The pot is made by the 'coil' technique and fired by simply stacking brush and wood around it. When it breaks, usually relatively soon after being manufactured, the pieces are used by the men as a grinding surface for preparing their hallucinogenic snuff powder. Clay pots were relatively common when I first began my field research, but have almost completely disappeared now. As we shall see below, only the members of a few villages made the pots and traded them to their neighbors.

Yąnomamö technology is very direct. No tool or technique is so complex that it requires specialized knowledge or raw materials, and each village, therefore, can produce every item of material culture it requires from the immediately available resources the jungle provides. Nevertheless, some 'specialization' in manufacturing and trade does occur, but the establishment of political alliances has more to do with this, as we shall see, than the actual distribution of resources: people create 'shortages' in order to have to trade with distant neighbors. Yąnomamö technology could almost be classified as that which would be more characteristic of hunters and gatherers, but the Yąnomamö are in fact horticultural.

Bowstaves, some 5 to 6 feet long, are always made from palm wood. One species grows wild, and the other, and preferred kind, is cultivated for its fruits. The wood of both is very dense, brittle, and hard. One cannot, for example, drive a nail into it. Bowstrings are made from the fibers of the inner bark of a tree. The bark is twisted into thick cords by rolling the fibers vigorously between the thigh muscle and the palm of the hand; the cords are so strong that one can use them, in a pinch, as hammock ropes. The bowstave is painstakingly shaped by shaving the stock with the teeth of a wild pig: the lower projecting teeth of this pig are worn razor sharp from eating, and the entire mandible is kept as a wood plane for making bows. The completed bow is oval or round in cross-section and is very powerful—comparable in strength to our own hunting bows. With age and use, they become brittle and often shatter when drawn too hard.

A pencil-shaped splinter of palm wood is also used for one type of arrow point: the curare-poisoned *husu namo* point. The splinter is weakened at about 1-inch intervals along its length by cutting partially through the wood; this causes it to break off inside the target, allowing the curare to dissolve in the bloodstream. While it is primarily used to hunt monkeys, it is also used in warfare. A monkey can pull an ordinary arrow out, but it cannot pull out a point that is broken off deep in its body. The curare gradually relaxes the monkey, and it falls to the ground instead of dying high in the tree, clinging to a branch. The Yąnomamö carry several extra curare points in their bamboo quivers, for they break off when they strike anything, and usually must be replaced after every shot. These arrow points are manufactured in large bundles—50 or 60—in several villages near Kąobawä's, and are prized trade items (Fig. 2–2). The poison comes from a vine that is leached in hot water; other vegetable ingredients are added to make it 'sticky' so it adheres to the wood. Men often wrap a leaf around the poisoned point to keep the rain from dissolving the poison as they travel. In some areas, other vegetable poisons are used, one of them being an hallucinogen. In a pinch, the men can scrape the poison off and get high by snuffing it deeply into their nostrils.

Fig. 2–2. Man painting curare poison on palm-wood arrow points. The poison is leached with hot water and painted on in many coats over glowing embers. The water is evaporated, leaving a sticky poison coating.

The arrow-point quivers—*tora*—which all men have dangling in the middle of their backs, are made from a section of bamboo, usually about 2 inches in diameter and about 15 to 18 inches long. A natural joint in the bamboo serves as the bottom; the open top is covered with the skin of some animal, usually a snake, monkey, or jaguar. The bamboo grows wild in large stands and some villages are known to 'specialize' in trading bamboo quivers. The quiver usually contains several arrow points, fibers, resin, and strings for repairing arrows and, occasionally, a magical charm. A piece of old bowstring is used to hang the quiver around the neck, whence it dangles in the middle of the back. A pair of *tomö nakö* (agouti-tooth) 'knives', used to trim the lanceolate-shaped, broad, bamboo arrow point—*rahaka*—is attached to the outside of the quiver, as is, occasionally, a fire drill made from the wood of the cocoa tree. One piece of cocoa wood, about 10 inches long and lanceolate shaped, contains several holes along the edges worn into the wood by the friction of the longer circular piece of wood that is rapidly spun between the palms of the hands. The lower piece is held secure by the foot, the other spun into it until the friction produces the glowing dust that is quickly fed tinder until a fire starts. Men sometimes work in pairs to generate fire with the drill, taking turns: as one finishes his downward spinning with his palms, the other starts at the top, and so on. The drill is wrapped in leaves to keep it dry. Today, matches in enormous quantities are provided as trade goods in those villages that have contact with outsiders, and these are traded far inland. Like the clay pot, fire drills are rapidly disappearing, even in the most remote villages.

Arrows are made from 6-foot-long shafts of cultivated cane. They are often assumed to be "spears" by people who see them in photographs.

Two long black feathers from the wing of the *paruri* (wild turkeylike bird) are attached as fletching in such a way as to cause the arrow to spin when shot. A thin fiber from a cultivated plant is used to attach the fletching, but white cotton thread traded in from missionaries is now commonly used in some villages. A nock is carved from a piece of hardwood, using the small agouti-tooth 'knife'. The nock looks like a golf tee when completed, except that it has a notch in it for the bowstring. It is stuck into the shaft behind the fletching and fastened with pitch and fine fibers wrapped tightly around the arrow shaft.

Three arrow points are commonly used and are interchangeable; 'spares' are often carried in the arrow-point quiver. The most effective point for killing large game such as tapir is a lanceolate-shaped point made from a section of bamboo. These are often painted with red, black, or purple pigments and some of them acquire a reputation and history if they have been used to take many animals or have killed men. These histories are recited in some detail when the point is traded to another owner, and much raising of eyebrows, clicking of tongues, and expressions of amazement accompany the transaction as the new owner praises his trading partner's generosity in divesting himself of a property so valuable and lucky. Bamboo points are fastened to the arrow shaft by simply pushing one of the sharp ends into the pith of the arrow cane as far as it will go, usually about one-fourth of the length of the point itself. The arrow shaft is prevented from splitting during this procedure by binding it tightly for about an inch or so with fine cord. The second most useful and effective arrow point is the curare-smeared, pencil-like palm-wood point (Fig. 2–2). These are weakened by cutting nearly through them every few inches or so along the axis, causing them to break off inside the animal, thus enabling the curare to dissolve and eventually kill the animal. The third kind of point is barbed and is used primarily for bird hunting. The barb is made from a sliver of bone, often a monkey bone. The barb prevents the arrow from coming out of the bird, and the weight of the shaft plus its unwieldiness keep the bird from flying away. A fourth kind of arrow point is made from a twig with many branching stems. It is usually fashioned on the spot in a few seconds and discarded after one or two uses. Small birds, often sought only for their decorative feathers, are shot with such points.

The Yąnomamö do not rely extensively on fish, but during certain times of the year fish are abundant and easily taken. One method is to simply wait for the rainy season to end. Then, areas of the jungle that have been flooded by the overflowing rivers begin to dry out, leaving pools of fish stranded. As the pools get shallow, it is a simple matter to wade into them and catch dozens of fish by hand.

Fish poisons made of wild lianas are used to poison small streams (Lizot, 1972). The men put the poison into the water upstream from where a small, mud dam has been made, and wait for the fish to become stupefied. They float or swim clumsily to the surface, stunned by the poison, where the women and girls scoop them up by hand or with large circular baskets (Fig. 2–3), biting the larger ones behind the head to kill them. Sometimes the women get shocked by eels while fishing, and the eel must be found and killed before the work continues.

The Yąnomamö use a splinter of a kind of reed—*sunama*— to shave their heads bald on the top and to trim their 'pudding bowl' bangs. A sliver of this reed is wrapped around the finger and scraped on the scalp, neatly cutting the hair off with no more discomfort than what would be associated with shaving

Fig. 2–3. Women collecting stunned fish with baskets in a small stream that has been dammed with brush and mud. The men put barbasco poison in the water upstream to stun the fish and the women catch them.

with a dullish razor blade. Men with large deep scars on their heads acquired from club fights present a somewhat grotesque image, especially when they rub red pigment on their scarred bald scalps. This enhances and exaggerates the scar and draws attention to it.

The size of the tonsure varies markedly from area to area. The Shamatari, for example, sport relatively small tonsures, about 3 inches in diameter. The Yąnomamö north and east of Kąobawä's village shave so much of their head that they look like they have just a narrow fringe of hair, like a black strap, wrapped around their heads just above the temples. Women wear the same hair style as men. If head lice become extremely noisome, they shave their heads completely, for it takes a considerable amount of time to 'groom' (delouse) someone. While grooming someone is also an expression of affection and friendship, it can become a tedious job. Children, in particular, are often shaved when lice become too much of a problem for parents to handle (Fig. 2–4). Amusingly, the Yąnomamö get 'revenge' on the lice by either eating them, or biting them to kill them. I recall the time when I was in elementary school that the county nurse had to come to school to delouse all the students, whether or not all of us needed it. Head lice are not all that far behind in our own culture's sanitation problems.

Hallucinogenic Drugs The jungle provides several highly prized plant products that are used in the manufacture of hallucinogenic snuff powders. The most widely distributed source of drugs is the *yakowana* tree, whose soft moist inner bark is dried and ground into a powder. To this are added snowy white ashes made from the bark of another tree. The mixture is moistened with saliva and kneaded by hand into a somewhat gummy substance, which is then placed on a piece of heated pot sherd (or, now, in some villages, the top from a gasoline drum) and ground into a fine green powder. But the more desirable hallucinogen is from the *hisiomö* tree, whose tiny, lentil-sized seeds are painstakingly skinned and packed into 10- or 15-inch-long cylinder-shaped wads and traded over a wide area. The tree has a spotty distribution, and villages located near natural groves tend to specialize in trading *hisiomö*. It is more desirable than *yakowana*, and more powerful. Like *yakowana*, it is kneaded with ashes and saliva and then pulverized into a green powder on a piece of heated pot sherd. A smooth stone, often a stone ax, is used to grind it into a powder. Several other plants are used to make hallucinogens: the Yąnomamö cultivate a variety of small bushes of the genus *justicia* and snuff these, but they are less potent and less desirable than the other two. All the drugs are referred to by a generic name when they are in powdered form: *ebene* (Chagnon, LeQuesne, and Cook, 1971).

The men usually make a batch of *ebene* every day; sometimes several different groups of men in a village each make their own batch. It takes quite a bit of kneading and grinding to produce a half cupful, enough for several men, depending on appetites and whether it is *hisiomö* or *yakowana*. The men paint themselves elaborately with red pigment, put on their fine feathers, and then gather around the front of the house of the host. A long hollow tube is used to blow the powder into the nostrils. A small amount, about a teaspoonful, is pushed by finger into one end of the tube to load it. The other end, to which a large, hollowed seed has been fashioned as a nostril piece, is put into a companion's nose. The green powder is then blown into the nasal cavity with a powerful, long burst of breath that starts slowly and terminates with a vigorous blast (Fig. 2–5). The recipient grimaces, chokes, groans, coughs, gasps, and usually rubs his head excitedly with both hands, or holds the sides of his head as he duck-waddles off to some convenient post where he leans against it waiting for the drug to take effect. He usually takes a blast of *ebene* in each

Fig. 2–4. Children delousing each other during a break from playing. Sometimes head lice become so numerous that it is simply easier to shave the children's heads bald.

Fig. 2–5. Blowing ebene *powder into another man's nostrils. The initial pain is severe, but the effects are eventually pleasant.*

nostril, sometimes two in each, and 'freshens' it with more blasts later. The recipient immediately gets watery eyes and a profusely runny nose—long strands of green mucus begin to drip from each nostril. Dry heaves are also very common, as is out-and-out vomiting. Within a few minutes, one has difficulty focusing and begins to see spots and blips of light. Knees get rubbery. Profuse sweating is common, and pupils get large. Soon the *hekura* spirits can be seen dancing out of the sky and from the mountain tops, rhythmically prancing down their trails to enter the chest of their human beckoner, who by now is singing melodically to lure them into his body where he can control them—send them to harm enemies or help cure sick kinsmen. (See the film *Magical Death*, listed in Appendix A, for a dramatic documentary of drugtaking and shamanism.)

Trade in *hisiomö* seeds was unexpectedly interrupted by changing warfare patterns while I was conducting field research in Kạobawä's village. The response to this by some individuals was fascinating, for it illustrated the kind of ingenuity that must lie behind the whole process of plant domestication. Rerebawä, who had grown very fond of the drug, took it upon himself to make sure that the source could not be interrupted by wars. He made several trips to an area far to the northeast where the tree abounded, and brought many seedlings back with him. Some of them he transplanted in his own village, and others he transplanted in Kạobawä's village. Yet others he traded inland, to men in the Shamatari villages. While many of the seedlings did not survive, some did—and later produced quantities of seeds. Whether or not they will manage to survive a long time in this microclimate remains to be seen, but the fact remains that he did attempt to domesticate a wild species and appears to have had some success at it. The Yąnomamö quickly disperse novel or more desirable varieties of other cultigens through trade, and when they discover such plants in distant villages, they generally try to get seedlings, cuttings, or seeds to bring home to their own gardens. For a while, the new variety or plant tends to be remembered as having come from a particular village, but over time people forget where it came from and tend to adopt the position that they have always had it. It should be recalled that the Yąnomamö are highly dependent on cultivated plantains, a domesticant that was introduced to the Americas after Columbus—yet they believe that they have always cultivated it, and have origin myths about it. Prior to plantains, the Yąnomamö were probably much more highly dependent on several other of their native Amazonian domestic foodstuffs (see below).

Shelter   All house construction materials are collected from the jungle: poles, vines, and leaves. The Yąnomamö make a sharp distinction, as do many humans, between 'domestic' and 'natural', that is, between Culture and Nature. The focal point of this distinction is the village and its surrounding garden. Things found here are *yahi tä rimö*: of the village, Culture. All else is *urihi tä rimö*: of the forest, Nature.

The village may be constructed of 'natural' things, but it becomes 'cultural' through the intervention of human effort and the transformation such effort entails. The permanent house and its central plaza is called the *shabono* and is probably one of the most labor-intensive products in the entire culture. A high degree of planning and cooperation is necessary to build a village, not to mention many days of work. Unfortunately, the *shabono* only lasts a year or two because the leaves begin to leak or the roofing becomes so infested with roaches, spiders, and other insects that it must be burned to the ground to get rid of them. The roaches can become so numerous that a constant buzzing noise can be heard, increasing in intensity when someone's head passes close to the roofing and alarms the bugs, or when someone places something—bows and arrows—into the roof thatch. Kąobawä's village was so infested at one point that every time someone would move, dozens of roaches would fall from the roof and scurry away. The roaches can get as large as small birds or be so tiny that they can manage to get between the elements in your camera lenses. For some reason, they just loved my Sony shortwave radio.

The *shabono* looks like a large round communal house to the untrained eye, but in fact it is a coordinated series of individual houses (Fig. 2–6). Each family builds its own section of the common roof. The men usually do the heavy work of fetching the poles for the frame, placing them into the ground or overhead, and weaving the thousands of leaves that go into the thatch. Women and older children also help in the thatching, as well as in gathering the necessary leaves and vines that constitute the major items in building the structure. If it is palisaded, the men do this heavy work.

Fig. 2–6. A small Yanomamö village from the air, located near the edge of the plantain garden and the Demini River.

The first step in building a new *shabono* is selecting the proper site. If the *shabono* is simply being reconstructed after burning the old one, the location might be either on that same spot, or a few yards away—as long as it is not in a depression and likely to be flooded in the rainy season. If it is a new location entirely, the primary consideration is the location of enemies and allies, and then, secondarily, the suitability of the land for gardens.

The four main posts of each house are sunk into the ground by digging holes with a stick and scooping the dirt out by hand. Two short poles, about 5 feet high at the back of the house, are set and then two long poles, about 10 feet high, are placed at the front. Front and back poles are about 8 to 10 feet apart to accommodate hammocks, which also determine how far apart the two front and two back posts are from each other.[2] Cross poles are then lashed to these, horizontal to the ground, near the tops of the upright posts. Long slender saplings are then placed diagonal to these, about a foot to 18 inches apart, and lashed to them with vines. These saplings are 20 to 30 feet long, and run from near ground level at the rear of the house, arching up, bending under their

[2]See my 1974 publication, which gives exact dimensions of a large Yanomamö *shabono* (Chagnon, 1974:257).

own weight into a gentle arc, and are 15 to 20 feet off the ground at their tips. Vines are then strung between the long saplings, perpendicular to them, about every 12 inches. These hold the long-stemmed leaves most often used in roofing—*bisaasi kä hena*, whence comes the name of Kạobawä's village, Bisaasi-teri: roofing-leaf people. Thatching work begins at the bottom of the roof. A long-stemmed leaf is slid under the second vine and bent over until it reaches down and rests on the first vine (Fig. 2–7). Another is placed a few inches away, bent over, then another, and so on. When one row that runs the entire length of the individual house is finished, a second, higher row is started. As the roof progresses, scaffolding made of poles and vines is erected to facilitate the work. The weight of the leaves bends the saplings even more, and support poles are added to hold up the overhang when the roofing is nearly completed. When club fights break out in the village, these support poles are often ripped out and used as clubs—and the roof often sags and breaks when this happens.

When each house is finished, the effect is a circle of individual houses, each separated from the next one by a few feet of open space. These spaces are then thatched over, and the village looks like one continuous circular roof surrounding the open plaza. Occasionally there will be an unroofed gap of a few feet to a few yards, and sometimes there will be a section of the village that is not connected to neighboring houses at either end. This makes the village appear to be composed of discrete sections, as it is, but the sections usually are not separated by open space in Kạobawä's area of the tribe. Elsewhere, to the north and east, Yạnomamö villages are seldom unified structures such as the kind just described. There, the individual sections of the village might even be double-gabled, that is, have double-pitched roofs on each house. This feature could possibly be introduced from the outside, since the Yạnomamö on the north and northeast periphery of the tribe have had much more contact with either the Ye'kwana (Carib-speaking Indians who have had long-term contact with European culture) or missionaries among the Ye'kwana.

The physical size of a village is a function of two important variables, at least in Kạobawä's area. First, and most obvious, the village is a function of how many people there are in the group. Because warfare is more common in this area of the tribe, villages tend to grow to a fairly large size before they can fission. They must contain at least 80 to 100 people in order to be able to fission, but they will sometimes grow much larger, as we will see in the next chapter. Obviously, a village with 400 people has to be larger than a village with 40 people. The second determinant of the physical size of a village is politics—the extent to which members of a village must enter into alliances and regular visiting with neighboring groups as part of their political strategy. This is a necessity in Kạobawä's area, and alliance obligations require that you invite all the members of your ally's village to visit you. To accommodate them, your village has to be physically larger than the space requirements of the permanent residents. Thus, the physical dimensions are such that accommodating an extra 100 or so visitors is not an impossibility. In a word, where alliances between villages are an inherent part of the political strategies of the

Fig. 2–7. Thatching the shabono *roof with leaves from the* bisaasi kä *hena plant.*

Yąnomamö, a village that housed 80 people would be physically larger than a village that housed 80 Yąnomamö in a part of the tribe where alliances of this sort were less important.

Elevation, and therefore temperature, also affect village construction. I visited Yąnomamö villages in the Parima highlands for several weeks in 1967, some of which were located at about 2500 feet elevation. I was puzzled by the fact that the *shabono* had large masses of banana leaves hanging down—almost to the ground—from the high point of the roof. I discovered why they did this on the first night I slept in such a village. The air temperature dropped to about 60 degrees Fahrenheit, and with the high humidity it felt like it was 40 degrees! The banana leaves kept the rising heat from the hearths from escaping too rapidly, but, unfortunately, also prevented the smoke from escaping. I felt like a smoked monkey each morning. But when you do not have clothing or blankets, you can learn to tolerate a good deal of smoke if it means keeping warm.

A new *shabono* is a pleasant place to be. It is clean, smells like fresh-cut leaves, and has a generally cozy, tidy appearance. It is like being in a new wicker hamper.

The wind, however, can be a destructive problem: it blows the leaves off and, if very gusty, will literally rip the roof off and blow the whole thing into the jungle. To remedy this chronic problem, the Yąnomamö throw heavy branches and poles on the outside surface to help hold the leaves down, but the most common defense is magical. The shamans rush forth and chant incantations at *Wadoriwä, hekura* (spirit) of the wind, pleading and enjoining him to stop blowing. He only cooperates occasionally.

When the Yąnomamö travel to another village or go on extended collecting trips in the jungle, they make a simpler house as mentioned above. It is essentially triangular in shape: two back poles and one front pole. They can erect one of these huts in a few minutes, and a whole group—all members of a village—can create a very homey camp of such huts in about half an hour. The roofing is usually made from the long broad leaf of the 'wild banana', *kediba*, a few of which suffice to make a waterproof roof that will last several days. Travelers run into such huts and simply string their hammocks up in them when it is time to camp, hoping that the roof will not leak. The roof always leaks, and if it rains, people spend most of the night in futile attempts to adjust and readjust the decayed leaves to keep the water out.

Permanent *shabonos* are often surrounded by 10-foot-high palisades if the residents have reason to believe they will be attacked by enemies. The palisade is made of logs, usually palm trees, and is erected a few feet behind the lower part of the roof. The logs are sunk into the ground a few inches and lashed together with vines. It is kept in good repair only if the threat of a raid is high; otherwise, people begin to pilfer the wood to cook with. Both the village entrances and the entrances through the palisade are covered with dry brush at night, the slightest movement of which makes enough noise to wake the dogs, and hence, the residents. Villages without palisades are more vulnerable, but people stack up their firewood under the low end of the roof in such a way that a nocturnal assassin could not easily take a shot at them from that vantage. In the darkness, all people look alike: the Yąnomamö made me stack my pack and any other containers, such as camera cases, against the back of the roof to add some personal safety, explicitly to thwart would-be raiders.

Hunting, Gathering, and Gardening

Wild Foods   The jungle provides numerous varieties of plant and animal food, some seasonal and others available at most times of the year, but access is often limited by rainfall. Groups of Yąnomamö could live entirely off the wild foods in their environment, but such groups would have to be relatively small and chronically migratory. Indeed, most of the villages in Kąobawä's area periodically go 'camping' for extended periods of time, usually breaking up into groups of about 30 or 40 people. During these times they subsist very heavily on wild foods, especially palm fruits and game, and time their camping trips to coincide with the ripening of wild fruits. They remain relatively sedentary at their temporary camps, but they usually 'hedge' their subsistence bets by bringing modest quantities of plantains with them from their gardens. Such camping trips are times of fun and relaxation for the Yąnomamö, for they can take a respite from gardening and delight in varying their diets by living off many kinds of wild produce when it is in season.

Generally, the most commonly taken game animals in Kąobawä's area are two varieties of large game birds that resemble our pheasant and turkey respectively (*mąrashi* and *paruri*), two species of wild pig, several varieties of monkeys, tapir, armadillos, anteaters, alligators (*caiman*), deer, rodents, and a host of small birds. Many varieties of insects, fish, larvae, and freshwater crabs are eaten with gusto and highly prized. In some areas, large snakes are also eaten, but are not considered to be very desirable—anacondas and boa constrictors in particular. Large toads and frogs are also eaten in some regions. Certain species of caterpillars are prized foods, as are the the fat white grubs of the insect that lays its eggs in the pith of palm trees, or the grubs that live in the seeds of many palm fruits. In the Parima area, some groups eat the flesh of jaguars, a habit that Kạobawä and his people consider to be peculiar. On the other hand, Kạobawä's people very rarely eat the flesh of the capybara, the world's largest rodent, which abounds in the lowlands and reaches 250 or 300 pounds: they look like giant beavers, but with no tails. Fish, as mentioned above, are taken in considerable abundance in certain seasons and, as introduced fishhooks and fishline become more common, are becoming increasingly important in the diet of those Yạnomamö who have access to fishing tackle.[3]

The Yạnomamö, in short, exploit a wide variety of animal protein resources and enjoy a high standard of living by world health standards (Neel et al., 1971). As more foreigners come into their area and and take up permanent residence, this situation will change quickly—and already has along the major river ways where permanent missions have been established, whose personnel hunt with guns, lights, and canoes both day and night and seine fish from the rivers with nets. The meat is often frozen in kerosene freezers and dispensed generously to the many visitors who are beginning to flock to the missions to 'see Indians'.

Vegetable Foods   Vegetable foods most commonly exploited by the Yạno-mamö consist of the fruits of several species of palm, fruits of several hardwoods, brazil nuts, tubers, seed pods of the feral banana, and a host of lesser items, including some very delicious mushrooms. Palm hearts can be eaten almost endlessly, and I have joined the Yạnomamö in orgies of palm heart eating in which 40 or 50 pounds among a dozen or so people was not uncommon.

Two of the most commonly eaten palm fruit are called *kareshi* and *yei*. The latter is about the size of a hen's egg, the former about half as large. Both fruits have a leathery skin on the exterior and a very large, hard seed on the inside. Between the skin and the seed is a thin layer of slimy, sticky, stringy flesh, somewhat sweet to the taste, that is sucked and chewed off the seed. The overall flavor of both, however, strongly resembles that of a grade of inexpensive soap, and my throat would often burn when I ate these fruits.

[3]The introduction of canoes and flashlights makes night hunting possible in those villages with chronic contact with missionaries, and the recent introduction of shotguns (after 1965) in these villages makes both night hunting and day hunting very efficient. Alligators (*caiman*), the *amota* (a rodent about the size of a small beaver), and tapir are relatively easily taken at night if canoes, flashlights, and shotguns are available. No shotguns were in the hands of any Yạnomamö in the Mavaca area when I began my field research in 1964. By 1975, members of at least 8 or 10 villages in that area experienced increased contact with missionaries and other outsiders to the point that some 40 shotguns could be found in these same villages. The situation in Brazil is even more dramatic, for used shotguns are so inexpensive in Brazil that they can be used extensively as trade goods, costing about as much as I had to pay in Venezuela for a steel ax head—about $5.00 or $6.00. Needless to say, the introduction of shotguns in some Yạnomamö villages has changed not only hunting patterns, but the warfare patterns as well, as we shall see below.

A third palm fruit, *ediweshi*, abounds in swampy areas. It is a tangerine color, about the size of a large hen's egg, and covered with hundreds of small scales not unlike fish scales. *Ediweshi* fruits look like tiny red hand-grenades. When the dry fruit first falls from the tree, it is very leathery and difficult to peel. The Yąnomamö usually throw the fruits into a pond of water, where most of them usually fall in the first place, and wait for them to be softened by soaking. Then the scaly skin can be scraped off with the fingernails. Underneath is a thin layer of yellowish, soft, sometimes slimy flesh that has a pleasant resemblance to the taste of cheese. It was great fun to go 'hunting' for *ediweshi* fruits with the Yąnomamö. We would probe around the knee-deep muddy water to find the fruit. When we accumulated a half-bushel or so, we would then gather around the pile and eat them and gossip. My general reaction to all the palm fruits just described is that it takes a tremendous number of them to get filled, and the effort required is enormous.

Wild honey is one of the most highly prized foods of all, and the Yąnomamö will go to great extremes to get it. Should someone spot a bee's nest, all other plans are dropped and honey becomes the priority of the day. One can usually assume that when someone returns to the village later than expected, he has been detained because he ran into a cache of honey.

Most honey—and there are many kinds—is harvested by ripping the combs out of the nest, often a hollow tree, and soaking wads of leaves in the liquid that remains in the nest. The honey-soaked leaves are rinsed in water. If nobody has a container with him, a shallow pit is dug in the ground, lined with broad leaves, and filled with water. They dip the combs into the watery pit and eat them, larvae and all. The watery liquid usually has large numbers of larvae and a few stunned bees floating on top, as well as much other debris. They dip the liquid out using cups fashioned from leaves, or, if they have a cooking pot, they pass it around, blowing the debris aside before drinking. Should the nest contain a large amount, they squeeze the honey-soaked leaves onto a pile of broad leaves and wrap it up to take home. Leaf-lined pits filled with water are also used to make other beverages, using palm fruits as the base. The fruits are skinned and kneaded by hand in the water until it is sweet enough, and the beverage is consumed by dipping cupfuls out of the pit.

One of the most ingenious gathering techniques is the process of collecting the large, fat palm-pith grubs. The Yąnomamö fell a large palm and eat the heart. Many days later, they return to the decaying tree and begin chopping it apart to get at the soft spongy pith inside. By then, a species of insect has laid its eggs in the pith and the eggs have developed into large grubs, some the size of mice! In fact, the grub looks like a housefly maggot, but a very large one. As they dig the pith out with sticks they run into the fat grubs, perhaps 50 or 60 of them in a good-sized tree. Each squirming grub is bitten behind its head and held tightly between the teeth. A strong pull leaves the head and entrails dangling from the teeth. These are spit out, and the remainder is tossed, still squirming, into a leaf bundle. Grubs damaged by the digging sticks are eaten on the spot, raw. Leaf bundles containing grubs are tossed onto the coals of the fire and roasted, rendering down into liquid fat and a shriveled white corpse.

The corpse is eaten in a single gulp, the fat enthusiastically licked from the leaves and fingers. I ate a number of different kinds of insects with the Yąnomamö, some of them quite tasty, but I simply could not bring myself to eat the palm-pith grubs. An experienced missionary who tried them said they tasted to him like very fat bacon, but I suppose anything fat that is cooked in a smoky fire would taste that way. The fascinating thing about palm-grub collecting is that it comes very close to being an incipient form of animal domestication, for the Yąnomamö clearly fell the tree with the intention of providing fodder for the insect eggs, and with the intention of harvesting the grubs after they mature to a desirable size.

Another interesting hunting technique has to do with taking armadillos. Armadillos live in burrows several feet underground, burrows that can run for many yards and have several entries. When the Yąnomamö find an active burrow, determined by the presence of a cloud of insects around the entry, an insect that is found only there, they set about smoking out the armadillo. The most desirable fuel for smoking out armadillos is the crusty material in old termite nests, which burns very slowly, producing an intense heat and enormous amounts of heavy smoke. A pile of this is ignited at the entry of the burrow and the smoke is fanned into the burrow. Other entries are soon detected as smoke begins to rise from them, and are sealed off with dirt. The men then spread out on hands and knees, holding their ears to the ground to listen for armadillo digging or movement in the burrow. When they hear it, they dig down into the ground until they hit the burrow and, hopefully, the animal. They might have to make several attempts, which is hard work—they have to dig two or more feet down before hitting it. On one occasion they had dug several holes, all unsuccessful—they even missed the burrow. One of the men then ripped down a large vine, tied a knot in the end of it, and put the knotted end into the armadillo entrance. He twirled the vine between his hands, gradually pushing it into the hole. When it would go no further, he broke it off at the burrow entrance, pulled it out, and then laid it along the ground along the axis of the burrow. They dug down where the knot was and found the armadillo on the first attempt, asphyxiated from the smoke.

Gardening Although the Yąnomamö may spend as much time "hunting" as they do gardening, the bulk of their food comes from cultivated plants. The Yąnomamö were persistently described by early visitors to the region as "hunters and gatherers," but that was a characterization based on misinformation or on the romantic assumption that a tribe so unknown and so remote simply had to exist in the "most primitive" conditions imaginable, and therefore *had to be* hunters and gatherers.[4] Approximately 80 to 90% of the

---

[4]Even more highly informed field researchers have erroneously perpetrated this misconception and have attempted to portray the Yąnomamö as hunters and gatherers to emphasize their 'primitiveness' or their 'pristine' quality, in spite of what their eyes could see. Thus, the Yąnomamö are occasionally referred to by some anthropologists, especially German or German-trained anthropologists, as "wildbeuter" or "hunters and gatherers" (e.g., Zerries, 1954; Wilbert, 1972; Becher, 1960).

food eaten by the Yąnomamö is from their gardens (Lizot, 1971c; Chagnon, 1968a [first edition of this book]), and their political, economic, and military activities reflect this fact in an overwhelming manner. Of their domesticated foods, plantains are far and away the most important item in their diet. To be sure, this horticultural emphasis must certainly be a post-Columbian phenomenon, but it would be reasonable to assume that prior to plantains they relied heavily on manioc, maize, and several indigenous varieties of cultivated tubers (see below).

The Yąnomamö are constantly aware of the potentials and suitability of the regions they hunt as future village and garden sites, for their warfare patterns dictate that they must eventually move their villages to such new areas. When I hunted with them, evening conversations around the campfire would eventually revolve around the merits of this particular area as a potential new garden site. Hunters are the ones who usually discover the regions that will be the future sites of their villages when a long move is required.

Land for a new site should not be heavily covered with low, thorny brush, since it is difficult to clear and burn. The larger trees should not predominate in an area, for too much labor would be required to fell them. Ideally, the new site should have very light tree cover, should be well drained and not be inundated in the wet season. It should be near a reliable source of convenient drinking water. One conception they have about potential new garden sites is implied in their word for savanna: *börösö*. Savanna to them is not merely a stretch of land that is treeless, but a jungle that has widely spaced trees that would be relatively easy to clear for gardening. They occasionally also refer to a potentially useful tract of jungle by the very name they use for a cleared garden itself: *hikari täkä*, a 'hole' in the jungle where a garden exists.

The first operation in making a new garden is to cut the smaller trees and low brush. The larger trees, *kayaba hii*, are left standing until the undergrowth is cleared. Then most of the larger trees are felled with steel axes and left lying on the ground for several weeks so the branches and leaves can dry out. Especially large trees are felled by chopping them down from scaffolds, which are built 10 or more feet above the ground: there the stump is not so thick and less chopping is required to fell the tree.

My older informants claimed that they did not have steel axes when they were younger and had to kill the big trees by cutting a ring of bark off the base of the stump with a crude stone or by piling brush and deadfall wood around the bases of the large trees. They burned the brush to kill the tree, which would then drop its leaves and allow enough light to reach the ground to permit their crops to grow. The dead trees were simply allowed to remain standing. Informants also claimed that making a garden was much more work in those days because a large area would have to be scoured in order to accumulate enough wood and brush to kill the larger trees with fire. Today steel axes are becoming so common that even the uncontacted villages enjoy relatively new ax heads that get traded into them via the intermediate Yąnomamö villages that link theirs to the mission posts whence most steel tools now come. Still, I have contacted remote villages where steel axes were not only rare, but so badly worn from previous use that at least 50% of the blade was gone. The rate at which steel tools and other Western items are now entering the region is nothing short of incredible. One Catholic missionary I knew very well, Padre Luis Cocco, gave the members of his village—some 130 people—over 3000 steel machetes alone in a 14-year period, plus hundreds of axes, aluminum cooking pots, knives, and hundreds of thousands of meters of nylon fishing line and an equivalent number of steel fishhooks. These items were quickly dispersed, through trade, to not only the villages immediately adjacent to his, but far inland to the most remote villages (Chagnon and Asch, 1976). Other mission posts where permanent contact with the Yąnomamö now exists provide large quantities of these same items to the Yąnomamö on both the Venezuelan and Brazilian sides of the border. Before the arrival of missionaries, the Yąnomamö appear to have gotten steel tools from the Carib-speaking Ye'kwana Indians to their north, who have been known to be in contact with Westerners for 200 years. The Ye'kwana, a people who have carried the art of dugout canoe building to a high degree of sophistication, would take trips as far away as Georgetown, Guyana, to trade with the English colonials there—long before Westerners penetrated their area to establish permanent contacts. Whole villages of Yąnomamö would go to the Ye'kwana villages to work for them for several months to earn steel tools and other items, tools that would eventually be traded further and further inland to the remote Yąnomamö villages whose members had never seen the Ye'kwana. A similar relationship between the northern Yąnomamö villages and the Ye'k-wana still exists, a relationship that has occasionally and erroneously been called 'slavery' (see Hames, 1978; Arvelo-Jimenez, 1971, for discussions of Ye'kwana/Yąnomamö political relationships).

I draw attention to the trade in exogenous items for a number of reasons. First, to make it clear that the Yąnomamö have had access to some steel tools for as long as 100 years, perhaps in some areas near the Ye'kwana for longer than that. This might possibly be important in understanding the rapid population growth that I have documented among several large clusters of Yąnomamö villages for the past 125 years—a "population explosion" that might be related to both the introduction of an efficient, productive cultigen—plantains—on the one hand, and steel tools that make gardening much more efficient and productive on the other. Second, I want to emphasize that 'uncontacted' as a description of some villages is a relative term: the residents of such villages might never have seen outsiders, but they and their ancestors might have had some benefits derived from exogenous items that were introduced into the New World by Europeans—such as steel tools and certain cultivated plants. Useful items often spread rapidly between cultures, a process that does not require direct contact, and such items often set about changes in the recipient cultures that transform them into new and different kinds of cultures. Classic examples of this process abound in the anthropological literature. For example, the nomadic equestrian buffalo-hunting cultures of the North American Great Plains region came into existence only after the introduction of firearms via the French and English traders in Canada and the introduction of horses via the Spaniards in Mexico (Secoy, 1953). Prior to this, the cultures of the Great Plains that we emphasize in both our anthropology textbooks and in our theatrical films simply did not exist in any form resembling what we now have fixed in our impressions. Again, many of the dramatic cultural processes and situations that are found in Highland New Guinea and in much of Micronesia and Polynesia owe their form and content to economies based on the cultivation of the sweet potato, a plant that was brought to these areas from the New World *after* the discovery of the Americas in the 16th century. Finally, many traditions and technoeconomic realities affecting Western European culture took form because of borrowed plant crops *from* the Americas. Karl Marx, for example, once mused that the Industrial Revolution could not have succeeded without the white potato, a cheap and efficient food for a large labor force: the potato came to Europe from the Andes. And what would pizza be like without tomato sauce, the tomato being another New World plant introduced to Europe after Columbus? Finally, I emphasize the almost staggering quantity of steel tools being introduced to the Yąnomamö by mission posts to answer a question I often get from sensitive but uninformed students and colleagues who find it morally questionable that I provided some steel tools to the Yąnomamö in order to conduct my field research, questions that often explicitly suggest that I, alone, am responsible for 'changing' or even 'ruining' Yąnomamö culture. The fact remains that the Yąnomamö (and all primitive cultures) will be exposed to acculturation processes in the complete absence of anthropologists, and the anthropologists have no control over this. We enter into the field situation long after the process has begun, and despite conscientious efforts to limit our own participation in it, have little alternative other than to trade exogenous items as part of the cost of being accepted and acceptable to the people we wish to study and understand. It would be almost impossible to enter Yąnomamö culture and not participate in some sort of reciprocity with them, and there is no reciprocal relationship that would not have some influence or impact on them. The only viable alternative to the fear of 'affecting' or 'having an impact on' the culture studied by the anthropologist would be to simply stay home and remain 'pure' while the culture disappears, being able to self-righteously point a finger at those who didn't stay home and who traded machetes for knowledge. But who would provide the ethnographic data that lies at the basis of our discipline if that were to be the proper course? The best that one can do is to simply attempt to minimize one's effects on another culture and try to be as unobtrusive as possible.

Thus, the Yąnomamö clear their trees with steel tools today, often not knowing the provenance of the tools they use or paying much attention to the question in the first place—other than "we got this ax from the Monou-teri" or "that machete came from the Yeisi-teri." They then plant these sites primarily with a crop that was introduced to the New World after Columbus (Reynolds, 1927).

The larger trees are usually felled toward the end of the wet season, although I have seen them do this kind of work at other times of the year, especially when military relationships imposed compelling schedules on them. In general, the clearing of the jungle tends to be a wet season activity and burning of the brush and smaller branches a dry season activity, but Yąnomamö gardening is far less 'systematic' than the slash-and-burn schedules found in many other parts of the world (see Conklin, 1961, for a useful bibliography on swidden farming; and Carneiro, 1960 and 1961, for an excellent analysis of swidden cultivation in the Amazon Basin). An adequate burning of the felled timber can be achieved even during the rainy season, provided that the fallen timber has had two or three days of sunshine in succession to dry it out. Only the smaller branches are burned, along with the brush and scrubby vegetation, and it is therefore not necessary to wait until the large trunks are dry. They are left lying helter-skelter on the ground and serve as 'boundaries' between patches of foodcrops owned by different families and as firewood.

Other Garden Products   Many kinds of additional foods and other nonfood cultigens can be found in most Yąnomamö gardens. Among the more important foods not yet discussed are several root crops. Manioc, a starchy root staple widely found throughout the Amazon Basin, is cultivated in small quantities by most Yąnomamö. They usually grow the 'sweet' variety, that is, a variety that contains little or no cyanic acid, a lethal poison that must be leached from the manioc pulp before it can be eaten (see Cock, 1982). When the pulp of the poisonous manioc is exposed to air, as it is when it is uprooted and peeled, the toxin oxydizes into hydrocyanic acid, related to the substance used in those states that use the gas chamber in capital punishment. The Yąnomamö are beginning to use larger and larger amounts of poisonous manioc in the north, where their villages are found near the villages of the Carib-speaking Ye'kwana, who have diffused both the plant and the proper refining techniques into the Yąnomamö area. In Kąobawä's area, the sweet manioc variety is dominant. It is refined into a pulp by rubbing the roots on rough rocks. The moist white pulp is made into thick 'patty cakes' about 10 inches in diameter, and then cooked on both sides by placing the cakes on a hot piece of broken pottery (Fig. 2–8). Ye'kwana cakes are much larger—up to 3 feet in diameter. In general, the Yąnomamö prefer foods that require little or no processing, a kind of 'take it from the vine, throw it on the fire' attitude that applies to both vegetable and animal food alike.

Three other root crops are also widely cultivated and provide relatively large amounts of calories in the Yąnomamö diet. One is called *ohina*, a South American variety of taro (*xanthosoma*). Sweet potatoes (*hukomo*) are also cultivated, as is another potatolike root known in Spanish as *mapuey* and in Yąnomamö as *kabiromö* or a slightly different variety called *ahä akö*. All these are usually roasted in the hot coals of the hearth, peeled by finger after cooking, and eaten with no condiments.[5]

---

[5]The Yąnomamö make a salty-tasting liquid from the ashes of a particular palm tree on rare occasions, and dip their food into it. It is probably calcium chloride rather than sodium chloride. When the Yąnomamö first taste salt, they detest it and claim that it 'itches' their teeth and gums. They gradually become addicted to it, and beg for it frequently.

Fig. 2–8. Kaobawä's younger brothers preparing packs of food at the end of a feast. These will be given to the guests to eat on their way home. Each pack contains vegetable food—cassave bread in this case—and smoked meat. Yąnomamö cassave bread is smaller and moister than that made by their Carib neighbors.

Perhaps another dozen food items of less importance are grown by the Yąnomamö, but not all of them are found in every garden. Avocados, papaya trees, and hot peppers are among the more important of these.

Several very important nonedible cultigens are also found in all or most Yąnomamö gardens. Arrow cane is grown for its long, straight shafts, which are dried in the sun and made into hunting or war arrows, exceptionally long by our standards: 6 feet. They are light and springy, but can be shot completely through the body of an animal or man.

Without a doubt, the most significant nonfood cultigen in any Yąnomamö garden is tobacco, to which men, women, and children are all addicted. They 'chew' rather than smoke their tobacco, but the chewing is perhaps better described as 'sucking'. Each family cultivates its own tobacco patch and jealously guards it from the potential theft of neighbors—a common problem when someone in the village runs out of tobacco, either by giving too much away to visitors in trade or having his crop fail. It is the only crop I saw in a Yąnomamö garden that is sometimes fenced off to remind avaricious neighbors that the owner is overtly and conspicuously protecting his crop from theft. The fence, a flimsy 'corral' of thin sticks stuck into the ground and laced together with vines, would not prevent theft: it is merely a proclamation that the owner is prepared to defend his tobacco plants with more than the usual vigor. I have even seen some Yąnomamö bury 'booby traps' in their tobacco patches to cause any poacher severe discomfort: very sharp, long splinters of bone were buried, and an unsuspecting intruder would have a painful sliver in his foot for a long time. Addiction to tobacco is so complete that even relatively young children—10 years old or so—are hooked. As a cigarette smoker myself, I can understand their plight when the tobacco runs out. They often 'bummed' cigarettes from me when this happened, but instead of smoking them they wrapped fine string around them to hold them together and stuck them between their lower teeth and gums and sucked contentedly on them, remarking how strong and *nakri* (powerful) my tobacco was. They prepare their own tobacco in a somewhat complex way. It is first harvested, selecting the individual leaves at the peak of maturity. The leaves are then tied together by the stems, 15 or 20 at a time, and hung over the hearth to cure in both the heat and the smoke of the campfire. Once dried, they are stored by making large balls, wrapped in other leaves to keep insects and moisture out. These balls of tobacco are traded to visitors. As needed, several leaves of the cured tobacco are removed from the ball, dipped in a calabash of water to moisten them, and then kneaded in the ashes of the campfire until the entire leaf is covered with a muddy layer of wood ashes. The leaf is then rolled into a short, fat, cigarlike wad, which is often bound with fine fibers to keep it in that general shape. The large wad is then, with conspicuous pleasure, placed between the lower lip and teeth, and the preparer reclines in his or her hammock with a blissful sigh and sucks on the gritty, greenish, and very large wad. They are also very sociable about tobacco: when someone removes his wad and lays it down for a second, another might promptly snatch it up and suck on it until its owner wants it back. The borrower may be a child, a buddy, a wife, a stranger, or, if willing, the anthropologist. Although I occasionally ran out of cigarettes during my fieldwork, I could never bring myself to suck either on a new or a used wad. It should be clear that tobacco usage among the Yąnomamö lends itself very effectively to the rapid spread of viruses and infectious diseases at both the village and regional level.

Cotton is also an important cultigen, for its fibers are used for hammock manufacturing as well as for 'clothing' (Fig. 2–9). One must have a fairly generous interpretation of the last word, since Yąnomamö 'clothing' is largely 'symbolic' and decorative. Indeed, some well-dressed men sport nothing more than a string around their waists to which they tie the stretched-out foreskins of their penises. As a young boy begins growing and maturing, he starts to act masculine by tying his penis to his waist string. The Yąnomamö use this cultural/ontogenic phase to quite accurately describe the age of young boys— "My son is now tying his penis up." A certain amount of teasing takes place at this time, since it is difficult to control the penis when you are young and inexperienced. It takes time to stretch the foreskin to the length required to tie it adequately and securely, and until that happens, it keeps slipping out of the string, much to the embarrassment of its owner and much to the mirth of the older boys and men around. Sometimes older boys and men accidentally get 'untied', causing great embarrassment—for it is like being *completely* naked.[6] A penis string is not comfortable. Take my word for it. Wherever

---

[6]So circumspect are the men about this that in the passion of a serious fight or duel they will cease hostilities momentarily should one of the contestants come untied. There is an amusing scene in our film *Yanomama: A Multidisciplinary Study* (see Appendix A) in which two men are pounding each other violently in a chest-pounding duel. The penis string of one of them comes untied and both, without any discussion, temporarily cease the duel until he gets his penis tied up again, at which point they resume slugging it out. Women, too, are very careful and modest despite the fact that they are dressed no more adequately than the men. Thus, a girl or woman will be very careful when rising from a sitting position, crossing her legs to conceal as well as she can her otherwise naked pubis.

Fig. 2–9. Cotton hammocks are made from a continuous strand of yarn wrapped between two upright posts. Cross 'woofs' are plaited in every few inches.

possible, as at mission posts, the men become rapidly accustomed to wearing short pants or loincloths and these become popular trade items very quickly. Men who wear pants stop tying their penises. It should not be assumed that *all* customs are enjoyed or liked by the practitioners, a topic of anthropological research that deserves far more attention than it has thus far received.

Most cultivated cotton is used for making hammocks. A continuous strand of spun cotton yarn is wrapped around two upright posts until the proper width of the finished hammock is achieved, and then cross-seams are plaited vertically every few inches to hold the strands in place (Fig. 2–9). When this is done, the posts are removed from the ground and the ends of the hammock are tied with stronger cotton yarn, giving a finished hammock about 5 to 6 feet long. Everyone wants to have a permanent cotton hammock, but since they are often given in trade, many people make do with a flimsier, less comfortable hammock made of vines. Women also use cotton yarn to make a small waistband that is quite pretty but covers nothing. Cotton yarn is also used to make armbands and a loose, multistring, halterlike garment that is worn by women crossed between the breasts and in the middle of the back. The women make, for men, a fat cotton belt that looks like a giant sausage; the men tie their penises to this. Men, women, and children wear single strands of cotton string around their wrists, ankles, knees, or chests. Apart from this, there is no other 'clothing'.

Finally, in some villages a variety of magical plants are cultivated, especially by the women. Most are associated with casting spells on others, spells that are often nonmalevolent as in the case of 'female charms' called *suwä härö*. Tiny packets of dusty powder, wrapped in leaves, are used by men to 'seduce' young women. The charm is forced against the woman's nose and mouth. When she breathes the charm, she swoons and has an unsatiable desire for sex—so say both the men and the women. The women also cultivate magical plants in some villages that allegedly cause the men to become tranquil and sedate. It is thrown on the men especially when they are fighting, the intended effect being to make the men less violent.

In villages to the north of Kạobawä's, people allegedly cultivate an especially malevolent plant that can be 'blown' on enemies at a great distance, or sprinkled on unwary male visitors while they sleep. A particularly feared class of these is called *oka* and is said to be blown through tubes at enemies, causing them to sicken and die. Kạobawä's group does not use *oka* but they insist that their enemies do. Their enemies, in turn, disclaim its use but claim that Kạobawä's group uses it. It is one of those harmful practices that you are sure the enemy employs but one that you yourself do not engage in. All Yạnomamö groups are convinced that unaccountable deaths in their own village are the result of the use of harmful magic and charms directed at them by enemy groups.

Slash-and-Burn Farming   Each man clears his own land. Adult brothers will usually clear adjacent portions of land and, if their father is still living, his garden will be among theirs. Thus, connections between males that are important for other social relationships to be discussed in a later chapter are also significant in the distribution of garden plots and land usage. The size of a plot is determined, in some measure, by one's family size and kinship obligations, but some men are poor planners and occasionally underestimate how much land they have to clear in order to plant sufficient food to take care of their family's needs. I once overheard a Yạnomamö headman, who was annoyed that one of the inmarried men in his village chronically had to borrow food from others, scold the man viciously as he inspected his garden: "This isn't big enough for your wife and children!" He warned, "You will have to beg plantains from others if you don't make it bigger! See that tree over there? Clear your garden out to there and you will have enough—and you won't have to beg from the rest of us later!" His tone of voice was such as to make it clear that future begging would be greeted with no small amount of reticence. One mistake is allowed, but persistent ones are not.

Headmen tend to make larger gardens than other men, for they assume a considerable responsibility for entertaining periodic groups of visitors that must be fed. They also contribute much more food to a feast when all the members of an allied village arrive to spend several days. Kạobawä's garden is much larger than those of other men. He is helped by younger brothers in some of the heavy work and by his wife's brother, a man who has no wife or dependent children—largely because he is something of a brute and a bit on the stupid and unattractive side. He is, however, an unflinching supporter of Kạobawä and will work indefatigably to help him garden. This man's son also helped Kạobawä in gardening, for he was eligible to marry any of Kạobawä's daughters, putting him into a relationship in which he 'owed' Kạobawä favors and service. The young man is Bäkötawä, the guide who abandoned me in the headwaters of the Mavaca River when I made first contact with Sibarariwä's group.

When the garden is ready to burn, the brush and smaller branches are stacked into piles and ignited. Other brush is added as it is ripped from the fallen trees. A man might have several such fires going in his garden, and each man burns his garden at a time most convenient for him. Sometimes the fires are placed around the large, fallen timbers, which dries them out and makes them easier to split into firewood, the collection of which is almost entirely the woman's task and the quantities of which are staggering. I had not anticipated that firewood could be such a major concern of the Yąnomamö or any Tropical Forest society, but very large quantities of firewood are needed—for cooking, for keeping warm at night, and for cremating the remains of dead people. Women spend a large amount of daily effort collecting firewood, and try to do so with minimal inconvenience and effort. Thus, a fallen timber in the garden plot—especially a species that splits easily—is jealously regarded and becomes a useful resource. Over time, the more useful large trees are gradually split, broken or chopped into firewood by the women and the garden gets 'cleaner' as it matures. A woman should not take firewood from the garden plot of a neighbor unless invited to do so. Firewood is not only valuable and important to the Yąnomamö, but somewhat to my own surprise, is a strategic resource in many other parts of the world as well (*National Academy of Science*, 1980).

Planting the newly-cleared and burned garden proceeds in one of two ways. If the site is at a considerable distance from the village, a great deal of strategic planning is involved as to crop mixture and maturity of the cuttings that will be transplanted. If the new garden is simply an extension of the old one, a different kind of strategy is involved, for the transport of seeds and cuttings is a small problem.

The Cultural Ecology of Settlement Pattern

Micro Movements of Villages and Gardens   Let us consider the first and simplest scenario of garden extensions. A Yąnomamö garden lasts about three years from the time of initial planting. As the garden becomes overrun with scrub vegetation and thorny brush and foodcrops nearly depleted, an extension is added to the garden by simply clearing the land around the periphery. At this point, the old garden is referred to as an "old woman"—unable to produce anymore. The new extension is called the "nose" and is added onto the "old woman" part as the latter is allowed to fall into disuse. The "old woman" part is also called the "anus" of the garden.

Some anthropologists during the 1950s and 1960s, when the theory of "cultural ecology" first began having a major impact on studies of cultural adaptation, argued that slash-and-burn gardens in Tropical Forest regions such as the kind occupied by the Yąnomamö had to be abandoned simply because the crops exhausted the soil nutrients and new, fresh land had to be brought under cultivation because of this problem. As the argument went, local villages in the Tropical Forest could not exceed a certain size limit, and complex cultural developments were impossible because the generally poor quality of the soils demanded chronic movement and relocation. In the 1950s, an anthropologist named Robert L. Carneiro decided to put this argument to an empirical test, using his own meticulous field research among the Kuikuru of the Brazilian Xingu area (Carneiro, 1960, 1961). His work literally overturned the 'poverty of the soil' argument that purported to account for village relocations in this kind of environment. By measuring crop yields in Kuikuru gardens, testing soil samples for declining fertility, and noting several measurable variables such as acreage required to support an average family or an individual, distance from the garden to the village that cultivators were willing to travel, and how long it took an old garden to regenerate new forest after being abandoned, he showed quite convincingly that Tropical Forest villages larger than 500 people were easily feasible, that villages did not have to move because of soil depletion, and that a high level of horticultural productivity could be maintained in the lands immediately surrounding a typical village. In short, he argued that whatever it was that lay behind the village relocations of tribes like the Kuikuru, exhaustion of soil nutrients was not a very persuasive explanation. Moreover, soil exhaustion could not be convincingly given as the explanation for why villages failed to exceed 500 people, or be used as an explanation of cultural inertia due to low productivity. Indeed, he was able to show that the Kuikuru produced more calories per acre than Inca farmers and did so with much less labor effort (Carneiro, 1961). Few people argue today that settlement relocation in the aboriginal societies of the Tropical Forest of Amazonia can be simply reduced to soil poverty—the issue is much more complex than that and many variables are involved in the decisions that lie behind village movements.

The short movements of gardens by the Yąnomamö can be thought of as "micro" movements and entail either the extension of an existing garden or the clearing of a new garden a few hundred or so meters from the existing garden. In either case, the planting of new crops is relatively easily accomplished, for the seeds and cuttings do not have to be carried very far. The reasons given by the Yąnomamö for making new gardens in this way are similar to those found among the Kuikuru studied by Carneiro and are also documented for other Amazonian cultivators: the vegetation that begins to grow up in maturing gardens is dense and usually very thorny, and therefore very unpleasant and tedious to clear and burn. This must be done by people who wear no clothing, and if you ever have to make your way through such vegetation in the buff, you will immediately understand the wisdom of avoiding such brush.

Figure 2–10 schematically illustrates "micro" movements of Yąnomamö gardening and how adjacent new land is brought under cultivation. Since, as I have described above, the *shabono* must be rethatched every two or three years, the movement of a garden a few hundred yards might also be the

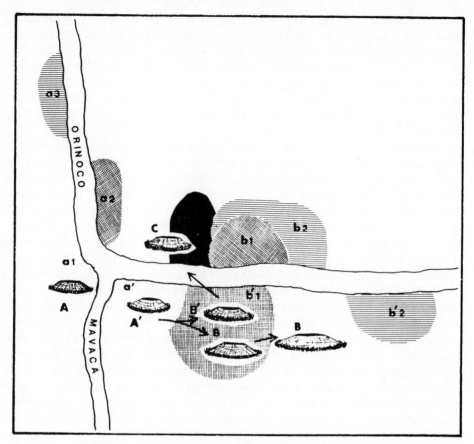

Fig. 2–10. "Micro" movements of Bisassi-teri between 1960 and 1968, showing how new gardens were added as extensions of older ones. When the Bisaasi-teri moved here, there were two shabonos on opposite sides of the Mavaca River, just a few hundred feet from each other (A and A'). Kąobawä's group (A') decided to make two new shabonos (B and B') when they extended their gardens, the first sign of a fission. Eventually one group (B') moved across the Orinoco to begin a separate existence (C). Kąobawä's group remained behind (B) and just a few hundred feet from the two other shabonos (from Chagnon, 1968c).

occasion to move the *shabono* as well—to keep it located conveniently near the food crops.

The Yąnomamö prefer to remain in one *general* area a long time, especially one that has a reliable source of game within a reasonable walk from the village. My research has revealed many cases of the same village remaining in one area for 30 to 50 years, leaving it only when the military pressures on them are overwhelming. A second attraction for remaining in the same general area has to do with the domesticated peach palm trees that produce very large crops of prized fruits every year. They continue to produce long after the garden is abandoned, so the Yąnomamö like to remain reasonably close to old, abandoned gardens to harvest these fruits. This palm is an exception to my earlier generalization that it takes a great many palm fruits to get a full belly.

Peach palm fruits (*rasha*) have a relatively small seed (some have no seed at all) and a very large amount of mealy flesh, about the texture of boiled potatoes, rich in oil, and very tasty. Families usually plant one or several of these trees every time a garden is cleared, and the trees produce very large crops of fruits for many years after the gardens have been abandoned (Fig. 2–11). Thus, by remaining in a general area, the peach palm crops can be easily and conveniently harvested, and yield enormous quantities of tasty, nutritious fruit.

Plantains, bananas, and manioc are cultivated by the generative process, that is, cuttings are transplanted: no seeds are sown. As a plantain 'tree' matures, it sends out underground suckers that sprout, each of which in turn can grow into a new productive 'tree'. Each mature plantain tree produces one bunch of fruits, often very large (depending on variety), and when this is cut, the plant is then useless and it, too, is cut to the ground to make room for the growing young suckers. The suckers are the next generation of plantain, for each will produce a new bunch of fruits at maturity. These can be transplanted when they are very small—a few inches high—or when they are very large—several feet high. The larger they are, of course, the heavier they are. But the larger they are, the sooner they yield their fruit. Thus, a man who wants to have a new crop of plantains soon will transplant large suckers, each weighing 10 pounds or more. But one does not want all the plantains to mature at the same time, for most of them will be wasted. Thus, a good garden has plantains in various stages of growth and nearness to maturity to insure that there will be reliable, abundant food all year long. Probably 80% of the calories from cultivated foods comes from plantains, and the gardens reflect that emphasis in terms of the proportion of land that is given to plantain cultivation. It takes about four months for a large sucker to yield a ripe bunch of plantains— perhaps six months for a small sucker to do the same.

Macro Movements of Villages and Gardens   The warfare pattern waxes and wanes in all Yąnomamö areas. Years may go by in some regions, particularly in the villages along the periphery of the tribal distribution, where no intervillage conflicts occur. In the interior of the tribal distribution, where all villages are surrounded by neighbors on all sides, as in Kąobawä's area, the periodicity of active wars is different in two ways. First, it is rare for long periods of tranquility between villages to occur: several years might pass without shooting difficulties with some neighboring group, but anything beyond that is not common. Second, once hostilities between villages erupts and someone gets killed, the contestants are locked in mortal relationships for many years and do not have the option of migrating away into a new, totally unoccupied area as do the villages on the periphery of the tribe. This essentially means that villages in Kąobawä's area have no choice but to develop political alliances with some neighbors, for it is impossible to move into distant land and escape from enemies, and it is unwise to 'leapfrog' past distant neighbors, for there are other, less known Yąnomamö beyond them who may be more difficult to deal with than one's immediate neighbors. But the distance between Yąno- mamö villages is very large in Kąobawä's area, so relatively long moves can be

Fig. 2–11. Rerebawä climbing a rasha *tree to harvest the fruit. He rests on one "A-frame" and pushes the second one up higher, climbs onto that one, and then pulls the lower one up. In this fashion he painstakingly reaches the top of the 75-foot tree and lowers the fruit bunch with a vine.*

effected—four or five days' walk—in order to escape from enemies and start a new garden elsewhere. I have characterized this situation as *social circumscription* (Chagnon, 1968b) similar in effect to Carneiro's (1961) "geographic circumscription." Carneiro argued that the world's major civilizations—Egypt, Mesopotamia, the Incas, and so on—all developed in regions that were circumscribed by deserts, the sea, or other geographical features that restricted expansion and therefore encouraged increasing intensification of land use within the developing region (Carneiro, 1961). He argued that this leads to increased complexity in social organization. My argument about "social circumscription" is similar, for Yąnomamö villages whose ability to move is restricted by the existence of neighbors on all fronts seem to be somewhat more complex in organization and much larger in population size than those on the tribal periphery where migration to virgin unoccupied lands is not impeded. Carneiro, in turn, adopted the notion of "social circumscription" into his general theory of the origin of the state (1970). The long moves made by the Yąnomamö are not provoked by horticultural techniques or the demands made on gardening from crop type, soils, maturity of gardens, or deterioration of the *shabono*. I call these *macro movements.* They are motivated by politics and warfare and must be understood in this context. The relevant 'ecological' variables here are human neighbors, not technology, economic practices, or inherent features of the physical environment as such. The 'cultural adaptation' in this is not so much to the 'sticks and stones' of the environment, but to one's neighbors.

Figure 2–12 gives a graphic illustration of how a macro move is effected when a group of Yąnomamö must abandon its currently producing garden and begin a new one at a long distance away. It will become increasingly clear why 'alliances' with neighbors is a kind of cultural adaptation that permits the Yąnomamö to have some flexibility in dealing with—adapting to—intervillage warfare and conflict. Chapter 6 describes this pattern in considerable detail, in the context of a specific war and settlement relocation.

The first phase in some macro moves is the recognition that continued residence in the village or area will lead to violent fighting in which someone near and dear to you (or you yourself) will be badly injured or killed—with clubs, machetes, axes, or arrows. All the members of a village might be united and act collectively in a move, the threat or danger being the presence of hostile enemies in other villages, enemies who begin raiding your group chronically and take a small toll per raid, but over time a toll that is significant. The constant fear and worry that raiders might be lurking outside is sufficient to increase the level of anxiety and tension in a village and disrupt the normal patterns of movement and social existence. When raiders are feared, nobody leaves the village alone. Even the women, who must collect firewood and water daily, have to be escorted the few yards to the garden or stream by armed men, who nervously keep their eyes peeled for telltale sounds and movements in the jungle, or the disturbance of birds in the distance, fidgeting with their nocked war arrows as the women collect the wood or water. During these times, people are even afraid to leave the village to defecate, and they are forced to do so on leaves, which are then thrown over the palisade. Several weeks or months of this is exhausting, and life could be more relaxed if one lived elsewhere, a greater distance from the known enemy. In other cases, there might be factions within the village, becoming increasingly hostile to each other, and increasingly violent in their arguments and duels, usually over sexual trysts and infidelity, but once started, easily provoked by snide comments, thinly veiled insults, or any one of a host of trivialities that ruffles someone's feathers the wrong way. As villages grow larger, internal order and cooperation become difficult, and eventually factions develop: certain kin take sides with each other, and social life becomes strained. There appears to be an upper limit to the size of a group that can be cooperatively organized by the principles of kinship, descent, and marriage, the 'integrating' mechanisms characteristically at the disposal of primitive peoples, a fascinating question to which we will return later. Suffice it to say here, kinship-organized groups can only get so large before they begin falling apart—fissioning into smaller groups. This size limit appears to be as much a function of the inherent properties of kinship and marriage alliance as it is a function of 'strategic resources'—the material things that sustain people and permit them to live in large social groups that are sedentary and fixed. One might, in this vein, view the long history of both our hunting and gathering ancestral past, as well as our more recent shorter history as cultivators, as a struggle to overcome the

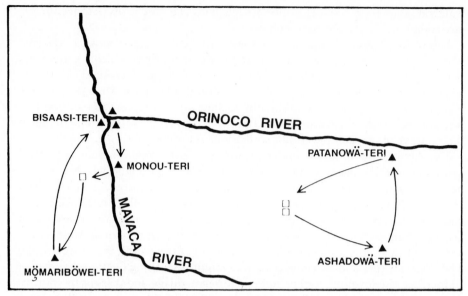

Fig. 2–12. How a new garden and village are established at a long distance (short-term "macro" movements) from the old garden and village (from Chagnon, 1968c).

limitations on group size imposed by the traditional principles of organization that mark most of our history: transcending kinship and adding new kinds of organizational principles. Many general discussions of our social past as hunters and early cultivators allude to the 'magic' numbers of 50 to 200 as the general community size within which our recent cultural and biosocial evolution occurred (see Lee & Devore, 1968), a maximal community size that was only transcended in the very recent past—within the last several thousand years.[7]

Thus, large villages eventually break up and subdivide into smaller villages, usually a bifurcation of the large group into two similar-sized smaller villages, occasionally into three. One of the groups retains possession of the existing, productive garden—or that portion of it that belongs to them—and the other faction must move away to clear, burn, plant, and begin life elsewhere in a new garden.

The distances between the recently fissioned groups can be small or large, depending on the precise nature of the confrontation that causes the fission. Thus, they may simply build two separate *shabonos* located only a few yards away from each other. This solution occurs when it would be hazardous for the larger group to fission and create two small, distantly located villages that would be easy prey to hostile neighbors who might otherwise avoid attacking the larger village or one of the two closely situated splinter villages. Such a solution or alternative is not possible, however, if the final confrontation that

[7]See Briggs (1983) for a summary of the remarkable rate at which large cities have emerged. Carneiro (1970) draws attention to the tremendous significance of the first development of supra local political organization of a nonkinship sort.

determines the split leads to the death of someone. Then, despite the number and determination of other enemies, the group *must* fission into two parts and one of the new groups must move far away and begin a new, separate garden.

Making a new garden from scratch and keeping well fed can be a problem if you must abandon your existing productive garden without warning. If, for example, 100 people from a village of 200 must suddenly pull up roots and immediately leave the group after a fight that led to the death of someone, they have only two choices. Either they can flee to a neighboring village that has been 'friendly' to them in past dealings and 'mooch' off them for several months, or they can tough it out by a combination of living extensively off wild foods and periodic visits to friendly villages where they rest, gorge themselves on their host's cultivated foods, and eventually depart, bringing as much cultivated food with them as they can carry or their hosts are willing to give them. Meanwhile, they are busy clearing a new garden and attempting to get crops producing as soon as possible. Here is where a 'cost/benefit' decision par excellence has to be made, for one must carry by hand all the cuttings and seeds that will be transplanted in the new garden. The issue is essentially a question of an early return of desirable foods, in which case you carry few but large plantain cuttings (Fig. 2–13), or a longer-term security of enduring desirable foodstuffs, in which case you carry larger numbers of smaller, lighter cuttings—but have to wait longer for them to begin producing. A compromise

Fig. 2–13. Plantains are transplanted by cutting 'suckers' from a larger plant. These produce within a few months if they are large, but the larger they are, the heavier. Transporting them a long distance is difficult and energetically expensive.

of sorts occurs with maize—less desirable than plantains, but its seeds are light, easily transported in large quantities, and the maturity time is short—two to three months. Thus, one can quickly get an abundant, early, low-effort crop into the ground in a hurry, have a surfeit of food for a spell, and wait for the plantains to start maturing. I have visited Yąnomamö gardens that had been established under these circumstances, and they are totally different from 'standard' gardens in the sense that the overwhelming fraction of the new garden is given over to maize cultivation. In time, plantains are gradually transplanted in large quantities and the garden shifts from mostly maize to mostly plantains.

The other important variable in such a move, also a function of the Yąnomamö dependence on garden produce, is the direction and precise location of the new site. Neighbors who are friendly are usually willing to provide plantain suckers for transplanting, and if it is impossible to return to the old garden to get such cuttings, the new garden must necessarily be located somewhere within a reasonable distance from a friendly neighbor who will provide the cuttings.

But the combination of variables can be quite mixed and complex. For example, the increase in village tensions might provoke some members of the group to begin clearing a new garden at a long distance away, anticipating the eruption of a fight that will inevitably cause a fission. One can, in short, predict the disaster and plan for it under some circumstances, and get a new garden under production prior to the final confrontation. If it never comes, the new garden is a convenient haven in which to 'camp out', and may serve, ultimately, just that purpose. A more common combination of variables entails a pattern, of the sort schematically represented in Figure 2–12, in which a newly formed fission group can sequentially exploit several human and natural resources: they can periodically return to their original productive garden to rest up, eat voraciously from their ripe crops, and leave, taking both food and cuttings with them, and camp out in their new garden where they work at felling or burning trees or planting crops, living off a combination of transported foods from their old garden and seasonally available wild foods and game. They might even send young men back to the old garden periodically to fetch more food, or to the village of a friendly neighbor, where supplies are begged. The entire group will follow a cyclical pattern of working in the garden, moving en masse to the village of an ally for a fortnight or so, thence to their producing garden, and back to the new garden.

But this pattern involves several kinds of risks. The first one is the risk of being attacked at the old garden or getting into a fight with the members of the group from which yours is now separating. If there were no such risk, the group would not have to move in the first place. The second risk is the dependency that one enters into with the allies who provide food, refuge, or both. The Yąnomamö are quick to take advantage of those who are vulnerable, and the 'cost' of getting food or accepting refuge from allies is usually the expected sexual license with which your wives, sisters, and daughters are treated: disadvantaged groups have to expect that the tendered friendship and support of an ally will invite some sexual advances from men of the allied village. This can be resisted only up to a point, and then one either is no longer welcome in the village or one must be prepared to overlook the chronic attempts of the hosts to seduce the women of the guests. The best solution is to visit allies for as short a time as possible, extract the maximum amount of economic and political aid in the available time, and then repair to either another ally or to one of the gardens, as shown in Figure 2–12.

Once a new garden is established and is yielding crops in a chronic, reliable manner, labor follows a more regular pattern. There is no peak harvest period, for plantains, if planted in the proper fashion, are ripening all year long. Peach palm fruits do, however, ripen all at once and large quantities of them are eaten at this time—February and March. Some trees produce a smaller crop in June and July.

The dry season (September through March) is the time for feasting, visiting other villages, trading, and for many groups, the time for raiding enemies. Garden activities are at a minimum at this time of year, but ambitious families will spend an hour or two each day weeding their gardens, transplanting plantain suckers, and burning small piles of brush and debris. In general, the Yąnomamö—and many other tribal peoples who rely on either hunting and gathering or on swidden agriculture— achieve an adequate, if not abundant, subsistence level with very few hours of work per day (Lee, 1968). So notable is this aspect of primitive economies that one distinguished anthropologist referred to hunters and gatherers as the 'original affluent society' (Sahlins, 1968a, b), stressing the fact that the difference between what they "need" and the "means" for achieving it is very small. In terms of absolute labor given to work this is equally true, for hunters and gatherers like the Bushmen of the Kalahari Desert 'make a living' on only a few hours per day (Lee, 1979) and Yąnomamö productive efforts are about the same (Lizot, 1971b; Hames, in prep.). By comparison, those of us in industrial society are condemned to a life of hard labor and overtime by the forces of the market!

Population and Village Dispersal over Time The micro and macro movements of Yąnomamö villages distribute the population and the villages thinly over the landscape. Immediate concerns for warfare and alliances with neighbors fix the villages with respect to each other at any given point in time as their respective members attempt to 'optimize' their garden and village locations. They want to be as far from active enemies as possible, but as close to current allies as they can be. With each village move, they also try to remain close to their ancient, abandoned gardens so they can continue to exploit their peach palm trees. And they do not want to make moves that entail severe deprivation caused by excessive labor (transporting cuttings a great distance) or catastrophic flight that leads to intense dependence on some erstwhile ally. Finally, some of the choices, as well as the timing of movements, are a function of the demographic properties of the village—especially the number of active, healthy adult males who will live in the new garden and village. These will be discussed in the next chapter.

The longer term patterns that result from the immediate decisions can be determined only by interviewing scores of old people who can recall all the gardens they lived in during their lifetimes and the major events that transpired there. Two of the most important events are the enemy/ally patterns that obtained at that site and the fissioning of larger groups into smaller ones. This information, when added to the genealogical information that links individual to individual by kinship and marriage ties, results in an overall settlement history of many villages, whose members are both historically and genealogically related to each other.

Figure 2–14 graphically represents the historical movements of several 'blocs' of Yąnomamö, based on approximately 125 garden relocations over a period of about 150 years. This is only a fraction of the information on garden relocation in my data files to date, but it is sufficient to illustrate the point that there is a dynamic relationship between population growth in local villages and the dispersal of both populations and the villages into which they subdivide. Figure 2–14 thus summarizes this in schematic terms, showing that it is possible to identify discrete 'population blocs' and describe the long-term migration pattern each follows. Figure 2–14 in fact identifies seven such population blocs (A through G). It is possible that as many as 30 or 40 such

Fig. 2–14. Long-term effects of "macro" movements of seven groups of Yąnomamö over a 125-year period. Populations grow and fission and move into new areas. In time, a given region will have as many as a dozen interrelated villages that derived from the same 'mother' village many years back. Kąobawä's population bloc is labeled "D"; his Shamatari neighbors are "F" (from Chagnon, 1968c).

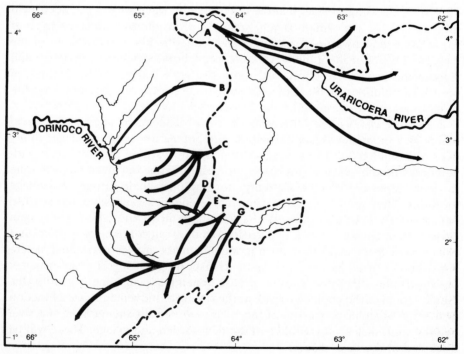

blocs could be identified among the Yąnomamö if the field research were conducted along the lines described here and elsewhere (Chagnon, 1974).

Only two of the seven population blocs shown in the above figure have been discussed above—the bloc to which Kąobawä's group belongs and the bloc that I have called Shamatari. I have designated Kąobawä's bloc as "Namowei-teri," the name of an ancient site where the ancestors of his group and the villages related to his lived nearly 100 years ago (Chagnon, 1974).

The current distribution of most of the villages in these two population blocs is summarized in Figure 2–15, which describes the geographical range of the villages in the two blocs. It is clear that the Shamatari bloc covers a much larger area. Yet the number of villages for each bloc is about the same (seven or eight each). But there are some major differences between them. Shamatari villages tend to be much larger than Namowei-teri villages. They average about 150 people per village, whereas Namowei-teri villages average closer to 80 or 90. Both figures are dependent on the year in which the census is taken, for fissions of large villages drastically alter average size in each population block (cf. Chagnon, 1974; 1975b; 1979a). The general pattern, however, is that Shamatari villages tend to be larger whatever the census year. Shamatari villages are also located much farther apart from each other. This seems to be due to two factors. First, the Shamatari have few neighbors to their south and therefore have more area into which they can pioneer. Second, warfare among the Shamatari seems to be somewhat more intense if mortality due to warfare can be used as a measure of intensity: approximately 30% of adult male deaths are directly attributable to warfare and mortal duels. In the Namowei-teri bloc this figure is about 25% (Chagnon, 1974). Finally, the maximum size to which the Shamatari villages grow is also different. Some of their villages have reached a population of close to 400 people before fissioning, whereas the Namowei-teri villages rarely reach a size of 200. The reasons for these differences appear to have something to do with the marriage and kinship patterns that occur in the two population blocs, patterns that I will discuss in more detail in Chapter 4. For the moment, I will simply suggest here that the differences in village size in the two population blocs is *in part* a function of the difference in warfare intensity, that is, the Shamatari villages grow larger before fissioning due to the slightly higher pressures of intervillage warfare.

The genealogical and settlement pattern information can be summarized in another fashion. Figure 2–16 schematically shows how both population blocs have come into existence through population growth and fissioning of larger villages into smaller ones. The genealogical and historical connections between the existing villages, both determined through field research using Yąnomamö informants, describe how the villages are related to each other. Note that in both population blocs there are 'questions' about other villages. For example, I know that there are other Shamatari villages beyond those I have personally contacted. These are still not known through firsthand visits to them. Still, I have rather complete genealogical data on some of them, at least for some of the older people who are known to live there. How large these

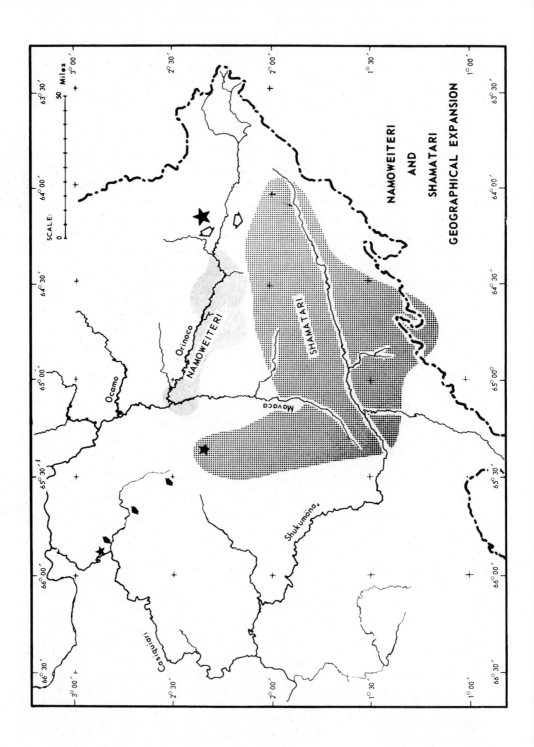

villages are and what the current kinship, family, and marriage patterns are can only be discovered by going there. For the moment, I simply know the villages exist, and where they fit in the political/historical/genealogical diagram given in Figure 2–16.

It should be clear now why a single Yąnomamö village cannot be considered in isolation from its neighbors. It fits into a historical matrix of kinship, descent, and political process. Some neighbors are well-known kin from whom you and your own covillagers separated at some recent point in time. Other neighbors are known to be "shomi"—different. Contact and alliance with these people leads to knowledge and familiarity with them and with their past, and highly advised men such as Kąobawä know a great deal about the history and fissions of the Shamatari villages. They have to, for the past relationships are good clues to what future relationships with them might be. Similarly, highly advised men among the Shamatari know a good deal about the history of Kąobawä's village. As is the case among all population blocs, there have been periods of war and periods of alliance between villages of the two blocs. Ironically, some of the consequences of war—abduction of each other's women— can be turned to advantage when a new alliance with an old enemy becomes a possibility. Men who are the sons of the abducted women use the kinship connection to her relatives in the enemy village as an entree to that village, and are called forth to make the initial visits. Thus, a man who has never seen any of his mother's kin during his lifetime will begin speaking with admiration and affection about his mother's brothers and how desperately he would like to visit these important kin. Through his visit a new period of alliance and peace might begin.

The Great Protein Debate: Yąnomamö Data and Anthropological Theory

The publication of the first edition of this case study in 1968 coincided with the rapidly developing emphasis in anthropology on what is generally known as cultural ecology theory. That theory explores the relationships between culture and environment in the broadest sense, attempting to demonstrate that the environment imposes limitations on the patterns that cultures can evolve and maintain and, in addition, seeks to identify the specific ways that cultures and human populations 'adapt' to their physical environments. The general theory has two components or dimensions. The first has to do with how the various parts of culture—kinship rules, descent rules, residence rules, economic practices, and so on—articulated with each other and 'functioned' to maintain the whole cultural system and how they influenced each other as the system changed over time. The second is borrowed from the field of general biology and has to do with the relationships of animal populations to their

Fig. 2–15. The geographical areas utilized by Namowei-teri villages and Shamatari villages. Much larger distances separate the Shamatari villages from each other and population density is expectedly lower there. Yet the warfare pattern appears to be higher among the Shamatari (from Chagnon, 1974).

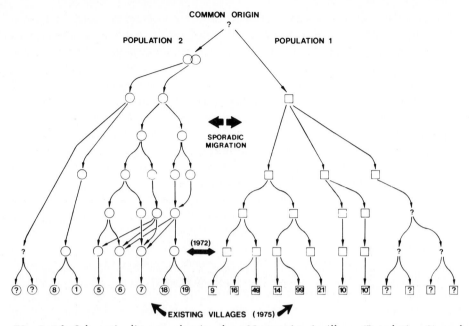

Fig. 2–16. Schematic diagram showing how Namowei-teri villages (Population 2) and Shamatari villages (Population 1) are related to each other historically (from Chagnon, 1979a).

resources and how certain critically important resources limited the growth and dispersal of populations and the densities that they might achieve given the fact that the resources might vary in abundance, predictability, desirability, and reliability. The addition of 'culture' to evolutionary ecology—that is, combining anthropological insights and understanding with general ecological principles—thus amounts to a kind of partial synthesis of anthropology and ecology and to an attempt to combine the best arguments of both.

The major emphasis in anthropology by those who are intrigued by this emerging synthesis is on the limitations or possible limitations that food and other critical resources impose on human population clusterings, the size to which they can grow, the densities they achieve, and the extent to which social and cultural institutions reflect the material (food/resources) substrate that all populations rest on. Most anthropologists would accept the general arguments, logic, and desirability of the cultural ecological approach and most of my own work is built on this general approach.

But the synthesis is proceeding faster and with greater enthusiasm than the facts warrant, and some of the logic is not carefully worked out. In addition, the portions of the argument that are borrowed from biology were borrowed at a time when biology itself was undergoing a major intellectual revolution that dramatically affected the whole field of ecology. One fundamental change in biology was the shift away from the argument that *whole populations* or species 'adapted' to their food and resource base to the argument that *individuals* within the population were the units of adaptation, and that the proper and theoretically most appropriate vantage in ecological studies was the individual and how the behavioral strategies (mating, foraging, social interactions) they adopted affected their personal chances of surviving and reproducing (Williams, 1966; Chagnon and Irons, 1979). In this view, the attributes of the population are the sum of the attributes of the individuals. There is, in short, a fundamental difference between a herd of fleet deer and a fleet herd of deer (Williams, 1966). The *group* is in a fundamental sense a sum of its *individual* parts. This is contrary to much of anthropological, if not philosophical, thinking. The *assumption* that human proclivities and behavior are the product of group selection can no longer be justified in any of the social sciences and this issue must now be reexamined in light of the important new discoveries in theoretical biology (see Williams, 1971, for a readable and comprehensive summary of these issues).

The argument over the 'group' versus the 'individual' perspective in the study of adaptation is now raging vigorously in the field of cultural ecology. Biologists have, however, generally concluded that the 'individual' perspective is the proper one. Whether that will be the ultimate conclusion in cultural ecology remains to be seen and these are very exciting theoretical times in anthropology as this issue is debated and the whole notion of culture is being critically reexamined. If man is 'group selected' it would appear that he is the only living organism for which that claim can be plausibly made. This is an astonishing and staggering claim, and brings us back to the intellectual milieu in which Darwin, in 1858, made the audacious argument that species were not immutable. It is nothing short of a challenge to reassess Man's place in Nature. But Man is the only living organism with culture, and that is the issue on which the debate will probably be resolved, for culture provides man with capacities and capabilities more complex and sophisticated than what other organisms are capable of.

One issue in the theoretical debate has to do with the extent to which 'protein' is the limiting resource par excellence in human cultural adaptations and human social behavior. My work on the Yąnomamö has been caught up in this debate, since some of the variables the protein 'argument' purports to explain are things such as warfare, infanticide, aggression, and population parameters, on all of which I have published extensively. Some of the most useful data needed to resolve the issue is Yąnomamö data, and therefore, the protein advocates have worked especially hard to make the Yąnomamö 'fit' the theory. I have, unfortunately, been less enthusiastic than they about the goodness of fit, since I collected the data and do not believe that it fits. I have also been skeptical about the assumptions and logic of the protein hypothesis because of the monocausal demands it makes, the failure of the data to fit the protein argument, and the devastating contradictions it contains in terms of the recent refinements in *biological theory*. The 'theory' of materialistic cultural ecology will now change radically to conform to its intellectual fount, biology, and Yąnomamö data will be one of the major reasons for this change.

The most prominent champion of the protein theory is an anthropologist named Marvin Harris, formerly of Columbia University, now at the University of Florida. We disagree a good deal and have 'debated' the protein issue publicly on a number of campuses. My data will not change. He refuses to change his protein 'theory'—at least not in one dramatic step. That is called "eating Crow," a high-protein diet eschewed by any concerned scholar. If his protein theory cannot explain the Yąnomamö, one tribe on which precisely the right kind of data exists that is germane to the theory, his theory is in serious difficulty. The Yąnomamö seem to be a critically important test case and thus they play an important role in the modifications that will occur in ecological theory. Although case studies are not usually the forum for explaining theoretical issues in anthropology, the issues are widely known to the public at large through several popular books written by Harris that, in my estimation, carefully edit Yąnomamö data to make the fit look better than it is. For this reason, I am discussing the 'protein' hypothesis in this case study. Students are often better judges of evidence and theory than the passionate advocates who produce both or either.

The argument began when I cautioned the protein advocates that the Yąnomamö did not suffer from a protein shortage and that their warfare (and warfare in any group) was too complex to reduce to a single variable such as protein scarcity (Chagnon, 1974). Professor Harris argued that the Yąnomamö probably were suffering from a per capita shortage of animal protein (Harris, 1974; Divale and Harris, 1976), as did several of his students (Gross, 1975; Ross, 1978). Harris seemed to take issue with my caution, for it challenged the more general proposition that many of the practices anthropologists documented in their field research among tribesmen and other kinds of societies were most likely responses to a scarcity of protein and should be interpreted as "adaptations." These included such things as the practice of female infanticide to regulate population size and thereby avoid overexploiting the game animals, or conducting warfare to keep people out of your hunting areas or adjacent lands that would be 'reserves' for future protein exploitation—or even why Hindus love cows but Jews and Arabs abhor pork (Divale and Harris, 1976; Harris, 1974). It seemed like a neat idea and Harris, as well as several of his students, pushed it as if it were the only or the most 'scientific' theory able to explain many cultural adaptations and the general evolution of culture from time immemorial (Harris, 1974; 1977). The theory began emerging as some of my first publications on the Yąnomamö appeared, and some of my observations were selectively perused to find 'evidence' of a protein shortage among the Yąnomamö. My several cautions were not only not taken seriously, but I soon found that I was some sort of villain for refusing to be 'scientific', to go along with the Columbia crowd and assert that it was all a question of protein shortage. Instead, I persisted in my insistence that this theory—any theory—had to be based on evidence, and none of my evidence on the Yąnomamö suggested that they were suffering from a shortage of protein. My demographic research had clearly demonstrated in a meticulous way that the Yąnomamö population was growing at a moderately high rate, which can hardly be taken as evidence that they had bumped up against the 'carrying capacity' of their environment. Indeed, that is the best evidence that the Yąnomamö have *not* yet reached the carrying capacity (Chagnon & Hames, 1979; 1980).

For most of my early research on the Yanomamö, I collaborated with a large team of very competent and distinguished medical researchers whose thousands of biomedical, epidemiological, and serological observations on several thousands of Yąnomamö led them to conclude that the Yąnomamö were one of the best nourished populations thus far described in the anthropological/ biomedical literature (Neel, 1970). This does not easily lend itself to the interpretation that their diet is marginal or deficient, and such a finding would cause some caution among scholars who might propose a dietary deficiency as the major driving force behind Yąnomamö warfare and infanticide.

As the Yąnomamö gradually came to be a popular 'textbook' culture and cited widely to exemplify specific aspects of tribal practices in general, the protein advocates found it more and more necessary to explain them away. Remarkably, their 'theory' began with the flimsiest of evidence. "Evidence" in the 1960s and 1970s was, unfortunately, rather loosely defined by the would-be "scientists" of the protein school. It often amounted to careful sifting of detailed ethnographic accounts to find suggestive statements about hunger, starvation, deprivation, or bad hunting luck that could, when stacked up in a pile, be used to make a circumstantial case for a 'theoretical' argument. Very often the original ethnographer did not provide statistical facts to accompany his/her statement, but even more remarkably, those who used the statements for 'scientific' arguments themselves never collected such information either. An enormous amount of 'science' was built on a nonempirical, anecdotal base. As one observer described their methods, it was "preemptive" theorizing (Neitschman, 1980). As far as Yąnomamö data goes, the protein advocates insisted that the onus of proof was on *me* to show that the Yąnomamö were *not* suffering from a protein shortage. The argument was that I had not actually weighed and measured the protein intake of the Yąnomamö, and until I had done so, they would refuse to accept my arguments to the contrary. Had they advocated Yak fat, trace elements, heavy metals, salt peter, or the absence of molebdenum in the diet as the cause of Yąnomamö warfare, it would presumably have been up to me to prove them wrong. That is what "preemptive" theorizing means.

To do my part to lay these concerns to rest forever, I agreed to meet with Professor Harris and his several supporters at Columbia University on the eve of my departure to the Yąnomamö in 1974 to continue my research. This expedition would collect, with the aid of several of my advanced graduate students accompanying me that year, the data that Harris and his supporters thought would empirically settle the issue. We discussed the matter at length and agreed that if the Yąnomamö consumed the equivalent of one Big Mac per day, a suggestion made by Harris himself, Harris would 'eat his hat'. A Big Mac contains about 30 grams of animal protein.

We left for the field the next day. The three students initiated their field research, one component of which was the determination of per capita protein intake per day. I will not go into some of the darker, ethical, and astonishing events that eventually transpired around this issue—at least not in this book—but simply report some of the results that we obtained. Table 2–1 summarizes the per capita protein consumption of the Yąnomamö, several other South American Indian groups, and selected industrialized nations—the latter data taken from tables in one of Harris' own textbooks. What it indicates is that the Yąnomamö are consuming large quantities of protein by comparison to even citizens in very affluent industrialized nations. Indeed, if a correlation between protein consumption and frequency, intensity, or seriousness of warfare exists at all, it is that protein *abundance*, not protein *scarcity*, correlates with fighting and warfare. One might even argue too much protein, not too little, causes war.

I have, in many publications, as I do again in this one, drawn attention to the fact that much of Yąnomamö fighting and conflict arises over sex, infidelity, suspicion of infidelity, failure to deliver a promised wife to a suitor—in a word, women. I explained Harris' theory of their warfare to the Yąnomamö: "He says you are fighting over game animals and meat, and insists that you are not fighting over women." They laughed at first, and then dismissed Harris' view in the following way: "Yahi yamakö buhii makuwi, suwa käbä yamakö buhii barowö!" ("Even though we do like meat, we like women a whole lot more!") Some protein advocates dismiss the suggestion that people will fight over sexual matters as 'labidinal speculation'. That is an ad hominem way of asserting that most of the theory of evolution by natural selection is, simply, labidinal speculation. And that, I submit, is not science. It is not only 'vulgar Marxism', it is also blind Marxism.

The assumptions behind the general ecological argument that all organisms, including humans, must eat to survive and how they satisfy nutritional needs sheds important light on their social activities and interactions are acceptable to most anthropologists, particularly those of us who advocate a 'scientific' view of human behavior and maintain that it can be explained in cause-and-effect terms. The extremes to which the protein advocates have carried the argument, however, are less acceptable. First, they simply dismiss or repudiate the significance of reproductive striving as a meaningful element in human social behavior—while simultaneously arguing that they are proposing an *evolutionary* view of human life. The basic fact is that evolutionary theory is not simply a theory about survival, it is a theory about survival *and* reproductive success. They are leaving out a major component by restricting it to survival alone. Second, even in the 'survival' component, they focus only on one item among a host of possible items: protein intake. Protein is treated almost as a mystical force, the inherent biological drive for which is alleged to produce all manner of adaptations and behaviors in humans that explain most everything that they do. In a peculiar sense, the argument seems to say you are what you eat, and the most important thing in your diet is red juicy meat. People seem to be seen, historically, as behaving almost as if they were inimically

TABLE 2–1   Comparative data on animal protein consumption per capita for some Amazonian tribes. In general, the only quantitative data that exists for Amazonian tribes clearly indicates that they are consuming more than adequate quantities of animal protein. These should be taken as very conservative estimates, since vegetable protein is not counted nor is the protein that is inevitably consumed by the hunters while they are on hunting trips. Data in parentheses indicates that either per capita or per adult consumption figure was missing in original source and was estimated by standard conversion factors from the original statistics, (revised from Chagnon and Hames, 1979). Figures reported by Harris (1975:430) indicated that the highest per capita animal protein consumption among developed countries is about 70 gm per day in Australia and New Zealand. The next highest level is for the United States and Canada at about 66 gm per day. Amazonian Indians do better than the U.S.S.R., the United Kingdom, Germany, Portugal, and Japan among developed countries, all of whose per capita consumption of animal protein falls below the figure 64.6 given in the table below.

Society	Per Capita	Per Adult	Source
Jivaro	79.3	(103.0)	Berlin & Markell, 1977
Jivaro	84.4	(116.2)	Ross, 1978
Yąnomamö	29.7	36	Lizot, 1977
Yąnomamö	51.9	77	Lizot, 1977
Yąnomamö	52	75	Chagnon & Hames, 1979
Wayana	(77.7)	108	Hurault, 1972
Boni	(82)	114	Hurault, 1972
Maimande	26.3	(36.2)	Aspelin, 1975
Bari	86.8	(119.5)	Beckerman, 1978
Ye'kwana	77.3	95.5	Hames, in prep
Siona-Secoya	64.3	96.7	Vickers, 1978
AVERAGES	64.6	88.8	

responding to a gigantic Paleo Mac Attack, and much of what they did was to satiate this urge. Evidence for the Paleo Mac Attack, unfortunately, usually amounted to preemptive anecdotalism. Any comment in an ethnographic monograph that alluded to meat being in less abundance than what the natives desired tended to be converted into evidence for widespread meat famine and starvation. One could as persuasively argue that a millionaire who complains about a 20% drop in his annual interest income is evidence of widespread poverty. What the protein intake actually was among the people who allegedly had extreme shortages of it *was never actually determined prior to theorizing*. It simply sounded so good to the ear, as 'mouthtalk' (Service, 1969) usually does, that its advocates apparently expected the anthropological community to accept it as if it were a hardnosed, rigorous idea or argument—detractors of which were cynically dismissed as 'softheads' who were non- or antiscientific.

But Harris and I do agree on one issue, the broader one. We agree that human behavior and cultural institutions can be explained scientifically and that the most satisfactory explanation will ultimately be an evolutionary one. I depart from him when the weight of evidence clearly shows that protein is *not* the central issue or single variable that magically explains everything—for no single variable can.

In a peculiar way, 'protein poverty' has been substituted for 'soil poverty', discussed above, and, like the 'soil poverty' argument, is withering when empirical studies of protein consumption have been brought to bear on the issue. Neither the research by Carneiro nor the research done on protein consumption argues that Amazon soils are rich or the forest a cornucopia of protein on the hoof or wing; both do effectively expose the weakness of grand arguments that are expressed as monocausality.

The Amazonian jungle evokes many kinds of reactions from people who try to portray it in a catchy phrase or in a few words. Casual visitors are impressed with its vastness, and with the serene beauty of the lush vegetation. For some of them it looks like a 'tropical paradise' and is portrayed as teeming with inexhaustable supplies of game, minerals, valuable undiscovered botanical and pharmacological treasures, and perhaps a hidden civilization or two. Others emphasize the dangers of its wildlife, such as jaguars, *caimans*, piranha fish, and both poisonous and constricting snakes, which are real enough and occasionally take a toll on the natives who dwell there. But Amazonia is far wide of the "green hell" that is usually given as the shorthand reference. Still others, often academically oriented, and perhaps motivated by a sense of duty to correct the 'tropical paradise' or 'green hell' image of novels and Hollywood films, go to some extreme to portray it as a desert, having little or no potential, a tough place in which to make a living. In recent years, national planners and optimistic businessmen, especially in Brazil, have promoted unrealistic conceptions of immense wealth in natural resources or potential grazing land for cattle and have set out on devastating enterprises to clear the jungle and turn it into pasture—pasture that feeds the herds for a year or two, and then is overrun by inedible vegetation and bakes hard from the relentless sun into a near desert, usless to humans and livestock alike, and forever taken from the native flora and fauna.

The fact of the matter is that Amazonia is a complex place and not a great deal of ecological research has been done there. That which has been done has also been ignored by planners and developers who, often wild-eyed, rush forth with designs to 'open it up' and harvest its putatively endless wealth.

Historically, the Amazon Basin was colonized by natives relatively late, long after agriculture had appeared and was flourishing in the Americas. The archaeological evidence is currently very spotty and of variable quality, but it does indicate that native cultures   spread throughout the Amazon forest long after native civilizations appeared in Mexico, Guatemala, and Peru. Population density appeared to remain relatively low all during the time periods documented archaeologically and ethnographically, save for those areas immediately adjacent to the larger rivers such as the Amazon. Very little is known about the peoples who lived deep in the jungle between the major rivers—the interfluvial 'foot' Indians of which the Yąnomamö are one example—but what little evidence we do have suggests that the adaptations, found both before and after Columbus, entailed the use of some cultivated foods. That is, true hunter/gatherers were rare in the deep forest. Perhaps this reflects a more correct view of the Amazon Basin, at least that portion of it away from the larger rivers: to prevail there requires at least some agricultural knowledge and skill. But with agriculture, relatively large native communities can develop and can remain sedentary, and can do so with little dependence on the abundant fish resources found in the local waterways. The Yąnomamö are one such example. Their diet is rich and highly varied, and they exploit a large number of animal species that assure both an abundant and a reliable fount of protein. Among most Amazon Basin Indians some forms of protein are more prized than others: tapirs are more enthusiastically sought and eaten than snakes. Some game is less predictable than other game in hunting. Hunting every-where, given native technology, is always a function of luck as well as a function of animal population density and biomass. I have hunted with the Yąnomamö on many occasions. On some, we had bad luck and brought home little or nothing, but on others we got so much we couldn't carry it all, had to terminate the hunt before we expected to, and brought enough meat home to feed the whole village. These kinds of trips are designed to take the most 'prized' kind of meat, for the Yąnomamö classify meat into a number of categories, one of which is specifically reserved for the kind of meat you are expected to give to visitors at ceremonial feasts. This includes tapir, spider monkeys, armadillos, *caimans*, paruri (turkey), alligator, and wild pigs. All else, in this context, is 'nonmeat', for it cannot be given at feasts, any more than we would invite guests for Thanksgiving dinner and serve them hamburgers or scrambled eggs. It is clear that the Yąnomamö are not suffering from a deficiency of protein in their diet, at least under aboriginal, noncontacted, nonacculturated conditions, and one should treat with extreme skepticism any argument that purports to explain either the broad features of their culture or the minute details as a mechanistic response to protein scarcity. That argument seems to rest largely on an assumption that is simply advocated with passion and has little empirical justification. It appeals to many of us in our culture, however, for we tend to think of protein as coming in lean, red, thick, juicy T-bone steaks or plump, corn-fed poultry. But for people who eat termites, grubs, bee larvae, and caterpillars with as much gusto as we eat lobster tails, such a view appears to be highly ethnocentric.

3/Myth and Cosmos

The Spiritual Environment

The comparative simplicity of Yąnomamö material culture contrasts sharply with the richness and ingenuity of their beliefs about the cosmos, the soul, the mythical world, and the plants and animals around them. One fascinating dimension of their intellectual world is the extent to which individuals can manipulate and elaborate on the ideas and themes, but within a set of limits demanded by orthodoxy and local versions of 'Truth'. Not only can individuals 'experiment' as artists and creators, but there is room for poets and verbal 'essayists' as well. Despite lacking a written language, the Yąnomamö have considerable freedom to turn a clever phrase or state something in a more sophisticated way than others are capable of doing. Some Yąnomamö play with their rich language and work at being what we might call literary or learned. The conception of primitive peoples having gruntlike languages whose poor vocabularies require lots of sign gestures is not only ignorantly wide of the mark, it is also ironic: the working vocabulary of most Yąnomamö individuals is probably much larger than the working vocabulary of most people in our own culture. While it is true that the absolute content of our language's vocabulary greatly exceeds the content of Yąnomamö vocabulary, it is also true that we know much less of ours than they do of theirs. When you do not have a written language you have to store more in your head. One might even suggest that the possession of a dictionary has made us lazy, for we can always 'look it up' if we can't remember it, and we probably tend to 'not remember' for that very reason. It is in this context that the often-heard Yąnomamö comment "I possess the Truth" makes a great deal of sense. To make the point as a Yąnomamö might do it, if we're so smart, why don't we have a word to describe that part of our body between the forearm and bicep? The best we can do is call it "inside elbow." The same for the "back knee." I can't imagine words more useful! The Yąnomamö have a rich vocabulary and a complex language—and they delight in making poetic use of them in their marvelous stories and sagas of the cosmos and of Man's place in it.

The Cosmos The Yąnomamö conceive of the cosmos as comprising at least four parallel layers, each lying horizontally and separated by a vague but relatively small space (Fig. 3–1). The layers are like inverted dinner platters: gently curved, round, thin, rigid, and having a top and a bottom surface. The edges of at least some of the layers are considered to be 'rotten' and somewhat fragile, as if to walk on them might be like walking on the roof of a badly deteriorated building. A good deal of magical stuff happens out in this region, a kind of netherland dominated by spirits, a place that is somewhat mysterious and dangerous. The most highly advised geographers and sailors in our own recent historical past had conceptions not markedly different, and Magellan was nothing short of relieved when his ships didn't fall off what was then thought to be the edge of a flat earth, a mere 470 years ago!

The uppermost layer of the four (there might be more according to some Yąnomamö) is thought to be 'pristine' or 'tender': *duku kä misi*. At present this layer is empty or void (*broke*), but many things had their origin there in the distant past: things tend to move downward in the Yąnomamö cosmos, falling or descending to a lower layer. Sometimes the uppermost layer is described with the term "old woman," as are abandoned, nonproducing gardens. The 'tender' layer does not play a prominent role in the everyday life or thoughts of the Yąnomamö, not even in their shamanism or myths. It is something that is just 'there' and once had a vague function.

The next layer down is called *hedu kä misi*: the 'sky' layer. The upper surface of *hedu* is invisible to us, but is believed to be similar to what we know on earth—it has trees, gardens, villages, animals, plants, and, most important, the souls of deceased Yąnomamö who are in some sense similar to mortal men. They garden, hunt, make love, eat, and practice witchcraft on each other. Everything that exists on earth has its replica or counterpart in *hedu*, as if *hedu* were a mirror image of life as mortals know it.

The bottom surface of *hedu* is what we on earth can actually see with our eyes: the visible 'sky'. Stars and planets are somehow or other 'stuck' onto this layer and move across it along their individual trails, east to west. Some Yąnomamö think the stars are fish, but they have a generally undeveloped set of astronomical ideas about the stars and planets and nothing that we would call named constellations. The bottom of *hedu* is conceived to be relatively close to earth, for I repeatedly was asked if I bumped into it when I took rides in airplanes.[1]

Man—Yąnomamö—dwells on 'this layer': *hei kä misi*. 'This layer' was created when a chunk of *hedu* broke off and fell downward. As all can plainly see, 'this layer' is characterized by jungle, rivers, hills, animals, plants, gardens, and so on, and is covered with people who are essentially slightly different variants of Yąnomamö—speaking a dialect of Yąnomamö that is 'wrong' or 'crooked'. Even 'foreigners' (*nabä* or, in some dialects in Brazil, *kraiwä*) are thought to dwell in *shabonos*, for foreigners are simply degenerate copies of real humans—Yąnomamö.

Finally, the surface below 'this layer', *heitä bebi*, is almost barren. A peculiar variant of Yąnomamö live there, a people called Amąhiri-teri. They originated a long time ago when a piece of *hedu* broke off and crashed to 'this layer',

---

[1] Airplanes were only rarely seen in 1964 when I began my fieldwork, for there were no airstrips in the Upper Orinoco region at that time. About that time, some missions began clearing airstrips for small, light planes, a process that rapidly accelerated in the following years—leading to an almost uncontrolled influx of curious visitors and tourists at some mission stations who could fly directly from Caracas.

THE COSMOS

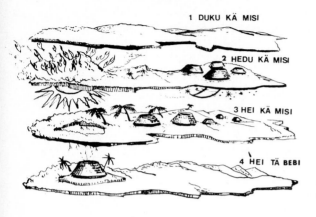

Fig. 3–1. The Yąnomamö cosmos: four parallel layers.

knocking a hole in it and continuing downward. It hit 'this layer' at a place where the Amąhiri-teri lived, carrying them and their village downward to the new layer. Unfortunately, just the garden and *shabono* of the Amąhiri-teri was carried downward and not their jungle, where they hunted. Thus, they have no game animals and have converted to cannibals: they send their spirits upward, to 'this layer', to capture the souls of children, which are carried down to their village and eaten. In some Yąnomamö villages, the shamans contest regularly with the Amąhiri-teri, attempting to thwart their cannibalistic incursions. The Yąnomamö have an almost morbid fear of becoming cannibals, almost as though humans are precariously close to an inherent predisposition to devour members of their own species, an act they find not merely repugnant, but a possibility that seems to them very real and must therefore be constantly opposed. Whenever I hunted with them and we shot a tapir, I would always cut off a thick juicy slice of tenderloin and fry it lightly on both sides—a rare steak that dripped juicy delicious blood as I cut it and ate it. This so disgusted and alarmed them that they could not bear to watch me eat it, and invariably accused me of wanting to become a cannibal like a jaguar, a disgusting eater of raw human flesh. For their part, they cook their meat so much that you could almost drive nails with it.

The Amąhiri-teri people lived at the time of the *no badabö*, the original humans. These original humans were distinct from living Man in that they were part spirit and part human, and most were also part animal—and the myths frequently explain how this transformation occurred. When the original people died, they turned into spirits: *hekura*. The term *no badabö* means, literally, "those who are now dead." In the context of myth and stories of the cosmos, it means "the original humans" or "those who were here in the beginning of time."

Myths: The Beginning of Time and the No Badabö   It is difficult, if not impossible, to get the Yąnomamö to explain how the first beings were created.

Myths: The Beginning of Time and the No Badabö   It is difficult, if not impossible, to get the Yąnomamö to explain how the first beings were created. They seem to assume that the cosmos began with these people present. Most of the *no badabö* had specific functions or roles in creative events that transpired after they themselves existed, events that, for example, explain the origin of certain animals or plants. They figure prominently in myths, and many bear the names of plants and animals useful or sometimes trivial to the Yąnomamö. The *no badabö* are the spirits of these living things, there being relatively little correlation between the mythical importance of some of them and the usefulness of the plant or animal whose name they bear.

Some of the characters in Yąnomamö myths are downright hilarious, and some of the things they did are funny, ribald, and extremely entertaining to the Yąnomamö, who listen to men telling mythical stories or chanting episodes of mythical sagas as they prance around the village, tripping out on hallucinogens, adding comical twists and nuances to the side-splitting delight of their audiences. Everybody knows what Iwariwä did, and that part cannot be changed. But *how* he did it, what minor gestures and comments he made, or how much it hurt or pleased him as he did it is subject to some considerable poetic license, and it is this that is entertaining and amusing to the listener. Occasionally the inspired narrator will go a bit beyond what is acceptable, a violation for which his own peers might good-naturedly forgive him, but a violation that people in other villages might object to, as they did when I taped the narrative and had people in other villages comment on it. "He's got it wrong! He's lying! It wasn't that way at all!" they would complain, adding that if I wanted the "truth," I would be well advised to consult with them. Usually the degree of objection to someone's narrative was a function of the degree of contempt they had for the members of the village in question—war and the orthodoxy of myth parallel each other. Most of the time it was a function of simple ethnocentrism and chauvinism: nobody does things quite as properly and faithfully as "my people," a conviction and sentiment almost all of us exhibit to some degree.

With my filmmaking colleague, Timothy Asch, I have produced a number of films that record specific myths and specific variants of some of the myths. These are easily and readily available through two major nonprofit distribution agencies (see Appendix A) and are widely used as supplements to this monograph. They capture something of the humor and wit of the storyteller, not to mention the humorous content of some of the myths themselves. They also reveal the high degree of dramaturgical skill of storytellers like Kąobawä and illustrate the qualitatively different impact that documentary film makes on people compared to the written word. It would be very difficult to capture the humor, subtlety, and wittiness of Yąnomamö myths without using motion picture film, a distortion of reality no more severe than writing it down with a pencil on a piece of paper, advocates of the latter occasionally being quick to criticize the use of film for recording myths. While we filmed quite a large number of the myths, only a few have been produced as final films to date. I should like, given this situation, to illustrate some of the other dimensions of

Yąnomamö myth by focusing here on themes and stories that are not available through the currently distributed films.

Sex is a big thing in Yąnomamö myths—the general relationships between men and women at the level of comparative status on the one hand and their relative biological attributes on the other. Sex is also a big thing in everyday life among the Yąnomamö, as it is elsewhere, and much of their humor, insulting, fighting, storytelling, and conceptions about humans revolve around sexual themes. If I were to illustrate the dictionary I have been patiently collecting on my field trips, it would be, as one of my puckish graduate students once commented, very good pornography! The proverbial Eskimos are proverbially alleged to have thousands of words for snow, the point being that vocabulary often reflects what is important in a particular culture. You would expect Eskimos to have a lot of words for snow. The Yąnomamö, by contrast, have no words for snow, but on the kind of argument posed here, one certainly would have no difficulty concluding that sex is their equivalent of snow if one had a representative dictionary of Yąnomamö language!

A few examples from their stories of the *no badabö* will suffice to illustrate the wit, humor, and themes in Yąnomamö intellectual life. Some seem to have 'morals' or 'lessons' in them while others purport to explain or 'justify' why things are the way they are in the mortal world today. Yet others seem to have no obvious point, such as the simple story of the exchange that Armadillo and Jaguar made with their teeth, each giving the other his own teeth, reversing their original roles and natures.

One of the themes that periodically crops up has to do with the relationships between men and women. Men are considered to be not only different from women, but superior in some regards to them. In this the Yąnomamö are not unique. And, as is sometimes found in the myths of other people, a peculiar intellectual struggle is implicit in the myths about male and female relationships. Levi-Strauss, the famous French anthropologist who devoted much of his brilliant efforts to creating a discipline dealing with the mythical themes of man, drew attention to this problem and has dealt repeatedly with it in his many publications. The problem is more general than just the relationships between the sexes, and has broadly to do with 'working out' via myths certain irreconcilable human beliefs and concerns. Thus, as the distinguished British anthropologist Edmund Leach succinctly put it in his scholarly but brief assessment of Levi-Strauss' view of the anthropology of myths (1970), it is a problem of the following order of magnitude. Humans often phrase, in ideological terms, the general proposition that men and women are more or less equal, no matter what other additional beliefs and attitudes they might have about the relative importance of males and females. But humans also explicitly condemn the practice of incest within the nuclear family. We have in these two statements the making of a contradiction that is hard to avoid and difficult to reconcile. If men and women are in fact equal, then they must have parents who are equal. Most creation stories begin with two individuals who people the earth with humans, but the only way that the first two people could be absolutely equal would be if they are siblings: brother and sister. If they are brother and sister, then all humans are the consequence of an original act of blatant incest, of brothers copulating with sisters. That's pretty distasteful in most cultures, but only some solve the problem by having a separate creation myth for women and men. It avoids the incest problem, but runs smack into a different one. If they are created separately, they are not therefore absolutely equal. That is how the Yąnomamö solve the problem: they have separate origins for women. The Christian Bible opts for a more incestuous solution: Eve was created from a portion of Adam's body, his rib, and therefore they somewhat incestuously go about creating the rest of us. A pre-Biblical account might have been adopted by the Bible, but wasn't: Adam set about his procreative work with a mate named Lilith, part human and part fabulous animal (Leach, 1970). The choice of the founders was probably a tough one, but we got the incest version. One of the Yąnomamö myths on the creation of Man is itself apparently ambiguous, for some Yąnomamö claim that only men were created in this story, the story of Moonblood (see the 16mm film listed in Appendix A, Chagnon and Asch, 1975), while other Yąnomamö argue that both men and women were created from Moon's blood. In the Moonblood story, one of the ancestors shot Moon in the belly. His blood fell to earth and changed into Men, but Men who were inherently *waiteri*: fierce. Where the blood was 'thickest', the men who were created there were very ferocious and they nearly exterminated each other in their wars. Where the droplets fell or where the blood 'thinned out' by mixing with water, they fought less and did not exterminate each other, that is, they seemed to have a more controllable amount of inherent violence. Because of this, humans are *waiteri*: fierce.

Those Yąnomamö who maintain that only males came from the blood of Moon also argue that females came from a kind of fruit called *wabu* in the following way.

Those created by Moon's blood were all males, and they had no women with whom to copulate. They went out collecting vines one day, and began pulling them from the trees. The headman of the group noticed that one of the vines had a newly opened wabu fruit attached to it, and the fruit had 'eyes' on it. He thought to himself: "Ummm. I'll bet that's what women look like!" and he tossed it on the ground. It changed immediately into a woman and immediately developed a large vagina. They continued to collect vines, not aware that the fruit had turned into a woman. As they dragged the vines home, the woman kept at a distance and would step on the ends of the vines, jerking the men off guard as she did, hiding behind trees when they turned back to look. She finally just stood on one of the vines, causing the men to screech to a halt. They turned and looked, and saw her. They were startled that she had a vagina—a very long and very hairy one. They stared at it and were overcome with lust. They rushed at her and all took a turn copulating frantically with her. They brought her back to the village and let all the men there have a turn copulating with her. Eventually she had a baby—a daughter, another, and another. As each daughter came out, everyone copulated with her and eventually there was an abundance of females, all descended from the *wabu* fruit, and that is why there are so many Yąnomamö today.

Jaguar Myths   A theme that repetitiously appears in Yąnomamö myths is about Man's relationship to Jaguar. In mortal form, the jaguar is an awesome and much-feared beast, for he can and does kill and eat men. He is as good a hunter as the Yąnomamö are, and is one of the few animals in the forest that hunts and kills men—as the Yąnomamö themselves do. He is in that sense like Man, but unlike Man, he is part of Nature, not of Culture. This distinction is fundamental in Yąnomamö conceptions, for the Yąnomamö separate themselves invidiously from the animals, and point out, as proudly as we do, that they have Culture and the animals do not. Thus, they bifurcate the world into 'things of the forest' and 'things of the village' (*supra*). The former is Nature; the latter is Culture. It is tempting to speculate about the distribution, in human societies, of this opposition and whence it comes and what it means. It seems to be an idea that is somewhat 'fixed' in human conceptions, a polarity that we can only with difficulty learn to view as a *continuous* scale of 'more natural' or 'more cultural'. There is probably not a single reader of this who has not been confronted with the kind of argument that pits 'learning' against 'instinct', or 'cultural' against 'biological'. It is 'in our heads' and it takes considerable effort to translate it into something more sophisticated than simply a Culture/Nature dichotomy, and there is some considerable evidence that 'cultures' must be very special and work very hard to break down this particular dichotomy—to the extent that one can say that cultures 'work' at anything. Be that as it may, the Yąnomamö pit Culture against Nature, as we often do, and see the cosmos in many contexts as an 'either/or' moiety. Thus, an animal, captured in the wild, is 'of the forest', but once brought into the village, it is 'of the village' and somehow different, for it is then part of Culture. For this reason, they do not eat their otherwise edible pets—such as monkeys, birds, and rodents—when they die, for to them, it is similar to cannibalism: eating something 'cultural' and therefore 'humanlike'. Nothing disgusted the Yąnomamö more than my matter-of-fact comments that we ate our domestic animals, such as cattle and sheep, and many a missionary gave up in frustration after having attempted to introduce chickens at mission posts. The Yąnomamö liked the roosters because they crowed at dawn, and kept them essentially for this aesthetic reason if they kept them at all, but would refuse to kill and eat them. They were 'of the village' and part of Culture. They did, however, have a different attitude toward eggs and ate them with gusto, for they were not quite the same thing as the chicken they produced, an attitude we also have when we discuss the moral implications of abortion: we allow for the fetus as being different from the being it creates, and are prepared, in some circles, to treat it differently in law and in medical practice.

Jaguar is peculiar to them, for he combines several human capacities while at the same time he is 'natural'. It is almost as if they both respect and fear jaguars, and the 'dual' nature of Jaguar might be viewed as a kind of contradiction of the sort that Levi-Strauss had in mind when he viewed myths as the intellectual vehicle through which such contradictions are reconciled. The many stories the Yąnomamö have about jaguars seem to all make the point, in one way or another, that Man is ultimately the master over Jaguar and can outwit him. Jaguar is usually portrayed as a large, clumsy, stupid and bungling beast—whatever he might be in real life. Indeed, the Yąnomamö are terrified at the prospect of having to spend the night in the jungle without fire, for they know that Jaguar hunts at night and they know that they are no match for him in this realm. I was awakened many times while I worked with the Yąnomamö and begged to go looking for some villager who failed to return by dark. They knew the villager had no fire drill or matches and were worried that jaguars might kill and eat him at night. I had to take them with my canoe and flashlights to help them find the wayward traveler, and the traveler was always very grateful that we found him before the jaguars did. I know how they feel, for I myself was stalked a number of times by jaguars, and on one occasion was nearly a meal for one of them. He walked into our camp at about 3:00 A.M. after our fire had gone out, and was sniffing me. Fortunately, I had given my flashlight to one of my guides, who awoke, shined the light on him, and he retreated quickly into the jungle as my guides hissed frantically into my ear: "Jaguar! Jaguar! Jaguar!" It is a word in Yąnomamö that I'll never forget, for the hot breath and the fearsome size of the animal is forever fixed to his name: *öra*.

Jaguar, then, is an ambiguous character to the Yąnomamö. He is like Man in that he hunts and is cunning and is so effective that one might say that the Yąnomamö are somewhat jealous of him. But in their stories about him, he is consistently portrayed as a stupid brute, constantly being outwitted by Man, and constantly subjected to the most scathing, ridiculous, and offensive treatments at the hands of Man.

Some stories are more oblique than others in this regard. In the story of the Jaguar named Kashahewä, or Hǫo, he is simply destroyed by men who use a palm-wood club called *himo*. These clubs are long, heavy, and sharpened at the upper edges, and made from a very dense, black, and heavy palm wood called *shidibasi*. They are slightly thicker than broom handles for most of their circular shaft, but widen out into a kind of skinny canoe paddle whose edges are very sharp. The Yąnomamö sometimes have duels with these clubs, which deal a severe and often fatal blow due to their heavy weight and sharpness. They are for hitting people on the head with the sharp edge forward. Jaguar, in a story in which he is known as Hǫo, has exterminated most of mankind. An old man in one of the villages is sleeping, snoring very loudly. Jaguar enters the village and carries his son off, who screams and protests that Jaguar is treating him like some common game animal. The members of the village— Shidibasi-teri (the wood used in the club)—decide to take a *himo* club to their neighbors, the Beribosihi-teri, knowing that Jaguar has been devouring them. But when they reach the village, they find that it has already been wiped out by Jaguar, and enormous buzzards are finishing off the human remains that Jaguar didn't eat. It is growing dark, and they become frightened. They flee to a nearby tree and climb it, for they hear Jaguar roaring and whining in the nearby jungle. They climb an *arausi* tree and, once at the top, begin to scrape and peel the bark off the trunk. They get out their fire drill and make a fire from the bark, fasten it to the tree, and sit in the highest branches, waiting for Jaguar. The brother-in-law of the snoring man has the *himo* club. He has a vine hammock, slung between the branches, and stands (sic) in it, watching for

Jaguar. Eventually Jaguar arrives, sniffing around, and climbs the tree after them. When he gets near the top, the man with the club wallops him soundly on the head, knocking him off the tree, and knocking him unconscious. Jaguar falls to the ground, eventually regains consciousness and climbs up again, and again gets clouted on the head by the *himo* club. Up and down, up and down, all night long. Meanwhile, they huddle closely around the fire and blow on it to keep it burning. Jaguar cannot make them out, and climbs close, peering at them, perhaps blinded by the fire. They smack him again with the club, and he falls to the ground again. Near dawn, Jaguar again climbs the tree. He gets almost up to them, stretches his arms out to catch them, and they hit him on the bridge of his nose with the sharp edge of the *himo* club. He falls again and lies motionless. It gets light and the forest is absolutely silent. Jaguar is motionless. One of them climbs down cautiously, and examines Jaguar, to see if he is breathing. Blood is oozing from his nostrils and the bees have begun to come for the blood. "Whaaa! He is dead! We got him!" they exclaim, and with that, depart. That is how the people of Palm-wood Village got him with a palm-wood club.

In another story, Jaguar is not at first given over to eating humans—he acquires the taste gradually. This story is interesting in the sense that it specifically discusses the use of red peppers as a form of 'chemical warfare', a tactic described by early Spaniards who observed Tropical Forest peoples 'smoking out' their enemies by burning red peppers upwind from them, the drifting smoke and toxic vapors driving the residents from their village, coughing and gagging. The present Yąnomamö do not use red peppers in this fashion, but the myth clearly indicates that they are aware of its potential for producing a very disagreeable and toxic smoke, a potentially fatal poison.

Jaguar has the name Käyäkäyä or Kräyäkräyä in this story—his name keeps changing. In this story, Jaguar's son-in-law (or nephew) actually begins the dastardly act of eating humans. Note that Jaguar is somehow mysteriously human, so eating humans is in fact an act of cannibalism. The son-in-law, Siroroma, saw some humans one day when they were hunting. He caught some game and then approached the wife of one of the humans, and gave her the meat. He copulated with her and got her pregnant. Her husband later began to suspect that he did not cause the pregancy and grew very suspicious. His wife told him that a bird named Kawamari gave her the meat, for she wanted to conceal the fact that she was pregnant by a jaguar. He went hunting, and when he returned, he discovered that his wife had more meat—another turkey. "What the hell is going on here?" he thought to himself. He began watching her more carefully, and eventually he heard a noise in the forest. It was Jaguar's son-in-law, Siroroma. The husband immediately concluded: "Haaa! He's the one who has gotten her pregnant!" He decided to get rid of Siroroma and set about all day long collecting firewood. He made a huge bonfire in the village, and then approached Siroroma, grabbing him in a tight bear-hug, and threw him into the fire to roast. But Siroroma turned into a liquid and quenched the fire, and then attacked the husband, squirting a stinging liquid into his eyes in the form of spit. He blinded him, and the husband fled in agony, rubbing his hands into his blind eyes. Siroroma, scorched by the fire, then decided to peel his own skin off, using his fingernails. He skinned himself on the spot and took his own pelt home, where he hung it up in his roof—where it still hangs to this day.

He looked very different with no skin. He went home, where he joined his father-in-law (uncle), Jaguar. On seeing the skinned nephew, Jaguar thought: "Hooo! My nephew has sent a wild pig home for me to eat!" Not knowing he was eating his own son-in-law, Jaguar devoured him voraciously and developed a craving for the flesh. He decided at that point to hunt this kind of game, and from that time on, Jaguar has hunted humans. But soon humans began to catch on to his designs and appetites. They began avoiding him. Jaguar took to living in caves, where he reared his family and fed them on human flesh.

He went to a human village called Wayorewä-teri, in the mountains. He sang his hunting song as he approached the village—"Käyäkäyä, Käyäkäyä, Käyäkäyä. . . . " He entered the village and found that all the adults were gone. They were away, hunting for *naö* fruits far from the village. Only an old woman, a large number of children, and a pubescent girl going through her first menses confinement were there. He entered and asked the old woman for water, and complained when he got it: it was stagnant. The old woman was the mother of the pubescent girl, and was mourning sorrowfully for the girl, for she knew the girl was hungry, but could not eat because of the menstrual taboos. Jaguar set his pack basket down, and the children grew apprehensive. He asked the old woman why there were no adults around, and he was told that they were out foraging for wild foods.

The story becomes very funny here, but there is no way to convey the sophistication of the humor in literal English translation. I'll change the names of the fruits and animals to try to get the humor across—at the expense of the accuracy of the proper identification of the actual species mentioned. I will also change a few body parts, for Yąnomamö and we have different views of what parts are more important. (The liver is more important to them than the heart, and "liverthrob" doesn't come out as well as "heartthrob" in, for example, a romantic passage; "my liver and shadow" doesn't grab us as much as "my heart and soul," but it would be a reasonable translation.) Jaguar's motive was to insult as viciously as possible and he tried to be as obnoxious as he could with his caustic retorts to the old woman.

"What kinds of food are they seeking?" he asked. "They went collecting peaches," said the old woman. "Hrumph! That will cause them to have fuzz all over their asses if they do that!" said Jaguar. "Well, they also mentioned that they wanted hardshell crabs," said the old woman. "Hrumpf! Their tits will turn into armour plating if they eat them!" said Jaguar. "Well, they also were after crayfish, too," added the old woman. "Hrumpf! Their peckers will turn pink and curl up if they eat any of them!" said Jaguar. "And they wanted to catch a few bullhead fish as well," said the old woman. "Hrumpf! That will cause them to have stringy tentacles growing from their snouts!" mused

Jaguar.[2] "Moreover, they plan to catch some striped fish," added the old woman.. "Hrumpf! They'll look like zebras when they eat them!" quipped Jaguar. "Some said they wanted a few eggplants," said the old woman. "Hrumpf! They'll break their assholes trying to pass an eggplant!" said Jaguar.

She went to the river to get him some fresher water, leaving the pubescent girl and the children unattended. When the old woman had gone, Jaguar immediately entered the girl's puberty hut and killed her. The old woman heard a noise, and hastily returned to the village, asking what the noise was about. "I was just fanning the fire!" lied Jaguar. The woman left, satisfied, and Jaguar immediately set upon the children, killing them as quickly as he could catch them, stacking up their tiny corpses in his pack basket. He thought he had gotten them all, and was about to leave when he noticed two rather strange things. They were children, but their heads were shaved clean because they had lice. Jaguar thought they were dogs and decided to bring them along, as pets, to his lair. He grabbed them and stuck them on top of his basket full of dead children, and left for his cave.

As he got close to the cave, he passed under a vine. The older of the two children grabbed the vine and swung off the basket into the trees. Jaguar noticed the sudden change in the weight of his load, and investigated. He tried to entice the child down, but the child would not comply, so Jaguar left him there and went on to his cave. Jaguar's cave was actually an armadillo den. (Recall that Jaguar and Armadillo exchanged teeth with each other.) He entered it with his basket of human flesh and began distributing it among his kinsmen. The child who had escaped into the trees fled home and told the adults what had happened. The adults decided to go after him and kill him. They set about collecting a large pile of red pepper and a large quantity of termite nest material. They mixed them together and set off for Jaguar's den. They found all the entrances to the den and covered them with dirt and brush. They put the mixture of peppers and termite nest material in the entrances and lit it.

Inside the den, Jaguar was distributing the meat: "Ahhh! Father has brought us some wild pigs!" exclaimed Jaguar's children.[3] They then cooked and ate the dead children. As they were eating, the parents of the victims were busily building fires in the red peppers and termite nests at the entrances to the den. The Jaguars ate, sucking the marrow from the bones, passing bits and morsels back and forth as in a feast: "This is for your sister!" "This is for your brother-in-law!" "This is for your mother!" Outside, the adults were blowing the acrid smoke into the cave. As it seeped in, the Jaguars inside began choking and coughing. There was smoke everywhere, and the Jaguars began getting delirious and screamed from the pain of the pepper smoke. They began dying in large numbers. Flashes of lightning came from the entrances to the den. There is a giant basket at that mountain now, and many red peppers grow there. The basket makes noises like the spirits do: "Dei! Dei! Dei! Dei!" That

[2]There is no way to easily render allusions to the forehead and the complexion of skin in Yąnomamö. It is the foulest of insults in their language, like telling someone to "fuck off!"

[3]The Mundurucu Indians of Brazil also equate hunting of pigs with killing of enemies (Murphy, 1960).

is how Kräyäkräyä began to eat humans. When Yąnomamö chant to the spirits today, only the spirits of the Kräyäkräyä come, for the original ones were all exterminated by the poison gas.

The story that most poignantly captures the cynicism and ambiguity the Yąnomamö have for Jaguar is the story of *misi*, the tortoise. Tortoises and turtles are slow moving and virtually helpless when their feet are not touching the ground. Indeed, some South American Indian groups 'store' turtle meat by capturing large numbers of them and just turning them upside down, where they squirm helplessly until it is time to cook them.

In the story of *misi*, the Original Beings from the village of Manakae-teri were traveling through the forest, hunting and collecting. They came upon a tortoise and were delighted: it would be their 'pet', their 'dog'. Little did they know that Jaguar was systematically exterminating everyone and that they would soon become his victims. Jaguar eventually came and began preying on them. They fled their village to escape his depredations, but before they did, they tied their tortoise by a vine and suspended him from the roof, as they always do with special possessions—to keep them dry and clean. He was thus helpless, dangling from the cord, unable to do anything but move his legs and head randomly and ineffectually. Jaguar approached the deserted village and entered it, looking for people to eat. He slowly wandered around the periphery, but the houses were empty. He eventually came to the house where *misi* was dangling from the rafters. *Misi's* head waved from side to side, and he made a helpless noise like "beek, beek, beek. . . . " Jaguar approached him to sniff, and *misi* grabbed his snout with his beak. He held on tightly as Jaguar struggled to free himself, tightening his bite the longer and more violently Jaguar struggled. He hung on to Jaguar's snout until Jaguar weakened and collapsed. He released his grip and Jaguar gasped his final breath. Jaguar's eyes gradually dulled and he died. *Misi* then packed his belongings (sic) and set off on a camping trip. On the way he came to the big river where his owners had made a palm-wood bridge and crossed. He caught up to the Manakae-teri, who were overjoyed to see their 'dog'. They examined him and discovered that he had been in a fight, for there was blood on his beak. They all went back to the village where they found the dead Jaguar and exclaimed: "Whaaa! Just look how big he is!" On hearing that, *misi* dropped dead. His owners were so grateful that he had killed Jaguar that they began mourning him. They decided to cremate his body and eat his ashes, reciting his exploits and achievements as they wept for him. Word reached other people that *misi* had died, and all requested gourds of his ashes so they, too, could honor him by drinking his ashes. The spirit of the Jaguar that *misi* killed now roams the forest and is meat hungry. He eats only agouti rodents today.

The irony of this story is that a simple, helpless turtle overcame and destroyed Jaguar, King of Amazonian Beasts. A stupid King of Beasts in myth alone.

The Twins Omawä and Yoawä   Several stories the Yąnomamö tell involve two paired male ancestors, Omawä and Yoawä (Yoasiwä). They do many things and are involved in the creation events that led to the distribution of many plants, animals, and customs the Yąnomamö are now familiar with. The two characters are somewhat of complementary opposites to each other—one is smart, beautiful, competent, and admirable while the other is stupid, ugly, a boob, and contemptuous. Sometimes there is a change of identities in the stories and the dumb one is the smart one and vice versa. Of all the fabulous events and situations that describe the activities of these two Original Beings, the story of the "Origin of Copulation" is the most humorous. In this story, Omawä is the attractive one of the two, and Yoawä the stupid one in the versions told by the Shamatari.

Yoawä went fishing one day. He tied bait to his fishing line and cast it into the river.[4] As he fished, he came upon a beautiful maiden. She was Raharaiyoma, daughter of the giant river monster, Raharariwä. There were no women at that time and Yoawä wanted to capture her so he could copulate with her. She was in the river, spinning cotton into yarn—and very sexy. "Wow! A real female! She has a beautiful vagina! I'd like to try it!" he said to himself. He knew she would not cooperate, so he decided to change into a small bird and lure her up to the surface where he could catch her. He decided to change into a bird that had a long beak and a combed head, in which form he fluttered above her trying to be seductive. She noticed him, and dismissed him with insults, saying he looked ugly with such a long snout and ridiculous apparatus growing out of his head. He then changed into a spotted, flecked bird and hovered above her, trying to be sexy. She again insulted him, for his skin was blemished with spots all over it. He tried several other bird guises, but failed each time and was dismissed with her biting insults. He was frustrated and angry, and went home in a huff. He threw his catch of fish onto the smoke rack and retired in disgust. His beautiful brother asked him in the morning why he let his fish cook to a black, charred inedible mess and why he was so moody. He explained that he was horny because he saw his first woman and could not seduce her. Omawä had compassion and explained a plan to catch the woman, for Omawä also grew horny. He insisted that Yoawä show him where she was, and the two of them set off to find her. She was still in the river, this time casually delousing herself. Again, Yoawä transformed himself into a small bird, but the woman dismissed him because he had ugly blemishes all over his body. He changed into another bird and was dismissed because his skin was too dark. He changed into a hummingbird, and she again dismissed him with insults, saying that his eyes were beady and he squinted. Yoawä then asked Omawä to help him. Omawä advised him to change into a small, minnowlike fish, which he did, and he hid in the water near her. Omawä then changed himself into a beautiful small bird with scarlet feathers and hovered above the woman. She was attracted and told her father that she wanted to catch this beautiful crimson bird and keep it as her pet. As she surfaced to reach for the bird, the two of them grabbed her, one on each arm, and dragged her from the water out onto the land. She screamed and struggled, but they

[4]The Yąnomamö claim that they used to fish with lines made of native fibers. They would tie a piece of bait to the string and wait for a fish—usually a small one—to swallow it. They would then pull the fish out of the water. I never saw them do it.

got her out of the water. Her father, the water monster, came to her aid, but they fled, dragging the woman with them until they escaped. They brought their sexy little trophy back home with them, and were anxious to copulate with her.

Their nephew lived with them—*Howashi*, the white monkey. He saw her vagina and the provocative pubic hair and was immediately overcome with lust. "Let me have her first! Let me have her! I'm horny as hell, and just look at that fantastic vagina!" They let him have the first turn. He passionately mounted her and stuck his penis into her vagina with a mighty pelvic thrust— and immediately screamed in agony, withdrawing his bloody stump: she had piranha fish inside her vagina and they bit the end of his penis off. He screamed and howled and fled into the forest, holding his bloody, amputated penis.[5]

Yoawä removed the fish from her vagina with a barbed arrow and then mounted her. He was consumed with lust, and made long, passionate pelvic thrusts. His penis went in deep and came back out rhythmically, and made a foul, disgusting noise: "Soka! Soka! Soka! Soka!" Omawä threw up his arms in despair, for such clumsy copulating, such foul noise, would anger people who might overhear it. He demanded that Yoawä cease and dismount so he could show him how to copulate in the proper manner. He then mounted as Yoawä observed. He copulated with slow, discreet pelvic thrusts and made no noise as he proceeded. "See? That is how to copulate properly, so nobody can hear your penis going in and out!" From that time on, people have been able to copulate discreetly.

The Soul   Yąnomamö concepts of the soul are elaborate and sophisticated. The 'true' or 'central' part of the soul is the will, or *buhii*. At death, this turns into a No Borebö, escapes up the hammock ropes and travels to the layer above. When it reaches the upper layer, it travels down a trail that has a fork in it. There, the son of *Yaru* (Thunder), a spirit named Wadawadariwä, asks the soul if it has been generous or stingy during mortal life. If the person has been stingy and niggardly, Wadawadariwä directs the soul along one path—leading to a place of fire: *Shobari Waka*. If the person was generous with his possessions and food, he is directed along the other path—to *hedu* proper, where a tranquil semi-mortal existence continues.

The Yąnomamö do not take this very seriously, that is, do not fear the possibility of being sent to the place of fire. When I asked why, I got the following kind of answer: "Well, Wadawadariwä is kind of stupid. We'll just all lie and tell him we were generous, and he'll send us to *hedu*!"

Another portion of the soul, the *no uhudi* or *bore*, is said to be released during cremation. It wanders around on earth and lives in the jungle. Some Yąnomamö claim that children always change into *no uhudi* and do not have a *no borebö* because their 'wills' (*buhii*) are *mohode*—innocent, unaware. It would appear that one's soul experiences an ontogeny that parallels human develop-

[5]Howashi monkeys (cappuchin) have penises that look like ten-penny nails: straight with a flattened head. This story explains how howashis got penises like that.

ment and that a certain amount of living has to occur before parts of the soul develop. Some of the wandering *bores* are malevolent and attack travelers in the jungle at night: they have bright glowing eyes and beat the mortal travelers with clubs and sticks. In 1968 I brought Rerebawä to Caracas for a few days—a hilarious but sobering experience for him—where he saw automobiles for the first time. As we drove along at night, the oncoming traffic with its bright pairs of headlights terrified him: it was a constant stream of *bore* spirits rushing at him at incredible speed and whizzing by (see Chapter 7).

The most critical component of the soul is known as the *möamo* and lies inside the thoracic cavity, near (perhaps even inside of) the liver. This portion can be 'lured' out and stolen, and is very vulnerable to supernatural attack if removed from the body. The person who has lost his *möamo* sickens and eventually dies, and the daily shamanistic attacks are usually directed at the *möamo* portions of the souls of enemies, or directed to recover this soul and return it to its owner (see 16 mm film *Magical Death*, p. 221).

In addition to multifaceted souls, all individuals have an animal counterpart, an 'alter ego', known as the *noreshi*. It is a dual concept, for the *noreshi* is not only an animal that lives in the forest, but is likewise an aspect or component of the human's body or psyche. People can 'lose' their *noreshi*.

A male inherits his *noreshi* from his father, but a girl inherits hers from her mother. Male *noreshis* are said to 'go above' and female *noreshis* 'go below'. Thus, certain monkeys and hawks are male *noreshi* animals and are found in high places, whereas snakes and ground-dwelling animals are female *noreshi* animals and travel low, a sexual superior/inferior equation. Kąobawä, for example, has the black spider monkey, *basho*, as his alter ego, which he and all his brothers inherited from their father: "We are of the *basho mashi*!" they would say, the "lineage" of the spider monkey. Kąobawä's wife, Bahimi, has the *hiima* (dog) as her *mashi*, which she and her sisters inherited from their mother. This Up/Down = Superior/Inferior = Male/Female duality occurs in other contexts, including very mundane ones: men tie their hammocks up high and women sleep in hammocks below them. When the campfire gets low, the men just dangle a foot over the edge of their hammocks, nudge their wives who unhappily grunt and sleepily throw another piece of wood onto the fire.

Noreshi animals duplicate the lives of their human counterparts. When Kąobawä or Rerebawäe go hunting, so too do their *noreshi* animals go hunting. When they sleep, so do their *noreshis*. If one gets sick, so also does the *noreshi*. A two-day trip for one is a two-day trip for the other.

While the human and his *noreshi* theoretically live far apart and never come into contact, it is said that misfortunes occasionally occur, as when a hunter accidentally shoots and kills his own *noreshi*—and thus dies himself. Moreover, if another hunter kills your *noreshi*, you, too, die. In a sense, hunting of game animals is like hunting and killing humans, for some of the animals are the *noreshi* of humans.

The close association the Yąnomamö make between 'soul loss' and sickness is best exemplified in the shamanistic practices of the men. They spend several hours each day, if they are shamans, chanting to their tiny *hekura* spirits, enjoining them to either attack the souls of enemies or help them recover souls lost by people in their own village. This is a constant battle, and the men take hallucinogenic snuff—*ebene*—daily to do contest with their enemies through the agency of their personal *hekura* (this is illustrated in my 1974 film *Magical Death*. See Appendix A).

But not all aspects of the soul are equally vulnerable. When I showed them pictures of themselves or other people, they called the photographs *noreshi*. They called tape recordings, in contrast, *no uhudi*. They seemed, at first, to be more anxious about photographs and cameras and, indeed, were very annoyed with my photographic attempts in the beginning. They initially threw dirt and stones at me and, on one occasion, threatened to club me with red-hot firebrands grabbed from the hearth. After about a year, they pretty much ignored my cameras, but a few would grumble from time to time. But they never objected to hearing tape recordings of their own voices and actually liked it—to the point that they would insist that I play back what I had recorded over and over again.

Endocannibalism   Anthropologists distinguish between two general kinds of cannibalism: that which entails the eating of other people, or exocannibalism, and that which entails the eating of your own people—endocannibalism. Neither form requires that the whole body be consumed and, in fact, most cannibalism entails the consumption of only selected parts. Most documented cases of cannibalism, except in extreme circumstances, are highly ritualistic and occur for religious or mystical reasons, although some of the advocates of the 'protein theory' have since the early 1970s attempted to argue that the widespread consumption of humans by some peoples, such as the Aztecs, was a response to acute protein shortage (Harner, 1977; Harris, 1977; cf. Ortiz de Montellano, 1978). The issue has to do with the 'ultimate' explanation of a hypothetical event. For example, a valiant warrior overcomes his equally valiant enemy in a mortal hand-to-hand contest. In celebration of his victory, he rips his enemy's heart out and ritually devours a portion of it to both honor his enemy and perhaps acquire some of his enemy's valor to add to his own. Is the valiant warrior short of protein, or is his act more sensibly interpreted as a symbolic gesture? Perhaps the best way to drive home the argument is to ask whether the taking of Holy Communion is evidence of a calorie shortage or a symbolic, mystical—and ritually cannibalistic—act of eating the 'body and blood' of a man called Jesus Christ? Holy Communion falls into a special category of cannibalism called theophagy, the Eating of Gods, and would make little sense if explained in terms of calorie or protein shortages. Most anthropophagy—the eating of men—is also like this.

The Yąnomamö are endocannibalistic anthropophagers—and that's a real mouthful! They eat portions of *their own* deceased: the ashes and ground bones that are left after a body is cremated.

When someone dies, say an adult, his or her body is carried to the clearing in the village and placed on a pile of firewood. More wood is stacked up around and on top of the body and ignited. The children and those who might be sick are asked to leave the village, for the smoke from the burning corpse can contaminate the vulnerable and ill. They often wash their bows and arrows after a cremation, for the smoke of the burning corpse can contaminate such possessions. On one occasion, I saw them also wash all the smoked meat the hunters had brought back for a feast, for it, too, had been contaminated by the smoke of a cremated corpse.

Someone attends the fire, making sure the body is entirely burned. When the ashes have grown cool, they are carefully and solemnly sifted. Unburned bones and teeth are picked out and placed into a hollowed-out log, prepared for the occasion. A close kinsman or dear friend of the deceased pulverizes the bones by grinding them with a short stout pole about 5 feet long. When the bones are all pulverized, they are carefully poured onto a leaf and then transferred to several small gourds, each with a small opening in it. The dust and ash that remains in the hollow log is rinsed out with boiled ripe plantain soup and solemnly drunk as the assembled, squatting relatives and friends mourn loudly and frantically, rending their hair with their hands and weeping profusely. The log is then burned. The gourds are carefully and tenderly stored in the roof of the kin's house, plugged shut with white down, and kept for a future and more elaborate ash-drinking ceremony that might be attended by kin who live in distant villages. At that time, a more elaborate ritual takes place: large quantities of boiled ripe plantain soup are made and the ashes are poured into gourdsful of the soup. The mixture in the gourds is passed around among close kin and friends and solemnly drunk while onlookers weep and mourn.

Children's corpses produce much less ash and bone, of course, and their remains are usually consumed by just the parents. More important adults who have many kin and many friends call forth a more elaborate ceremony, and many people partake of their ashes. In normal cases, the entire remains are consumed in a single event. However, men who have been killed by enemy raiders are treated in a special fashion. Only women drink their ashes, and they do so on the eve of a revenge raid. Thus, the ashes of men who have been killed by enemies may remain in a village for several years—until his kin feel that his death has been avenged. One prominent man I knew, the headman of his village, was killed by raiders (see Chapter 6) in 1965. Ten years later gourds of his ashes were still in the rafters of his brother's house, and his group continued to raid the village that killed him—despite the fact that they had managed to kill several men in revenge.

Should many people die at one time, as during an epidemic, the bodies of the deceased are taken into the jungle and placed in trees, wrapped with bark and wood. After they decompose, the remaining flesh is scraped from the bones and the bones are burned, stored in gourds, and later drunk.

Finally, as one of the myths above suggests, some prized pets are cremated, especially good hunting dogs. The bones are buried afterward, not eaten. The bodies of ordinary dogs are discarded a short distance from the *shabono*, sometimes before the dog is dead.

Shamans and Hekura   The word *shaman* is a word from the Arctic tribe, the Siberian Chuckchee, and has been widely used to describe men and women in any tribal society who manipulate the spirit world, cure the sick with magic,

Fig. 3–2. Three shamans chanting to the hekura *spirits while curing sick people.*

sucking, singing, or massaging; diagnose illness and prescribe a magical remedy; and generally intercede between humans and spirits in the context of health versus sickness (Fig. 3–2).

Among the Yąnomamö, only men become shamans. It is a status or role that any man can aspire to if he so chooses, and in some villages a large fraction of the men are shamans. They are called *shabori* or *hekura* in Yąnomamö, the latter word being used also for the myriad tiny, humanoid spirits they manipulate.

One must, however, train to be a shaman. This entails a long period of fasting, a year or more, during which the novice loses an enormous amount of weight. He literally looks like skin and bones at the end. An older man or older men instruct the novice in the attributes, habits, songs, and fancies of the *hekura* spirits. During the period of fasting, the novice must also be sexually continent, for the *hekura* are said to dislike sex and regard it as *shami*—filthy. Novices attempt to attract particular *hekura* into their chests, a process that takes a long time and much patience, for the *hekura* are somewhat coy and fickle, apt to leave and abandon their human host. The interior of a shaman's body is a veritable cosmos of rivers, streams, mountains, and forests where the *hekura* can dwell in comfort and happiness. Only the more accomplished shamans have many *hekura* inside their bodies, and even then they must strive to keep them happy and contented. Once you are on good terms with your *hekura*, you can engage in sex without having your spirits abandon you. I sometimes suspect that the older men have put one over on the younger men by insisting that it is good to be a shaman and that all of them should try it— and then insisting that they have to forsake women for extended periods of time. It is an effective way to reduce sexual jealousy in the village, one of the chronic sources of social disruption. I have been confidentially told by young men that they didn't want to go through the shamanism training because it required sexual continence.

There are hundreds—perhaps thousands—of *hekura*. They are all small, but vary in size from a few millimeters to an inch or two for the really large ones. Male *hekura* have glowing halos around their heads called *wadoshe*, a kind of palm-frond visor that the Yąnomamö sometimes make and wear. Female *hekura* have glowing wands sticking out from their vaginas. All are exceptionally beautiful, and each has his or her own habits and attributes. Most are named after animals, and most came into existence during some mythical episode that transformed some original Being—one of the *no badabö*—into both an animal and its *hekura* counterpart. The *hekura* are often found in the hills, or high in trees, often suspended there, but they can also live under rocks or even in the chest of a human. Many of them have special weapons used to strike or pierce souls (Taylor, 1974). Some are 'hot' and some are *naiki*—meat hungry. Some are both hot and meat hungry, and these are the ones sent to devour the souls of enemies. All of them have individual trails they follow when their human hosts call to them. The trails lead from the sky or the mountains, or even from the 'edge of the universe', to the human host's body. There, the trails enter the feet of the human and traverse the body until they terminate in the thoracic cavity where villages, forests, and mountains can be found. The *hekura* come out of their mountains and lairs, reeling and dancing, glowing as they come, fluttering around in ecstasy, like a swarm of butterflies hovering over a food patch. Once they are there, they are subject to the designs of their human host, who sends them to devour enemy souls—especially children's souls—or to help their hosts cure sickness in the village.

The shamans have to take hallucinogenic snuff—*ebene*—to contact the spirits, but adept shamans with great experience need very little—just a pinch is enough to get them going, get them singing the soft, melodic, and beautiful songs that attract the spirits. The *hekura* require beauty, and most shamans decorate their chests and stomachs with *nara* pigment, don their best feathers, and make themselves beautiful before calling to the spirits. The *hekura* have their own intoxicant, a magical beverage called *braki aiamo uku*, that they take when their human counterparts are snorting *ebene*.

As the *ebene* takes effect, the shamans begin singing louder and louder, often screaming, but always melodically and expertly. They recite the deeds of the *hekura*, the time of creation, the songs, and habits of the *hekura*, and explain many marvelous and fabulous events. Since this happens every day, most people in the village appear to be ignoring what is going on, but most of them are consciously or unconsciously listening to the songs and stories. Someone might even interrupt to add a correction to a slurred or inaccurate statement of 'mystical truth', or remind the shaman that he forgot to make a specific and characteristic gesture when he got to a certain spot in his mythical account. This is generally how the mythical times are revealed publicly, and often just snippets of the story are told, but all know what the whole story is. Sometimes the inept younger men take too much hallucinogen and 'freak out', as if they had overdosed (Chagnon and Asch, unpublished 16mm film).

The men take *ebene* almost every day in the villages I have lived in (Fig. 2–5). Taking *ebene* is noisy, exciting, and dramatic. It is sometimes unpleasant and nauseating as well, for the blast of *ebene* powder each man takes into his nostrils produces vomiting and profuse discharges of nasal mucus, laden with green powder. In their stupor the men simply ignore this, and the long strands of green mucus drip down their chins onto their chests, or dangle and sway from their noses until they smear it all over their faces—or fall with a plop to the ground.

It is sometimes dangerous as well, for the trances are often the occasion for men to relieve the frustrations that have been building up. The Yąnomamö attitude seems to be that one is not quite responsible for his acts if he is in communion with the *hekura* and high on *ebene*. Thus, one occasionally sees timid men use the opportunity to become boisterous and at times violent— running around the village in a stupor, wild eyed and armed, threatening to shoot someone with an arrow or hack someone with a machete. The same men would be unlikely to do this when sober, and I have always suspected that one of the primary functions of the daily hallucinogenic bouts is to give otherwise frustrated men a quasi-acceptable means through which they can work off their pent-up antagonisms and have, if only briefly and artificially, a moment of passion they might not otherwise be able to enjoy. When they become *waiteri* on drugs, people pay attention to them, chase them, disarm them, attempt to calm their tempers, and entreat them to calm down and stop being 'fierce'. Most of them allow their concerned peers to disarm them and calm them down, for they appear to be aware that carrying the event too far will strain credulity and invite less compassionate responses. Thus, the timid can, for a moment, be fierce and feared and can have their moment of ferocious passion, whether or not they would be able to meaningfully hold that status when sober. Even some of the stringent avoidance taboos are overlooked if people are intoxicated on *ebene*. Thus, sons-in-law can touch, talk to, and caress their fathers-in-law, something that would be unthinkable if both were sober. It is almost as if the psychological dimension of socially tripping out is a release valve for pent-up emotions and strains that the workaday life imposes and generates.

But it can also get out of hand and be antisocial. In a village to the north of Kąobawä's, one of the men decapitated another with a single blow of his machete, provoking a violent fission in the village and a long war between the two related groups. It is not, in my estimation, irrelevant that the decapitated man was a chronic opponent of his killer and that there had been a long history of argumentation between them. I myself was nearly shot by a wild-eyed young man who was high on *ebene*, a man with whom I had had a disagreement earlier that day (Chagnon, 1974).

The Yąnomamö cosmos parallels and reflects the mortal world that men know, understand and dwell in. When they die, they repeat life again elsewhere, in the layer above, hunting, collecting, gardening, making love, and making war. In *hedu* as it is on earth.

4/Social Organization and Demography

Introduction

In this chapter I will discuss the daily social life and social organization of the Yąnomamö from several vantages, for there are, indeed, a number of acceptable and widely used approaches to the understanding of social organization in primitive society. I will focus primarily on the fascinating problem of village fissioning among the Yąnomamö and how this reflects the "failure of solidarity," the inability of villages to be held together by kinship, marriage, descent from common ancestors, and the ephemeral authority of headmen such as Kąobawä. It would appear that primitive societies can only grow so large at the local level—the village in this case—if internal order is provided by just these commonly found integrating mechanisms.

I will also counterpose two points of view that are widely found in the field of anthropology. One of the approaches is the so-called "structural" approach, which focuses on ideal models of societies, models that are based on the "rules" of kinship, descent, and marriage. These are highly simplified but very elegant models, but they do not explain much about the actual behavior of individuals in their day-to-day kinship roles or their actual marriage practices and life histories. Another approach is the so-called "statistical model" approach, which derives from large amounts of actual behavioral facts, but yields less elegant, less simplified models. However, such models conform more to reality. I prefer the latter, for they lead to a more satisfactory way to understand individual variation and therefore the ability to predict social behavior.

A poignant way of illustrating the difference in approach is an anecdote I once heard the famous French anthropologist Claude Levi-Strauss use to justify his interest in ideal models and "structures." He likened social and cultural anthropology to a kind of science that studies crustaceans. It is legitimate, and even meritorious, to concern oneself with the shell of the organism itself. Levi-Strauss preferred to consider the shells: they are attractive, symmetrical, pleasant to handle, and pleasant to think about. But he acknowledged that there were other ways of studying this life form. One could focus on the slimy, amorphous, rather unpleasant animal that lives in the shell—such as an oyster or slug. That, too, was a legitimate and meritorious endeavor, and he had no objection if others pursued that kind of approach.

The issue, of course, has to do with the extent to which the shell and the amorphous animal inside it make much sense when considered alone and separately. My own view is that the animal is not as amorphous as it appears and itself has some structured integrity. My view is also that there has to be some kind of causal relationship between the animal and the type of structure it generates in the form of a pretty shell. The shell in this analogy is "social structure." The amorphous animal inside it is "social behavior."

Daily Social Life

Male-Female Division   A number of distinctions based on status differences are important in daily life. Perhaps the most conspicuous and most important is the distinction between males and females.

Yąnomamö society is decidedly masculine. Female children assume duties and responsibilities in the household long before their brothers are obliged to participate in useful domestic tasks. For the most part, little girls are obliged to tend their younger brothers and sisters, although they are also expected to help their mothers in other chores such as cooking, hauling water, and collecting firewood (Fig. 4–1). By the time girls have reached puberty they have already learned that their world is decidedly less attractive than that of their brothers. Most have been promised in marriage by that time.

Girls have almost no voice in the decisions reached by their elder kin in deciding whom they should marry. They are largely pawns to be disposed of by their kinsmen, and their wishes are given very little consideration. In many cases, the girl has been promised to a man long before she reaches puberty, and in some cases her husband actually raises her for part of her childhood. In short, they do not participate as equals in the political affairs of the corporate kinship group and seem to inherit most of the duties without enjoying many of the privileges.

Marriage does not enhance the status of the girl, for her duties as wife require her to assume difficult and laborious tasks too menial to be executed by the men. For the most part these include the incessant demands for firewood and drinking water, particularly the former. Women spend several hours each day scouring the neighborhood for suitable wood. There is usually an abundant supply in the garden within a year of clearing the land, but this disappears rapidly. Thereafter, the women must forage further afield to collect the daily supply of firewood, sometimes traveling several miles each day to obtain it. It is a lucky woman who owns an ax, for collecting wood is a tedious job without a steel tool. The women can always be seen at dusk, returning to the village in a procession, bearing enormous loads of wood in their pack baskets (Fig. 4–2). Good planners will spend a great deal of time collecting wood on some days so that they can take a vacation from this chore on others. If a woman locates a good supply of wood near the village, she will haul as much as she can and store it rather than let it be taken by her covillagers.

Fig. 4–1. Young girl baby-sitting for her mother.

Women must respond quickly to the demands of their husbands. In fact, they must respond without waiting for a command. It is interesting to watch the behavior of women when their husbands return from a hunting trip or a visit. The men march slowly across the village and retire silently into their hammocks. The woman, no matter what she is doing, hurries home and quietly but rapidly prepares a meal for the husband. Should the wife be slow at doing this, the husband is within his rights to beat her. Most reprimands meted out by irate husbands take the form of blows with the hand or with a piece of firewood, but a good many husbands are even more severe. Some of them chop their wives with the sharp edge of a machete or ax, or shoot them with a barbed arrow in some nonvital area, such as the buttocks or leg. Many men are given to punishing their wives by holding the hot end of a glowing stick against them, resulting in serious burns. The punishment is usually, however, adjusted to the seriousness of the wife's shortcomings, more drastic measures being reserved for infidelity or suspicion of infidelity. Many men, however, show

Fig. 4–2. Women returning from the garden at dusk with loads of firewood.

their ferocity by meting out serious punishment to their wives for even minor offenses. It is not uncommon for a man to injure his errant wife seriously; and some men have even killed wives.

Women expect this kind of treatment. Those who are not too severely treated might even measure their husband's concern in terms of the frequency of minor beatings they sustain. I overheard two young women discussing each other's scalp scars. One of them commented that the other's husband must really care for her since he has beaten her on the head so frequently!

A woman usually depends for protection on her brothers, who will defend her against a cruel husband. If a man is too severe to a wife, her brothers may take the woman away from him and give her to another man. It is largely for this reason that women abhor the possibility of being married off to men in distant villages; they know that their brothers cannot protect them under these circumstances. Women who have married a male cross-cousin have an easier life, for they are related to their husbands by cognatic ties of kinship as well as by marriage. Bahimi is, for example, Kạobawä's Mother's Brother's Daughter (MBD) and their marital relationship is very tranquil. He does punish Bahimi occasionally, but never cruelly. Some men, however, seem to think that it is reasonable to beat their wife once in a while "just to keep her on her toes."

A young man in Monou-teri shot and killed his wife a few years before I conducted my fieldwork. Even while I was there, a man in one of the villages shot his wife in the stomach with a barbed arrow. Considerable internal injury resulted when the arrow was removed. The missionaries had her sent out by airplane to the Territorial capital for surgery. Her wound had gotten infected, and the girl was near death by the time the incident came to their attention. Another man chopped his wife on the arm with a machete; the missionaries in that village feared that the woman would lose the use of her hand because some of the tendons to her fingers were severed. A fight involving a case of infidelity took place in one of the villages just before I left the field. The male culprit was killed in the club fight, and the recalcitrant wife had both her ears cut off by her enraged husband. A number of other women had their ears badly mutilated by angry husbands. The women wear sticks of cane in their pierced ear lobes; these are easily grabbed by the husband. A few men jerked these so hard that they tore their wife's ear lobes open.

It is not difficult to understand, then, why many Yąnomamö women have such a vindictive and caustic attitude toward the external world. By the time a woman is 30 years old she has "lost her shape" and has developed a rather unpleasant disposition. Women tend to seek refuge and consolation in each other's company, sharing their misery with their peers.

A woman gains a measure of respect when she becomes old. By then she has adult children who care for her and treat her kindly. Old women also have a unique position in the world of intervillage warfare and politics. They are immune from the incursions of raiders and can go from one village to another with complete disregard for personal danger. In this connection they are sometimes employed as messengers and, on some occasions, as the recoverers of bodies. If a man is killed near the village of an enemy, old women from the slain man's village are permitted to recover his body.

Still, the women have one method by which they can exercise a measure of influence over village politics. All women fear being abducted by raiders and always leave the village with this anxiety at the back of their minds. Women always take their children with them, particularly younger children, so that if they are abducted, the child will not starve to death because of the separation of the mother. They are therefore concerned with the political behavior of their men and occasionally goad them into taking action against some possible enemy by caustically accusing the men of cowardice. This has the effect of establishing the village's reputation for ferocity, reducing the possibility of raiders abducting the women while they are out collecting firewood or garden produce. The men cannot stand being belittled by the women in this fashion, and are forced to take action if the women unite against them. This is clearly the case in the film *The Ax Fight* (Asch and Chagnon, 1975).

Child-Adult Division   Despite the fact that children of both sexes spend much of their time with their mothers, the boys are treated with more indulgence by their fathers from an early age. Thus, the distinction between male and female status develops early in the socialization process, and the boys are quick to learn their favored position with respect to girls. They are encouraged to be fierce and are rarely punished by their parents for inflicting blows on them or on the hapless girls in the village. This can be seen in one of the scenes in the film *A Man Called Bee* (Chagnon and Asch, 1974a). Kạobawä, for example, lets Ariwari beat him on the face and head to express his anger and temper, laughing and commenting on his ferocity. Although Ariwari is only about 4 years old, he has already learned that the appropriate response to a flash of anger is to strike someone with his hand or with an object, and it is not uncommon for him to give his father a healthy smack in the face whenever something displeases him. He is frequently goaded into hitting his father by teasing, being rewarded by gleeful cheers of assent from his mother and from the other adults in the household.

When Kạobawä's group travels, Ariwari emulates his father by copying his activities on a child's scale. For example, he erects a temporary hut from small sticks and discarded leaves and plays happily in his own camp. His sisters, however, are pressed into more practical labor and help their mother do useful tasks. Still, the young girls are given some freedom to play at being adults and have their moments of fun with their mothers or other children.

But a girl's childhood ends sooner than a boy's. The game of playing house fades imperceptibly into a constant responsibility to help mother. By the time a girl is 10 years old or so, she has become an economic asset to the mother and spends a great deal of time working. Little boys, by contrast, spend hours playing among themselves and are able to prolong their childhood into their late teens if they so wish. By that time a girl has married, and many even have a child or two.

A girl's transition to womanhood is obvious because of its physiological manifestations. At first menses (*yọbömou*), Yạnomamö girls are confined to their houses and hidden behind a screen of leaves. Their old cotton garments are discarded and replaced by new ones manufactured by their mothers or by older female friends. During this week of confinement, the girl is fed by her relatives; her food must be eaten by means of a stick, as she is not allowed to come into contact with it in any other fashion. She speaks in whispers, and then only to close kin. She must also scratch herself with another set of sticks. The Yạnomamö word for menstruation translates literally as "squatting" (*roo*), and that fairly accurately describes what pubescent females (and adult women) do during menstruation. Yạnomamö women do not use the equivalents of tampons or sanitary napkins. They simply remain inactive during menstruation, squatting on their haunches and allowing the menstrual blood to drip on the ground. However, women are menstruating relatively infrequently, for they are pregnant or nursing infants much of their lives. After her puberty confinement, a girl usually takes up residence with her promised husband and begins life as a married woman.

Males, on the other hand, do not have their transition into manhood marked by a ceremony. Nevertheless, one can usually tell when a boy is attempting to enter the world of men. The most conspicuous sign is his anger when others call him by his name. When the adults in the village cease using his personal name, the young man has achieved some sort of masculine adult status. Young men are always very touchy about their names and they, more than anyone else, take quick offense when hearing their names mentioned. The Yạnomamö constantly employ *teknonymy* when a kinship usage is ambiguous. Thus, someone may wish to refer to Kạobawä in a conversation, but the kinship term appropriate to the occasion might not distinguish him from his several brothers. Then, Kạobawä will be referred to as "father of Ariwari." However, when Ariwari gets older he will attempt to put a stop to this in an effort to establish his status as an adult. A young man has been recognized as an adult when people no longer use his name in teknonymous references. Still, the transition is not abrupt, and it is not marked by a recognizable point in time.

Finally, the children differ from adults in their susceptibility to supernatural hazards. A great deal of Yạnomamö sorcery and mythological references to harmful magic focuses on children as the target of malevolence. Yạnomamö shamans are constantly sending their spirits (*hekura*) to enemy villages. There, they secretly attack and devour the vulnerable portion of the children's souls, bringing about sickness and death. These same shamans spend an equal amount of time warding off the dangerous spirits sent by their enemies. Children are vulnerable because their souls are not firmly established within their physical beings and can wander out of the body almost at will. The most common way for a child's soul to escape is to leave by way of the mouth when the child cries. Thus, mothers are quick to hush a bawling baby in order to prevent its soul from escaping. The child's soul can be recovered by sweeping the ground in the vicinity where it most probably escaped, calling for it while sweeping the area with a particular kind of branch. I once helped gather up the soul of a sick child in this fashion, luring it back into the sick baby. One of the contributions I made, in addition to helping with the calling and sweeping, was a dose of medicine for the child's diarrhea. A consequence of this set of attitudes about the vulnerability of children is that much of the village's activity with respect to shamanism and curing is directed toward the children.

Daily Activities   Kạobawä's village is oval shaped. His house is located among those of his agnatic (related through male ties) kinsmen; they occupy a continuous arc along one side of the village. Each of the men built his own section of the village, but in such a way that the roofs coincided and could be attached by simply extending the thatching. When completed, the village looked like a continuous, oval-shaped lean-to because of the way in which the roofs of the discrete houses were attached. Each house, however, is owned by the family that built it. Shararaiwä, Kạobawä's youngest brother, helped build Kạobawä's house and shares it with him. He also shares Koamashima, Kạobawä's younger wife. Kạobawä's older wife, Bahimi, hangs her hammock adjacent to Kạobawä's most of the time, but when there are visitors and the village is crowded, she ties her hammock under his in order to be able to tend the fire during the night. Ariwari still sleeps wih his mother, but will get his own hammock soon: he is nearly 4 years old. His parents are afraid he will fall into the fire at night and get burned, since he is still a little too young to sleep alone.

Daily activities begin early in a Yạnomamö village. One can hear people chatting lazily and children crying long before it is light enough to see. Most people are awakened by the cold and build up the fire just before daybreak.

They usually go back to sleep, but many of them visit and talk about their plans for the day.

The entrances are all covered with dry brush so that any movement of people through them is heard all over the village. There is always a procession of people leaving the village at dawn to relieve themselves in the nearby garden, and the noise they make going in and out of the village usually awakens the others.

The village is very smoky at this time of day, since the newly stoked campfires smolder before they leap into flames. The air is usually very still and chilly, and the ground is damp from the dew. The smoke is pleasant and seems to drive away the coolness.

Clandestine sexual liaisons usually take place at this time of day, having been arranged on the previous evening. The lovers leave the village on the pretext of "going to the toilet" and meet at some predetermined location. They return to the village by opposite routes.

This is also the time of day when raiders strike, so people must be cautious when they leave the village at dawn. If there is some reason to suspect raiders, they do not leave the confines of the upright log palisade that surrounds the village. They wait instead until full light and leave the village in armed groups.

By the time it is light enough to see, everybody has started preparing breakfast. This consists largely of roasted green plantains, easily prepared and steaming hot. Leftover meat is taken down and shared, the men usually getting the tastiest portions. The meat is hung over the fire by a vine to keep the vermin off it and to preserve it.

If any of the men have made plans to hunt that day, they leave the village before it is light. Wild turkeys can be easily taken at this time of day because they roost in conspicuous places. During the dry season the *hashimo* (a kind of grouse) sing before dark and can be readily located. If any were heard the night before, the men leave at dawn to stalk them.

Tobacco chewing starts as soon as people begin stirring. Those who have fresh supplies soak the new leaves in water and add ashes from the hearth to the wad. Men, women, and children chew tobacco and all are addicted to it. Once there was a shortage of tobacco in Kąobawä's village, and I was plagued for a week by early morning visitors who requested permission to collect my cigarette butts in order to make a wad of chewing tobacco. Normally, if anyone is short of tobacco, he can request a share of someone else's already chewed wad, or simply borrow the entire wad when its owner puts it down somewhere. Tobacco is so important to them that their word for "poverty" translates as "being without tobacco." I frequently justified my reluctance to give away possessions on the basis of my poverty. Many of them responded by spitting their wads out and handing them to me!

Work begins as soon as breakfast is completed; the Yąnomamö like to take advantage of the morning coolness. Within an hour after it is light the men are in their gardens clearing brush, felling large trees, transplanting plantain cuttings, burning off dead timber, or planting new crops of cotton, maize, sweet potatoes, yuca, or the like, depending on the season. They work until 10:30 A.M., retiring because it is too humid and hot by that time to continue with their strenuous work. Most of them bathe in the stream before returning to their hammocks for a rest and a meal.

The women usually accompany their husbands to the garden and occupy themselves by helping with planting and weeding. In this way the men are sure that their families are safe and that the women are not having affairs with other men.

The children spend a great deal of time exploring the wonders of the plant and animal life around them and are accomplished biologists at an early age. Most 12-year-old boys can, for example, name 20 species of bees and give the anatomical or behavioral reasons for their distinctions—and they know which ones produce the best honey. An 8-year-old girl brought me a tiny egglike structure on one occasion and asked me to watch it with her. Presently it cracked open and numerous baby cockroaches poured out, while she described the intimate details of the reproductive process to me.

The younger children stay close to their mothers, but the older ones have considerable freedom to wander about the garden at play. Young boys hunt for lizards with miniature bows and featherless arrows. If they can capture one alive, they bring it back to the village and tie a string around it. The string is anchored to a stick in the village clearing and the little boys chase it gleefully, shooting scores of tiny arrows at it (Fig. 4–3). Since lizards are very quick and little boys are poor shots, the target practice can last for hours. Usually, however, the fun terminates when an older boy decides to make an end to the unhappy lizard and kills it with his adult-sized arrows, showing off his archery skills to the disgruntled small fry. Sometimes the children catch live bees and tie light cotton threads to their bodies, allowing them to try to fly off dragging the string behind them. The bees have difficulty flying and move very slowly, with the string sticking straight out behind them as the frantically beating wings hold it straight. The children then chase the bees with sticks, trying to knock them down. Sometimes the children will be organized by older men, who teach them how to go on raids. They usually sneak up on an effigy made of leaves and shoot it full of arrows on the command of the older men, and then 'flee' from the scene.

Most of the people rest in their hammocks during the heat of midday, although they will collect fruits and other wild foods from the surrounding area, if any are in season. They avoid being in the direct rays of the midday sun.

If the men return to their gardening, they do so about 4:00 P.M., working until sundown. Prior to that they usually gather in small groups around the village and take hallucinogenic snuff, chanting to the *hekura* spirits as the drugs take effect (see the film *Magical Death*, Chagnon, 1973). This usually lasts for an hour or two, after which the men bathe to wash the vomit or nasal mucus off their bodies. When I first lived with the Yąnomamö, Kąobawä did not participate in drug taking. He began doing so when a group of Protestant missionaries began having a strong impact on his group in the late 1960s (see Chapter 7). Most of the men do take drugs and enjoy doing it, despite the associated unpleasantries of vomiting and the pain that follows the blast of air as the powder is blown deeply into the nasal passages.

Fig. 4–3. Little boys practicing archery with a lizard that is tied by a string.

Whatever the men do for the afternoon, however, the women invariably search for firewood and haul immense, heavy loads of it to their houses just before dark.

The biggest meal of the day is prepared in the evening. The staple is plantains, but frequently other kinds of food are available after the day's activities. Meat is always the most desirable food and is always considered to be in short supply as is frequently reported elsewhere in the Tropical Forest—almost irrespective of its actual abundance. For example, the Siriono Indians of Bolivia would gorge themselves on monkey meat and then later complain of being meat hungry, thereby drawing attention away from the possibility that they might have some extra meat to share (Holmberg, 1969). It is a happy occasion, however, if someone should kill a tapir, for then a large number of people will get a share, depending on their kinship ties. Hunters who kill tapirs are supposed to give all the meat away and eat none of it themselves. They usually give it to their brothers-in-law or father-in-law, and the sharing is done by them.

Both sexes participate in the cooking, although the women do the greater share of it. Men do all the cooking at feasts, a ceremonial occasion (see Chapter 5 for a description of a feast). Food preparation is not elaborate and rarely requires much labor, time, or paraphernalia. Spices are never used, although the salty ashes of a particular kind of tree are sometimes mixed with water to form a condiment of sorts. The food is dunked into the salty liquid and eaten (see footnote 5, Chapter 2).

Everyone eats in his hammock using his fingers for utensils. Some meals cannot be eaten from a reclining position, so the members of the family squat in a circle around the common dish. For example, large quantities of tiny fish are cooked by wrapping them in leaves and cooking them in the hot coals. When the fish are done, the package is spread open, and everyone shares its contents.

Animals are rarely skinned before cooking. They are merely put over the fire after their entrails have been removed, and roasted—head, fur, claws, and all. Most of the fur is singed off in the process of cooking. Small animals are dismembered by hand. Large ones are cut up with knives or machetes before smoking or roasting. The head of a monkey is highly prized because the brain is considered a delicacy. Monkey is one of the more common meats, so that this delicacy is enjoyed rather frequently by the Yąnomamö.

By the time supper is over it is nearly dark. The fires are prepared for the evening; if someone has allowed his own fire to go out during the day, he simply borrows two glowing sticks from a neighbor and rekindles his own hearth. The entrances to the village are sealed off with dry brush so that prowlers cannot enter without raising an alarm. Before retiring to their hammocks, the Yąnomamö first sit on them and wipe the bottoms of their bare feet by rubbing them together. This rubs off most of the debris that has accumulated on them during the course of the day. Everyone sleeps naked and as close to the fire as possible. Despite the inevitable last-minute visiting, things are usually quiet in the village by the time it is dark.

Things are not always quiet after dark. If anyone in the village is sick, a shaman will chant to the malevolent spirits most of the night to exorcise them. Or, should anyone be mourning a dead kinsman, he or she will sob and wail long after the others have fallen asleep. Occasionally, a fight will break out between a husband and wife, and soon everybody in the village will be screaming, expressing opinions on the dispute. The shouting may continue sporadically for hours, dying down only to break out anew as someone gets a fresh insight into the problem. Once in a while someone gives a long, loud speech voicing his opinion of the world in general. This is called *patamou* by the Yąnomamö—to 'act big'. Those who are interested may add their own comments, but the audience usually grumbles about the noise and falls asleep.

Status Differences and Activities   Daily activities, except those concerning gardening and visiting, do not vary much from season to season. Much of the variation that does occur is a function of one's age or sex, as was shown above.

Other status differences do exist and account for some variation in the activities of particular individuals. Rerebawä, for example, is an outsider to Kąobawä's group and had no intention of joining the village as a permanent resident. Consequently, he did not participate in the gardening activities and had considerably more spare time than other married men. He spent this time hunting for his wife and her parents, one of his obligations as a son-in-law. He was quite dependent on them for the bulk of his diet because they provided him with all his plantains. He is quick to make reference to his hunting skills and generosity, perhaps to draw attention away from the fact that he did not cultivate food for his wife and children. He was able to avoid making a garden because of his status as a *sioha*—an in-married son-in-law. He intended to return to his own village as soon as his bride service was over. But his in-laws wanted him to stay permanently so that he would be able to provide them with meat and garden produce when they are old. They have no sons to do this for them and even promised Rerebawä their second daughter on the condition that he remain permanently in the village. They prevented Rerebawä from taking his wife and children home by keeping at least one of the children with them when Rerebawä went to visit his own family. They knew that his wife could not bear to be separated permanently from her child, and Rerebawä invariably brought her back home so that she could be with the child.

By Yąnomamö standards he did enough bride service and deserves to be given his wife. Also, by their standards he has lived in the village so long that he should be obliged to make his own garden. But he was in a position to legitimately refuse to do this because he discharged his son-in-law obligations well beyond what was expected of him.

Kąobawä, on the other hand, has the special status of being his group's headman. Apart from this, he is also some 20 years senior to Rerebawä and has many more obligations and responsibilities to his larger number of kin. Rerebawä, in addition to initially refusing to make a garden, thought nothing of taking a week-long trip to visit friends, leaving his wife and children with her parents. His attitude toward the children, compared to Kąobawä's, was rather indifferent when Rerebawä was younger. For example, Kąobawä had planned to accompany me to Caracas to see how 'foreigners' live until Ariwari began crying and appealed to his father's paternal sensitivities. Kąobawä stepped out of the canoe, took off the clothing I had loaned him, and picked up Ariwari. "I can't go with you," he explained. "Ariwari will miss me and be sad."

Kąobawä thinks for the others in the village, many of whom are not able to perceive some of the less obvious implications of situations. In political matters he is the most astute man in the group, but he so diplomatically exercises his influence that the others are not offended. Should someone be planning to do something that is potentially dangerous, he simply points out the danger and adds parenthetically, "Go ahead and do it if you want to, but don't expect sympathy from me if you get hurt." Shararaiwä, his youngest brother, planned to take a trip to a distant village with me. I knew that the two villages were not on particularly good terms with each other, but they were not actively at war. Kąobawä arrived at my canoe just as we were about to depart and asked me not to take Shararaiwä along, explaining that the Iyäwei-teri might possibly molest him and precipitate hostilities between the two groups. Shararaiwä was willing to take a chance that my presence would be sufficient to deter any potential trouble, but Kąobawä would not risk it.

On another occasion a group of men from Patanowä-teri arrived to explore with Kąobawä the possibility of peace between their two villages. They were brothers-in-law to him and were fairly certain that he would protect them from the village hotheads. One of the ambitious men in Kąobawä's group saw in this an opportunity to enhance his prestige and made plans to murder the three visitors. This man, Paruriwä, was a very cunning, treacherous fellow and quite jealous of Kąobawä's position as headman. He wanted to be the village leader and privately told me to address *him* as the headman. On this occasion Kąobawä let it be known that he intended to protect the visitors. For the better part of the day the village was in a state of suspense. Paruriwä and his followers were not to be found anywhere; a rumor spread that they had painted themselves black, were boasting of their fierceness, and were well armed. Kąobawä and his supporters, mostly his own brothers and brothers-in-law, remained in the village all day, their weapons close at hand. Late in the afternoon Paruriwä and his men appeared in their black paint and took up strategic posts around the village. He himself held an ax. He strutted arrogantly up to the visitors holding his ax as if he were ready to strike. The village became very quiet, and most of the women and children fled nervously. Neither Kąobawä nor the Patanowä-teri visitors batted an eyelash when Paruriwä approached, although the others were visibly nervous and sat up in their hammocks. It was a showdown. But instead of striking the visitors with the ax as he appeared to suggest he was going to do, he invited one of them out to chant with him. Within seconds all three of the visitors had paired off with members of Paruriwä's group and were chanting passionately with them, explaining the reasons for their visit and giving their justification for the state of hostilities.

The crisis had been averted because of Kąobawä's implied threat that he would defend the visitors with force. A number of men in Paruriwä's group were visitors from Monou-teri; their headman had been killed a few months earlier by the Patanowä-teri. When Paruriwä failed to go through with his plan, they left the village in a rage, hoping to recruit a raiding party in their own village and ambush the visitors when they left.

Kąobawä realized that the visitors would not be safe until they got back home, since the Monou-teri would attempt to intercept them. He visited me that night and asked me to take the visitors back to their village at dawn in my canoe, knowing that I had already planned a trip there for the immediate future. After I agreed to accelerate my own plans, he proceeded to give me instructions about the trip: I should not stop to visit at any of the villages along the Upper Orinoco River, for all of them were at war with the Patanowä-teri and would shoot my companions on sight. The Patanowä-teri men lay on the floor of my canoe and covered themselves with a tarp when we passed these villages. The people on the bank shouted curses at me for not stopping to visit and give them trade goods. At this time the Patanowä-teri were being raided by about a dozen different villages. We had to cover part of the distance to their village on foot, proceeding very cautiously because of the danger of raiders. At one point the men showed me the spot where a Hasuböwä-teri raiding party had killed a Patanowä-teri woman a week earlier. Thus, Kąobawä not only protected the visitors while they were in his village but he also arranged a "safe-conduct" for their return.

Kąobawä keeps order in the village when people get out of hand. Paruriwä, for example, is particularly cruel to his four wives and beats them severely for even slight provocations. None of his wives have brothers in the village, and few people are courageous enough to interfere with Paruriwä when he is angry. On one occasion Kąobawä was holding a feast for the members of an allied village. His preparations were being duplicated by an equal effort on the part of Paruriwä, an obvious attempt by the latter to show that he was also a leader. Some of the visitors arrived early and were visiting in Paruriwä's house. He commanded one of his wives to prepare food for them, but the woman moved a little too slowly to suit him. Paruriwä went into a rage, grabbed an ax, and swung it wildly at her. She ducked and ran screaming from the house. Paruriwä recovered his balance and threw the ax at her as she fled, but missed. By this time, Kąobawä had seen the ax go whizzing over the woman's head; he raced across the village in time to take a machete from Paruriwä before he could inflict much damage with it. He did manage, however, to hit her twice before Kąobawä disarmed him, splitting her hand wide open between two of her fingers with one of the blows.

On another occasion one of Kąobawä's brothers took too much drug and became violent. He staggered to the center of the village with his bow and arrows, while people ran frantically out of their houses to avoid being shot. Kąobawä managed to disarm him and hid his weapons.

During the several club fights that took place while I was in the field on my first trip, Kąobawä stood by with his bow and arrows to make sure that the fighting was kept relatively innocuous (Fig. 6–1). In one of the chest-pounding duels, he managed to keep the fight from escalating into a shooting war by making sure that everybody in his group took a turn in the fighting. (See Chapter 5 for a description of the fight.) On this occasion his group was being trounced by their opponents, largely because only a few of the men were doing all the fighting for Kąobawä's group. These men were forced to take several turns in rapid succession, while a large number of men stood by and watched. The fighters wanted to escalate the battle into a duel with axes, hoping to intimidate their opponents into conceding. Kąobawä quickly forced the idle men to participate in the chest pounding, thereby distributing the punishment a little more evenly and reducing the possibility of a bloodier confrontation.

After the duel was over, Kąobawä coolly discussed the fight with the leaders in the opponents' group, explaining that he did not intend to raid them unless they raided first. A number of men in the village, notably Paruriwä and some of his followers, shouted threats at the departing opponents that they would shoot them on sight should they meet again. Paruriwä frequently boasted like this, but rarely put himself in a position that was potentially dangerous. He later ran into a party of hunters from the above-mentioned group while he was leading a raid against the Patanowä-teri. Instead of shooting them on sight as he threatened to do (they could have shot back, as they were armed), he traded arrows with them and rapidly retreated. He boasted in the village how he had terrified these men. I later visited their village and learned that Paruriwä was the one who was terrified. They themselves continued to hunt, while Paruriwä fled for home.

Kaobawä's personality differs considerably from Paruriwä's. Where the former is unobtrusive, calm, modest, and perceptive, the latter is belligerent, aggressive, ostentatious, and rash. Kaobawä has an established status in the village and numerous supporters, whose loyalties are in part determined by their kinship ties and in part because he is a wise leader. Paruriwä is attempting to share in the leadership and does not have a well-established position in this respect. It is obvious who the real leader is: when visitors come to Upper Bisaasi-teri, they seek out Kaobawä and deal with him, no matter how ambitiously Paruriwä attempts to emulate his position. Paruriwä does not have as many living brothers in his group as Kaobawä has, so his "natural following" is somewhat limited. In addition, two of his brothers are married to actual sisters of Kaobawä and have some loyalty to him. Paruriwä, therefore, has very little means with which to establish his position, so he is given over to using bluff, threat, chicanery, and treachery. This he does well, and many of the young men in the village seem to admire him for it. He has gained the support of some of these men by promising them his wives' yet unborn daughters. Remarkably enough, some of them cling to these promises and do his bidding. He is, in short, a manipulator.

Finally, one of Kaobawä's most unpleasant tasks is to scout the village neighborhood when signs of raiders have been found. This he does alone, since it is a dangerous task and one that is avoided by the other men. Not even Paruriwä participates in this. It is for this reason that many headmen are killed by raiders: they are exposed to more risks than most men.

Kaobawä has definite responsibilities as the headman and is occasionally called upon by the nature of the situation to exercise his authority. He is usually distinguishable in the village as a man of some authority only for the duration of the incident that calls for his leadership capacity. After the incident is over, he goes about his own business like the other men in the group. But even then, he sets an example for the others, particularly in his ambitions to produce large quantities of food for his family and for the guests he must entertain. Most of the time he leads only by example and the others follow if it pleases them to do so. They can ignore his example if they wish, but most of the people turn to him when a difficult situation arises (Fig. 4–4).

Social Structure

One learns, after many months of living with people such as the Yanomamö, that there are 'abstract' rules and principles they can invoke to explain or justify the social interactions in which they participate. It is difficult to explain precisely how a fieldworker acquires this knowledge, for it is a gradual process. It is very much as we learn the 'rules' in our own culture. Most of us cannot, for example, explain precisely how it is that we came to 'know' that having sex with a sister or brother is 'bad', but almost all of us know that it is. But anthropologists are aware, when they go into the field to study tribal

Fig. 4–4. Kạobawä, the quiet unpretentious headman.

societies, that there are usually 'rules' about proper behavior and that these rules are often phrased in the contexts of (a) kinship, (b) descent, and (c) marriage. We therefore at least know where to begin looking for the 'rules' and 'principles', even if we cannot always say precisely how it is we 'learned' what they were. One such rule, for example, is about 'who you should marry'. It was difficult for me to get the Yạnomamö to state this in some sort of abstract way as a general 'principle' or 'rule'. I had to establish the 'rule' in a more indirect way, such as asking individual men, "Can you marry so-and-so?" The answers, when pieced together, allowed me to formulate a general rule that they themselves take to be so self-evident that they can't imagine that others do not 'know' who to marry. Answers to that question would take the form, for example, of: "What? No! I can't marry so-and-so! She is my *yuhaya* (daughter of my child or sister; granddaughter)!" Or, "No! She is my *tääya* (daughter; brother's daughter)!" Eventually, I learned all the kinship terms that both men and women used for their kin and who among them was a prohibited spouse. I also learned, in this fashion, that men could marry only those women they put into the kinship category *suaböya*. By collecting genealogies that showed who was related to whom in specific ways, it was then possible to specify any man's 'nonmarriageable' and 'marriageable' female kin. As it turned out, men could marry only those women who fell into the category of kin we would call "cross-cousins." These are, from a man's point of view, the daughters of his mother's brother or the daughters of his father's sister. Figure 4–5 shows the difference between "cross-cousins" and "parallel cousins." The rule, therefore, is that the Yạnomamö marry bilateral cross-

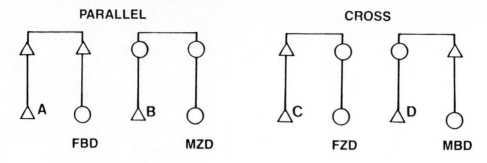

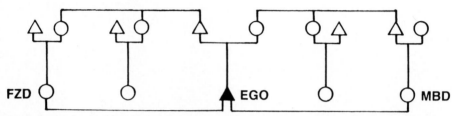

Fig. 4–5. In Yąnomamö society, men can marry their FZD or their MBD—their cross-cousins. They can not marry their FBD or their MZD, who are parallel cousins and classified as 'sisters'. The upper half of the diagram shows parallel and cross-cousins and the relationship of men (A, B, C and D) to the female cousins. The bottom half shows an "egocentric" kinship diagram and how the four female cousins are traditionally diagrammed.

cousins. Bilateral means "both sides," that is, father's *and* mother's side of the family. From their vantage, the rule is, "We marry our *suaböya*." In a very real sense, they say, "We marry our wives"——and to ask "Whom do you marry?" seems somewhat peculiar to them. They marry their wives, as real people are supposed to do.

The interesting fact here is that their 'marriage rule' is at once embedded in the kinship terminology itself as well as existing as a 'principle': we marry *suaböya*. Their kinship system literally defines who is and who is not marriageable, and there are *no* terms for what we would call 'in-laws'. In a word, everyone in Yąnomamö society is called by some kinship term that can be translated into what we would call 'blood' relatives. To be sure, they 'extend' kinship terms to strangers who are nonkin. Kąobawä calls Rerebawä by a kinship term, but they are not related. The analyses below will indicate how kin and nonkin are treated. The fascinating aspect of their society is that *all* neighbors are some sort of kin and therefore social life takes place in a kinship matrix. Nobody can escape it, not even the anthropologist. Kąobawä, for example, calls me *hekamaya*—nephew (sister's son). Rerebawä calls me *aiγä*—older brother. Everyone gets placed into some sort of kinship matrix which, to a large degree, specifies 'in principle' how one is expected to behave vis-a-vis his or her kin of specific categories. Both Kąobawä and Rerebawä *know* I am not their sister's son or older brother respectively, but I must necessarily be put into *some* kinship category so that a general basis of proper and expected social behavior exists. To be outside of the kinship system is, in a very real sense, to be inhuman or nonhuman: real humans are some sort of kin. It is in this sense that anthropologists say that primitive society is, to a large degree, organized and regulated by kinship.

The 'discovery' of one principle often helps you to identify and understand other principles. I knew, for example, that they had warm affectionate attitudes about men that they called by the term *shoriwä*. These men, it turns out, are brothers of the women you have married, will marry, or could marry—they are also your male cross-cousins. Similarly, the easily detected warm relationship of a man to his mother's brother (Fig. 4–6) is also comprehensible in terms of the marriage rule: you can marry his daughter.

These general rules or principles also exist for notions of descent from distant ancestors—and are discovered by the anthropologist in essentially the way just described for 'discovering' kinship rules. For the Yąnomamö, descent through the male line is more important than descent through the female line, especially as regards general principles of marriage. Patrilineal descent defines as members of one group—called a patrilineal lineage (or, simply, patrilineage) all those individuals who can trace descent through genealogical connections back to some male ancestor *using only the male genealogical connections*. Figure 4–7 shows a patrilineage and who 'belongs' to it. The general Yąnomamö rule about marriage, insofar as it can be phrased in terms of a descent rule, is simply

Fig. 4–6. Ariwari being fondled by his mother's brother, a very special kinship relationship among the Yąnomamö.

that everyone *must* marry outside of his or her own patrilineal group. The Yąnomamö patrilineage is, therefore, an *exogamic* group—all members must marry outside of it into a different patrilineage. Kąobawä is in a different patrilineage than Bahimi, who is his cross-cousin. In Yąnomamö society, one's cross-cousins will always belong to a different lineage but parallel cousins will always belong to your own lineage.

An "Ideal" Model of Yąnomamö Society   Structural anthropologists, such as Levi-Strauss, are fascinated with the 'structures' that can be drawn to represent, in shorthand fashion, individual societies. They use as the basis of the 'models' or 'structures' abstract rules or principles of the sort just described: rules about kinship, descent, and marriage. One can use such models as beginning points to make more detailed observations about other social phenomena, or one can compare the ideal models themselves. These models, in the analogy given at the beginning of this chapter, are the 'symmetrical shells' that are fun to manipulate and consider.

Figure 4–8 gives the ideal model of Yąnomamö society, based on their 'general principles' of patrilineal descent, bilateral cross-cousin marriage and the classification of bilateral cross-cousins as 'wives'. The model is at once elegant and incorporates all of the important 'rules'. It shows, in effect, that Yąnomamö society can be represented as being bifurcated into two intermarrying 'halves' or 'moieties'. One half, the Xs, gives women to the other half, the Ys, and receives in return the women that they will marry. Each person belongs to the patrilineage of his or her father, and all men are marrying women who are *simultaneously* their Father's Sister's Daughters (hereafter FZD) *and* their Mother's Brother's Daughters (hereafter MBD). Such models are heuristic and useful, for they suggest additional lines of inquiry to the field researcher, and they state very simple principles that enable the observer to take a 'holistic' view of the social organization.

Such models can be used, in turn, to phrase other general questions and summarize other social processes, such as village fissioning. Consider how this kind of model can elegantly represent the fissioning of a larger Yąnomamö village into two smaller ones, as shown in Figure 4–9. Village A contains two patrilineages, X and Y, each subdivided into four 'cadet' sublineages 1, 2, 3, and 4. Figure 4–9 only shows the male members for purposes of simplicity. In

Fig. 4–7. A patrilineage: members are indicated by solid coloring and belong to the patrilineal descent group of their fathers.

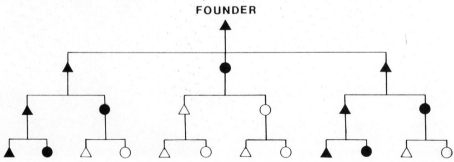

FOUNDER

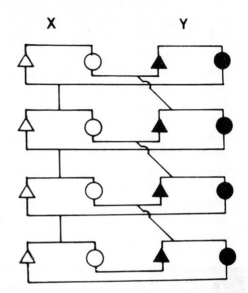

Fig. 4–8. "Ideal" model of Yąnomamö social structure, showing two lineages (X and Y) that exchange marriageable women. Each man marries a woman who is simultaneously his MBD/FZD.

Village A, the cadet lines of both lineages that are drawn opposite to each other exchange marriageable females: X-1 gives its females to Y-1 and gets females in return from them. In fact, the marriages are arranged by these 'cadet' segments for the younger males and females in them: older brothers and the father make arrangements to give their sisters and daughters to men in the 'cadet' segment of the opposite lineage. Theoretically, any male of lineage X can marry any female of lineage Y, but past marriage exchanges tend to keep particular cadet lines 'bound' to each other in a long-term obligation to exchange only their own females with each other. Notice also that the cadet lines 1 and 2 are genealogically 'closer' to each other than either is to cadet line 3 or 4. Patrilineal descent, plus the Yąnomamö kinship classification system, would require all men of the same generation in the same lineage to call each other by "brother" terms. But the men in cadet line 1 of lineage X are 'actual' brothers (they have the same father) to each other, whereas the men in cadet line 4 of lineage X are their distant (parallel) cousins. They are, as the diagram is drawn, second cousins. They are, in a very real sense, *competitors* with them for all the marriageable women in the opposite lineage. Whereas actual brothers are cooperative, 'distant' brothers (parallel cousins) are competitive. A good deal of the competition can be nullified by faithfully giving your sisters and daughters to the men in the cadet lineage with whom your immediate group members have traditionally exchanged women.

As Village A grows in size, internal conflicts will increase among its members and it will eventually fission into two groups: Villages B and C. Notice how, in the diagram, the cadet lines 1 and 2 of lineages X and Y remain together in Village B and separate from their distant cousins, who go into Village C. Each new village contains members of both lineage X and lineage Y, and the cadet lines are still 'bound' to each other by marriage ties. In this fashion, the members of a lineage are distributed in several villages. Kąobawä, for example, has "brothers" in Lower Bisaasi-teri, Monou-teri and Patanowä-teri—but they are, in fact, his 'parallel cousins'. His actual brothers are in his own village; the model shown in Figure 4–9 helps make clear, in 'ideal' terms, how this comes about. Over time, Village B fissions, producing two new villages, D and E, as shown in Figure 4–9. Village C continues and does not fission.

Figure 4–9 summarizes, in ideal terms, some of the important rules and processes that can be documented in Yạnomamö culture. It does this clearly and efficiently and enables us to get a good overall picture of how their social system 'works' in ideal terms. Like Figure 4–8 above, it simplifies a great deal of otherwise confusing information by ignoring what *particular* individuals did in their marriages or what the actual lineage composition of *specific* villages is. The particulars of what individuals do in marriage or how actual villages are comprised in terms of descent group membership is, in the oyster analogy, the basis of the *statistical* representations that can be drawn.

It is to these kinds of data that we will now turn. It is important to point out beforehand that very different kinds of field research *could* be entailed in the two different approaches. It is, for example, quite possible for a field researcher to do a 'structural' analysis of information provided by a few key informants or even a single informant. This situation is often unavoidable, particuarly when a formerly large tribe has been reduced to a small population by epidemics and where the demographic underpinnings of social organization

Fig. 4–9. How local descent groups 'pair' with each other and remain bound when larger villages fission into smaller ones. In this fashion, larger lineages (X and Y in this drawing) are distributed among several villages (D, E, and C' in this diagram).

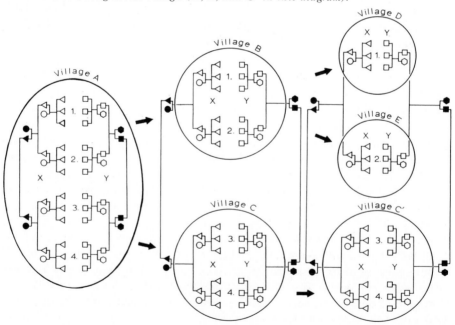

have all but disappeared. But where there are large numbers of people and where the ravages of epidemics and acculturation have not yet had a marked effect on tribal social organization, a 'statistical' approach is not only possible, but highly desirable and can be conducted simultaneously with a structural study. This usually entails a more thorough and exhaustive collection of genealogical data, actual marriages and marriage dissolutions, and the reproductive histories of both males and females. The first chapter of this case study described some of this kind of field research.

The Demographic Basis of Social Behavior

I will illustrate the 'statistical' approach by focusing on the question of solidarity as it relates to the process of village fissioning.

Anthropologists have long been concerned with the problem of 'social solidarity'. The famous French anthropologist Claude Levi-Strauss dealt with this issue at great length in his now classic 1949 work *Elementary Structures of Kinship*, taking up themes on solidarity and reciprocal exchanges developed by his predecessors Marcel Mauss (1925) and Emile Durkheim (1938 [1895], 1933 [1893]), and applying them to kinship and marriage patterns that were commonly found in the primitive world. The arguments can be thought of as essentially what provides the 'binding force' or 'cohesion' in primitive societies, the 'attraction' between both individuals and groups of individuals that permits them to live together amicably in large groups.

Yąnomamö village fissioning can be viewed in this context, for they grow to a certain size and then fission into smaller, more cohesive villages. One might even think of the process of village growth and fissioning as the 'failure' of solidarity in a certain sense, for the forces or principles that keep its members together in cooperative wholes fail to do so beyond a certain size limit. While there are many variables that affect village size—ecological, demographic, military, and social—much of the internal cohesion in Yąnomamö villages is generated through kinship relationships, marriage ties, and the charisma that particular individuals, such as Kąobawä, contribute to social amity and organization (Chagnon, 1975b).

Let us look at marriage patterns in a statistical way and try to relate this evidence to the problem of explaining why particular Yąnomamö villages are able to grow to a large size—300 or more people—while others seem to be unable to grow beyond a size of 125 or so people. The overall pattern of village size is as follows. The cluster of villages to which Kąobawä's belongs differs from the cluster of Shamatari villages to the south in several important ways. In Kąobawä's area, his village and those to which his is related historically and genealogically (the Namoweiteri villages; see Figure 2–16 of Chapter 2 and discussion) seem to fission at a lower size limit than the Shamatari villages. Could it be that there is something about the patterns of marriages in the two groups of villages that helps explain this difference? If so, what do you look for in marriages?

This question is actually an extension of one of the major questions posed by Levi-Strauss, who argued that whole *systems* of marriage were, as systems, capable of greater or lesser ability to promote solidarity (1949). The Yąno-mamö 'system' described in the previous section of this chapter was one of the three major systems discussed by Levi-Strauss, but one that he dismissed as being as 'inherently' capable as some other systems of marriage of promoting social cohesion and solidarity. Instead of considering the whole system, let us extend his argument and examine the specific types of marriages *within the specific system*. In other words, irrespective of the 'system's' comparative potential for promoting solidarity, let us see if there is a different kind of marriage pattern within Shamatari villages than within Namoweiteri villages: both groups have the same overall system or set of rules, but individuals within them may either use them differently or are better able to marry specific kinds of cousins simply because they have more of them to begin with.

Such an exhaustive statistical examination requires the use of the computer, into which is coded all of the genealogical, marital, and reproductive data that were collected in the field. Each individual is an 'Ego' about which some 20 different pieces of quantitative information are known, such as approximate year of birth (hence, age), birthplace (garden where born), mother's name, father's name, names of all spouses, order in which spouses were married, how many children Ego had by each spouse, village of residence of every Ego if alive, or place of death for each Ego if dead, and so on (Chagnon, 1974). The computer searches each Ego's relationships and builds up an exhaustive genealogy or pedigree from the field data provided to it. It compares Ego to his or her spouse and spells out precisely all genealogical connections if any exist, that is, tells precisely how each person is genealogically connected to his or her spouse. Most spouses in Yąnomamö villages are genealogically related to each other, but some are not. The analyses described below show how this is taken into consideration. The reciprocal marriage exchanges described above in elucidating the 'ideal' model usually result in spouses being related to each other in many complex ways, as is the case in Figure 4–10, which shows the marriage of one man to two women. Table 4–1 describes the genealogical connections. This example immediately reveals a problem that has to do with classifying particular consanguineal marriages, for each 'relationship loop' in the example specifies a kind of cross-cousin relationship between the man and his wives. Thus, it is difficult to characterize this man's marriages as examples of "FZD" or "MBD" types, for each marriage is both. Most Yąnomamö marriages raise the same general problem, a methodological question that is real and important, but one that is beyond the scope of this case study. Here, we will simply focus on the numbers and kinds of connections between related spouses to get the general picture of patterns in the Namoweiteri and Shamatari villages.

The 'ideal' model presented above (Fig. 4–8) represents each man as marrying a woman who is simultaneously his MBD and FZD. In actual practice, this rarely happens, largely because of demographic reasons to be raised in the next section. What does happen is that men marry women who are sometimes FZDs or sometimes MBDs. However, there are many different types of both if you consider the precise genealogical connections between

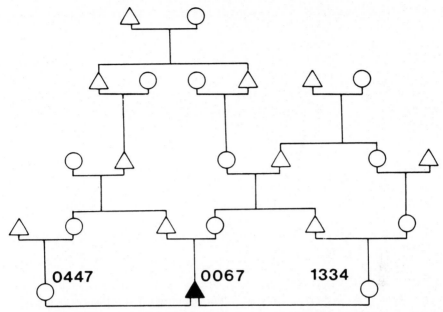

Fig. 4–10. Genealogy of a man's relationships to two wives. See Table 4–1 for the genealogical specifications and relationship coefficients.

spouses. Figure 4–11 gives some illustrations, showing how half-relationships between siblings and degrees of remoteness of cross-cousins can combine and yield a variety of cross-cousins that are "FZD" and/or "MBD" to the male Ego (only matrilateral cross-cousins are illustrated in Figure 4–14). It is these possible permutations and combinations that I have in mind when I speak of 'patterns' or 'types' of marriage within the general Yąnomamö system of marriage with Bilateral Cross-Cousins. The question, then, is about the relative frequency and type-distribution of some of these types in actual Yąnomamö villages and whether or not Shamatari villages have more or fewer of certain of the types compared to Namoweiteri villages.

Figure 4–12 presents the comparison of such types for both the Shamatari villages (pooled together) and the Namoweiteri villages (pooled together), giving the distributions of *all* of the 'genealogical loops' between men and all of their spouses. In other words, it is not the distribution of individual marriages, but the distribution of relationship types for all marriages. Thus, the marriage of Ego 0067 to his two wives discussed above is represented in this distribution as 10 different types, not as just two individual marriages. It is the overall pattern that is of interest here, simply to get a broad view of differences between the two populations in the types of connections men have to their wives.

What emerges in Figure 4–12 is that marriages in the two populations follow markedly different patterns. In the Shamatari villages, men tend to be more often related to their wives as *first* cross-cousins of both the FZD and the MBD types than are men in the Namoweiteri villages: they are marrying *closer* cross-cousins. This logically means, of course, that they marry proportionately

TABLE 4–1 Genealogical specifications and coefficients of relatedness between Ego 0067 and spouses 0447 and 1334.

Spouse	Genealogical Relationship	Coefficient of Relationship
0447	FFDD	0.0625
	FMDD	0.0625
	MMFFSSDD	0.0039
	MMFMSSDD	0.0039
	TOTAL	0.1328
1334	MFSD	0.0625
	MMSD	0.0625
	MFFDDD	0.0156
	MFMDDD	0.0156
	FFFFSDSD	0.0039
	FFFMSDSD	0.0039
	TOTAL	0.1640

fewer second or third cross-cousins. What is suggested by these data is that the maximum size to which a village might grow is somehow related to the fact that men in those villages tend to marry 'close' cousins more often than do men in Namoweiteri villages. A whole series of reasons why this might be true can be raised, but most of them are demographic in genre. One reason, not demographic, is that men might be 'trying harder' to marry close cross-cousins in the Shamatari village, but this essentially means that their *parents*, who arrange the marriages, are actually the ones who are 'trying harder'. This, in turn, comes to a question of how and to what extent the members of local descent groups enter into and continue reciprocal marriage exchanges over several generations. Thus, the question of 'trying harder' to 'follow the rules' is actually a much more complex question. In fact, all men 'try hard' to find a wife and most men are delighted if they get any at all, and in this sense, they cannot be plausibly viewed as 'trying to follow the marriage rules'. If anything, as we shall see in a moment, they can more properly be thought of as trying to break the marriage rules when the rules get in the way—as they do. The frequency distributions seem most plausibly to be a major consequence of the demographic attributes with which each village begins its career, the role that polygynous marriage plays in generating a 'genealogical' pattern that is conducive to high frequencies of cross-cousin marriage of various types, and the strategies individuals use to give women to men in particular other groups as a means of making sure that they will get at least some women back for their brothers and sons.

Polygyny, Genealogical Structures, and Close Kinship   It is easy to marry a cross-cousin if you have a lot of them to choose from. When this happens, the frequency distribution of cross-cousin marriage types will be high, as it is among the Shamatari. But why should the Shamatari men have more cross-cousins than Namoweiteri men? The answer to that question essentially boils down to a question about the frequency of polygyny and, through polygyny,

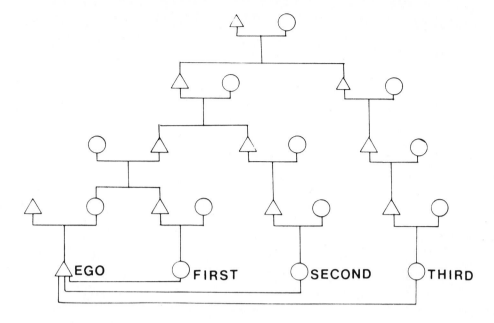

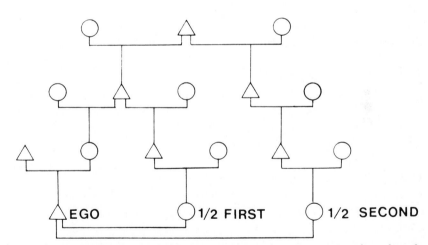

Fig. 4–11. Degrees of cousinship and half cousinship. The upper portion shows how first, second and, third cousins are genealogically related to Ego. The lower half shows how half first and half second cousins are related to Ego. In Yąnomamö marriage, all these relationships would be classified, simply, as 'cousins' and marriages with them would be legitimate. The main point is that the term 'cousin' does not mean only full first cousin but includes larger numbers of more remote cousins.

the sometimes spectacular reproductive accomplishments of specific Yąno-mamö men. Polygyny in a society with patrilineal descent has very different consequences for social organization than polyandry in a society with matrilin-eal descent: one man with 10 wives can have many more children than one woman with 10 husbands, and these physiological differences have profound

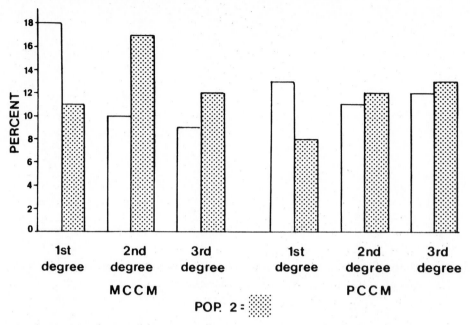

Fig. 4–12. Distribution of frequencies of cross-cousin marriage by degree (first, second, and third cousins) and laterality (matrilateral and patrilateral), for all marriages among living adults in the Shamatari (Population 1) and Namowei-teri (Population 2) villages. Shamatari men marry their full first cross-cousins more often than do Namowei-teri men—on both sides of the family (patrilateral and matrilateral).

implications for understanding lineage size and interlineage marriage exchange practices in societies like the Yąnomamö.

There was a particularly accomplished man in the Shamatari population several generations back named "Shinbone." Some of his children are still alive today, so he is still well known to many people who knew him personally. Shinbone had 11 wives, by whom he had 43 children who survived long enough for people to be able to recollect them. His children, of course, were all siblings or half-siblings to each other and therefore the males among them had many sisters to give away in marriage—in exchange for women they (or their sons) could marry. There were two or three other men like Shinbone around at the time, men with many wives and many children, but none rivaled Shinbone in reproductive performance. By entering into marriage alliances with these men and their sons, members of his descent group became 'bound' to each other in long-term marriage exchanges. If you consider how Shinbone's grandchildren are related to each other, it is clear that they are all siblings, half-siblings, or full or half-cousins of either the parallel or cross varieties. Thus, his grandchildren had many cross-cousins to choose among as potential spouses and it was relatively easy for them to 'follow' the rules of cross-cousin marriage (Fig. 4–13).

While there were some men in the Namoweiteri population who did very well at getting extra wives and, as a consequence, producing large numbers of

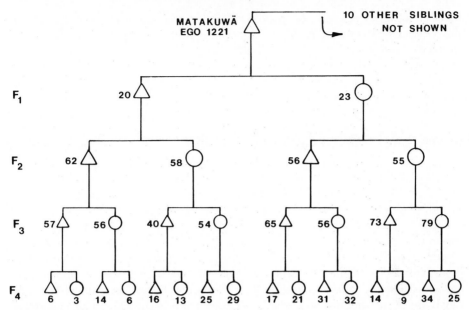

Fig. 4–13. All descendents of 'Shinbone' (Ego 1221) grouped by sex. He had 20 sons and 23 daughters (F₁ generation). The 20 sons in turn had 62 sons and 58 daughters, and so on. (Overlap in the F₃ and F₄ generations is not removed; descendants in generations F₅ and F₆ are not shown.)

children, none did nearly as well as Shinbone or some of his Shamatari peers. In effect, the Shamatari population had fewer male founders, but they produced more children, than was the case in the Namoweiteri population. Another way of saying this is that there are more lineages in the Namoweiteri population, because there are more male founders. This, ultimately, is reflected in the lineal composition of villages and therefore the machinations of men who arrange marriages for their children: they can choose among a larger number of other lineages for future wives, but this results in the creation of more conflict and opportunism. In a hypothetical sense, if you belong to Lineage Y and got a girl from Lineage X several years ago for your son, there is a temptation to give one of your daughters to someone in Lineage Z if they have a girl they are willing to exchange with you at that moment and will not do so otherwise. This gets the men in Lineage X angry. The more lineages there are, the more this is likely to happen. The long-term promises are often subverted by short-term opportunities that lead to conflict. In a formal and statistical sense, the best long-term game to play is to be faithful to your partners and remain bound to them, even if it means giving away more girls at any specific point in time than you get back at that point. An occasional alliance with another group can be 'sneaked in' from time to time, depending on specific situations and the charisma of the individuals involved: some are better than others at pulling this off.

One consequence of the marriage-arranging relationships between members of the larger lineages such as Shinbone's is that villages are characterized by overall higher amounts of kinship relatedness between *all* individuals, not just between married individuals. The computer procedures described above to show how spouses are related can be used to show how *any pair of individuals* is related. As might be expected, the Shamatari villages also differ from the Namoweiteri villages in patterns of relatedness: individuals have more relatives and are more closely related to their relatives than is the case in Namoweiteri villages. This is of great interest to anthropologists, particularly in the context of theories of solidarity. Some anthropologists argue that kinship, rather than marriage alliance, provides the solidarity and amity that keeps groups cohesive whereas others insist that it is the marriage bonds—the so-called "alliance versus descent" argument between Edmund R. Leach (1957) and Meyer Fortes (1959; see Keesing, 1975, for an overview of some of the arguments) and other prominent anthropologists.

Table 4–2 shows what this means in terms of descendants. Shinbone's father (the actual founder) is designated as Ego 1222. If you examine the genealogies of just the living residents in all the Shamatari villages, you will see that a very large fraction of all the Shamatari can trace descent, either through males or females (called "cognatic" ties), back to Shinbone's father. In some villages, as much as 90% of the population is descended from Ego 1222. In all Shamatari villages combined, Ego 1222's descendants amount to about 75% of the entire population. If the number of descendants from Namoweiteri ancestors is examined in the same way for the current residents in Namoweiteri villages, a different picture emerges: smaller fractions of the Namoweiteri villages are descended from specific founders.

When you examine this using the computer procedure described above, the results clearly show that members of the Shamatari villages are, on average, more closely related to each other than are members of Namoweiteri villages. Table 4–3 summarizes this information for census year 1972.

This is done by taking one individual in a particular village, say Kąobawä in Upper Bissasi-teri, and comparing him to all other individuals in the village to search for common ancestors. Thus, the search will show he is related to Bahimi, his wife, in several distinct ways—including the above-mentioned Mother's Brother's Daughter way. The computer measures each genealogical relationship loop to Bahimi, using a statistic known as the *coefficient of relatedness*, a statistic commonly used by population geneticists (Wright, 1922) and breeders to describe and study inbreeding. The result is that a very precise metric statement can be used to discuss "close" or "remote" kinship. Brother/Sister, Father/Child, Mother/Child combinations are associated with a a coefficient of relatedness of $F_g = 0.5000$, i.e., 1/2. This means, among other things, they share about 50% of their genes in common. Half-siblings are related by $F_g = 0.2500$, since they have only one parent in common. First cousins (parallel or cross) are related by a coefficient of relatedness of $F_g = 0.1250$, i.e., share 1/8th of their genes in common. The more remote the relationship, the smaller the value of the coefficient of relatedness.

Continuing with Kąobawä as the focal point, after comparing him to Bahimi and recording his relationship coefficient for her, we then compare him to another person, then another, and another until we have compared him to

TABLE 4–2   Descendants in six Yąnomamö villages from three founders, showing the number and percent of descendants in each village through the male line (lineal) and through both the male and female line combined (cognatic).

Village	Size	Founder 1222				Founder 2936				Founder 2967			
		Lineal	%	Cognatic	%	Lineal	%	Cognatic	%	Lineal	%	Cognatic	%
09	97	48	49	92	95	7	7	52	54	11	11	52	54
14	119	20	17	91	77	35	29	97	82	27	23	93	78
16	116	56	48	107	92	2	2	39	34	5	4	50	43
21	95	4	4	92	98	7	7	80	84	74	78	89	94
49	77	23	30	52	68	20	26	38	49	26	34	58	75
99	37	5	14	18	49	5	14	33	89	1	3	21	57

everyone in the village, including people like Rerebawä to whom Kąobawä is *not* related: F_g = 0.000 in these cases. We can then take two kinds of averages for Kąobawä: his average relatedness to just those people who are his demonstrable kin (F_g CON(sanguineal)) and his average relatedness to *all* residents, the unrelateds being included in the statistic (F_g ALL). There will always be some difference between the values of F_g CON and F_g ALL, since there are always a few 'strangers' in each village, such as in-married sons-in-law or women who were abducted from distant villages. Where the difference between these two statistics is relatively small, the individual (such as Kąobawä) is surrounded by people who are mostly kin. Where the difference is large, the individual is surrounded by many 'strangers' and few kin. As might be expected, the difference between F_g CON and F_g ALL for Kąobawä (not shown) is relatively small, but the difference between F_g CON and F_g ALL for Rerebawä (not shown) is very large—his only kin in the village are his own children.

After comparing Kąobawä to all the residents of the village, we then compare the next person on the list to all others and get, in turn, an average relatedness coefficient for that person. This continues until every person in the village has been compared to all others. These values can be plotted on a distribution of the sort shown in Figure 4–14, which describes this analysis for one of the Shamatari villages. An average of these values can also be taken. For the village shown in Figure 4–14, that average is close to F_g = 0.1000, nearly equivalent to the value associated with full first cousins (F_g = 0.1250). Thus, in that village an average person is related to others drawn at random as approximately a first cousin. Note, however, that there is a variance away from the mean in Figure 4–14: some people are much more closely related to others in the village and some are much less closely related to others.

A fascinating problem emerges once 'closeness' and 'remoteness' of kinship is measured. It makes possible much more finely detailed questions about the relationship of 'close kinship' and the quality of life an individual has in his or her local village. Anthropologists have long argued that 'closeness' of kinship affects the overall amity and quality of relationships, making them warmer, more enduring, more likely to be peaceable—kind as in kin. The measurements can be used to make predictions. For example, if you know that

TABLE 4–3   Average relatedness in villages of both the Shamatari (Population 1) and Namowei-teri (Population 2) population blocs. See text for definitions of F_gAll and F_gCon. Average mean relatedness in the Shamatari villages (Population 1) is higher (revised from Chagnon, 1979a).

Village Comparisons

Village	Size	Average Mean Relatedness		Average Mean Relatedness	
		F_gAll	S.D.	F_gCon	S.D.
Population 1 9	97	.111	.018	.124	.019
14	119	.106	.018	.117	.017
16	116	.092	.014	.112	.029
21	95	.167	.024	.172	.023
49	77	.098	.019	.127	.025
99	37	.167	.034	.186	.034
Population 2 1	100	.067	.018	.137	.052
5	127	.063	.013	.102	.043
6	94	.060	.011	.106	.021
7	116	.071	.015	.101	.021
8	122	.060	.015	.127	.054
18	147	.071	.011	.087	.022
19	78	.090	.013	.106	.025

Population Comparisons

Population 1: N = 542		.118	.025	.133	.027
Population 2: N = 784		.068	.014	.108	.038

Kąobawä calls 10 men by the term meaning "brother," would you expect him to 'act the same' toward all of them if some were real brothers, others were half brothers, and yet others parallel cousins? The kinship term "brother" itself wouldn't be much help to you, especially if you took it to mean 'in principle' a relationship between men that is 'amiable'. I have made tests of this kind. For example, when a village fissions, where do all the "brothers" go? The answer is that the close ones (measured with the F_g statistic) remain together and the distant ones go to a different village (Chagnon, 1981). Or, in a fight, people take sides in proportion to the closeness of relationship measured by the F_g statistic, not by 'what they call' each other (Chagnon and Bugos, 1979). While they might be related to the people they are fighting, they are *more closely related* to the people they are helping and defending. Statistical analyses of the kind described here help to sharply focus attention on where to begin looking: they can identify individuals who, as a category, have very few kin around them and then explore the details of their social interactions—sharing, cooperating, getting along with others, taking sides in fights, and so on—and then compare these with individuals who have many kinsmen in the same village. One area where this is demonstrably important is in getting a wife, for marriages are arranged by parents and elder male kinsmen for both males and females. We will return to this fascinating issue in a moment. Here, however, I

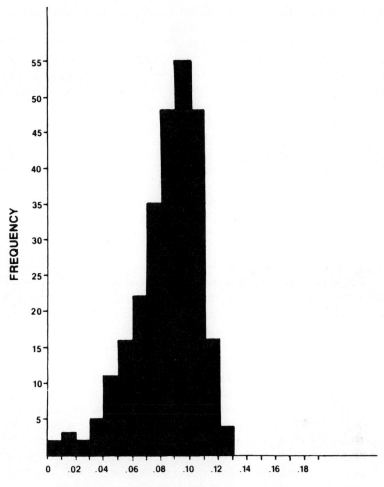

Fig. 4–14. Distribution of average coefficients of genealogical relatedness in one large Yąnomamö village. Some people (less than 3%) are related to few or no co-residents and some people (about 5%) have a very high average relatedness (0.1300) to everyone in the village. The mean average relatedness in this village is about 0.1000, indicating that any pair of individuals drawn at random is likely to be related by a value of F = 0.1000. This is a relatively high average relatedness.

want to illustrate how closeness of kinship measured by the coefficient of relatedness is associated with village fissioning.

A number of larger villages have fissioned during my study of the Yąnomamö. It was therefore possible to make the above calculations for the village prior to fissioning, and then make new calculations in each of the new villages that resulted from the fission. The results show that village fissioning keeps close kin together but separates them from more distant kin. This, so far, has been an invariable pattern. Table 4–4 shows the statistics on one such fission, indicating that average relatedness (both F_g CON and F_g ALL) in the prefission villager was *lower* than it was in either of the newly formed fission villages: close kin stay together. To paraphrase the argument by the distinguished British anthropologist, Meyer Fortes (1969), kinship is the rock-bottom of social amity and should be thought of as prescriptive altruism. In a word, this is about solidarity and cooperation.

Shamatari villages are larger than Namoweiteri villages. As in the case of the marriage patterns described above, the kinship patterns—kinship closeness, to be precise—are also different. The Shamatari are more closely related to each other within villages than are the Namoweiteri, that is, the average values of F_g are higher in Shamatari villages. Table 4–3 gives the data that shows this. Hence, in addition to marriage pattern difference, there is also a difference in degree of relatedness which, along with marriage ties, seems to enable their villages to grow larger: closeness of kinship seems to promote greater amity and solidarity.

Kinship Rules, Reproduction, and Rule Breaking   I mentioned above that many Yąnomamö seem to break the rules, especially kinship and marriage rules. The arena in which this is most conspicuous is incestuous marriage. Recall that the Yąnomamö define only one category of women as marriageable: all others are prohibited and considered to be incestuous (*yaware*). Their definition of incest is broader than ours, but includes our prohibitions as well. Let me give an example of how this comes about.

Figure 4–15 is an example of a case of incest that led to a fight in Kąobawä's village and, ultimately, to the fission of his group from the Lower Bisaasi-teri. The man marked "A" is in Kąobawä's father's generation and, indeed, is called "father" by Kąobawä—they are in the same lineage. "A" is the headman of Lower Bisaasi-teri. This man had several sons and he wanted to find them wives. He cleverly redefined the woman labeled "B" in the diagram as his "sister," thereby moving her up one whole generation: he was supposed to call her by a "niece" term, and did so most of his life. Since she was now his "sister," his sons were eligible to marry her daughters—they were their father's "sister's" daughters (FZD)—but in "classification" only. One of them did marry one of her daughters as shown, thus leading to a big fight and a fission. The issue had to do with taking marriageable females out of the mate pool that other men were eligible to marry into and they, of course, objected strenuously. Some people went along with the new kinship fabrication—those who had something to gain. Others did not—those who had something to lose. The manipulator's son was the right age to marry his forbidden wife, who was also of marriageable age.

This example illustrates a problem of much larger proportions in Yąnomamö society. Incestuous marriages, by the Yąnomamö definition, are very common and are accompanied by manipulations of the kinship classifications of the kind just described. While genealogical information and knowledge cannot be changed, kinship classifications can—and a lot of Yąnomamö do it. Much of it appears to be done in order to increase someone's chances of

TABLE 4–4   Average mean relatedness among individuals before and after a fission in one large Yąnomamö village. Values for average mean relatedness among individuals in the three new villages created by the fission were higher. Fissioning leads to the creation of new villages whose members are more closely related to each other (revised from Chagnon, 1980).

	Village	Size	F_gAll	F_gCon
Before Fission:	Old 16	268	0.0790	0.0956
After Fission:	New 16	127	0.0880	0.1001
	New 09	55	0.1345	0.1402
	New 49	68	0.1075	0.3553
	Others*	18		
	TOTAL	268		

*Includes several people who died after the fission and several young men who went to other villages to find wives there.

finding a wife in a situation where it is difficult for men to find wives (Chagnon, 1972; 1974; 1979a; 1982; Fredlund, 1982).

The source of this problem lies, in large part, in the reproductive attributes and histories of individuals. Women marry young and therefore begin producing children while young. But their reproductive lifespan is relatively short—20 years or so. Men marry later, begin producing later, but their potential reproductive lifespans are very long. Men such as Shinbone had children that differed in age by at least 50 years. One consequence of these facts is that generation length through females is relatively short compared to generation length through males. The net result is that the absolute ages of individuals gets out of synchrony with their generational identities. People will have brothers or sisters that are younger than their grandchildren. Since Yąnomamö kinship classifications utilize generational position, something must give: girls are ready for marriage at puberty and boys shortly thereafter. No right-thinking Yąnomamö would sit patiently for 50 years until his sister's daughter is old enough to marry one of his sons. What gives is the kinship classification, which means that people manipulate it and change it—to their

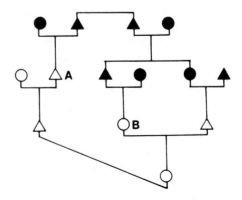

Fig. 4–15. An example of an "incestuous" marriage and manipulating kinship classification with matrimonial gain in mind. Ego A originally called B by the correct term meaning 'niece' but arbitrarily changed his classification of her to a term that meant 'sister.' This enabled A's son to marry B's daughter as shown, since she was terminologically his 'father's sister's daughter'. A good deal of fighting and conflict resulted, for it removed A's daughter from the legitimate mate pool of other men.

advantage. In short, the demographic and reproductive attributes of the Yąnomamö population can never be compatible with or synchronized to the kinship-defined proper marriage partners. They *must* break the kinship rules to make the actual marriage practices work (Chagnon, 1982). One fascinating implication of this is that probably *nobody* in a Yąnomamö village classifies relatives according to the ideal rules laid out in their Iroquois kinship terminology (see Glossary). This is likely to be true in *any* society where kinship classifications define marriageable partners and where the reproductive lifespans of males and females are markedly different.

Let me conclude this chapter with an illustration that emphasizes the "structural" attributes of Yąnomamö kinship as distinct from the "metric" attributes. I described above that a fundamental distinction in Yąnomamö kinship has to do with separating cross-cousins from parallel cousins. Metrically, there is no difference between these kinds of cousins (if paternity is certain): both are related to Ego by $F_g = 0.1250$. The point I am trying to make is that only some dimensions of Yąnomamö social behavior can be understood by measuring close versus distant kinship relationships. The 'kind' of kinsman is also important. This distinction includes cross versus parallel and matrilateral versus patrilateral distinctions whose implications are not metrically appreciable. However, one can examine these "structural" differences in quantitative terms: is having more matrikin more important than having more patrikin in, say, finding a wife?

Figure 4–16 is an analysis of the kinds of kin that adult men have in all Yąnomamö villages, broken down into patrikin, matrikin, ascending generation kin, and own generation kin. The adult men are divided into three categories: those with several wives (polygynous men), those with only one wife (monogamous men), and those with no current wife (single men). By using the computer, one can show the distribution of the various kinds of kin each kind of man has surrounding him in his own village. What emerges in the figure is that matrimonially unsuccessful men have fewer matrikin, fewer ascending generation kin, and fewer own generation kin. Thus, finding a wife is not simply a question of having a lot of kin, or being related to a lot of people, but more a question of having the right *kinds* of kin. It is self-evident that if you have few ascending generation kin you are less likely to easily find a wife, for marriages are largely arranged by people in the ascending generation on your behalf: how many 'allies' you have there is a measure of their political influence and, therefore, their ability to make marriage arrangements for you. The relative shortage of matrikin for men who are unmarried is partially explained by marriages in ascending generations in which a woman comes into the village from some distant group. This happens when females are abducted, or when girls are given amicably in marriage between allied villages. The net result for their sons is that they have few or no matrilateral kin in their village of residence, which appears to decrease the chances of their finding a wife.

These examples should indicate that Yąnomamö social life and social organization is much more complex and variable than what is implied by an examination of just the ideal rules or principles and what, in turn, these lead to as ideal structural models. The 'statistical' approach reveals very large numbers

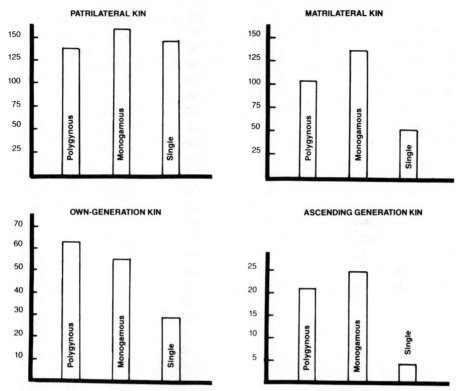

Fig. 4–16. Types of kin, numbers of kin, and marital success among males. When males must depend on kin to help them find marriageable girls, the numbers and types of kin they have becomes critically important. By definition, single men are unsuccessful. The reason is primarily their lower numbers of kin on their mother's side of the family and in the ascending and own generation. All men in this figure are 25 years old or older. The Y axis represents average numbers of kin.

of problems and issues about the relationship of individuals to "society" and how individuals must come to grips with the rules that are said to regulate their behavior. In one sense, the statistical dimensions of social life validate and confirm broad features of the ideal models, but they go far beyond that and help us better understand and appreciate how specific individuals develop strategies in their social interactions with those who surround them. It is, I believe, in this arena that the study of human social behavior is the most fascinating and rewarding. I am, like Levi-Strauss, stating a preference. I think the amorphous critter that generates the perfect shell is more interesting and more challenging than the shell it generates. I also believe that its often imputed "shapelessness" is not only greatly exaggerated, but is far from the truth. It has a shape and form that can be discovered. But that takes quite a bit of extra work. The shell part, by comparison, is a piece of cake. For me, its meager substance is more noticeable than its agreeable flavor. And, as in eating cake, one feels hungry shortly afterward. The perfect shells might be fun to think about, but they aren't very satisfying as food—for thought or for explaining. That is *my* preference.

5/Political Alliances, Trading, and Feasting

Yąnomamö feasts take place only when one sovereign group entertains the members of another allied group. Feasts, in brief, are political events. To be sure, economic and ceremonial implications are also significant, but these are relatively minor when compared to the functions of the feast in the context of forming alliances. The chief purpose of entertaining allies is to reaffirm and cultivate intervillage solidarity in the intimate, sociable context of food presentations, thereby putting the ally under obligation to reciprocate the feast in his own village at a later date, bringing about another feast and even more solidarity.

I will describe in this chapter some of the relationships between trade, economic specialization, historical ties between groups, warfare, and intervillage marriage exchanges, all of which are intimately connected and interact with each other in the process of developing political alliances.

I described in Chapter 2 how the members of independent villages cultivated friendships with each other in the process of establishing themselves in a loose network of allied villages. I then showed in Chapter 4 how Kąobawä's followers were related to him and how he, in turn, was related to the members of several other villages. Now I will take up some of the political consequences of the historical ties and how they shape and mold the nature of specific contemporary relationships between Kąobawä's group and those which have political dealings with it. To illustrate this, I will describe the details of a particular feast in the context of the political ties, both historical and contemporary, existing between Kąobawä's group and the guests at the feast. First, however, I will comment on Yąnomamö alliances in general.

General Features of Alliances

One of the expectations and implications of alliance is that the partners are under obligation to provide shelter and sustenance to each other whenever one of them is driven from his village and garden by a powerful enemy. The beleaguered partner may be obliged to remain in the village of his host for a year or longer, approximately the length of time required to establish a new plantation and productive base from which an independent existence is possible. Twice in the recent history of Kąobawä's group they were driven from their gardens by more powerful enemies and were forced to take refuge in the village of an ally. In each case the group remained with the ally for a year or so, moving away only after their new garden began producing. In both cases, the hosts demanded and received a number of women from Kạobawä's group without reciprocating in kind, a prerogative they exercised from their temporary position of strength. The longer the group takes advantage of a host's protection, the higher is the cost in terms of women, so visitors always make an attempt to establish their gardens as quickly as possible and move into them as soon as they begin producing. Without allies, therefore, the members of a village would either have to remain at their single garden and sustain the attacks of their enemies or disband into several smaller groups and join larger villages on a permanent basis, losing many of their women to their protectors. The jungle simply does not produce enough wild foods to permit large groups to remain sedentary, and the threat of warfare is such that smaller groups would soon be discovered by their enemies and attacked.

Because of the ever-present risk of being driven from one's garden, no Yạnomamö village can continue to exist as a sovereign entity without establishing alliances with other groups. Warfare is attended by a bellicose ideology which asserts that strong villages should take advantage of weaker ones and coerce them out of women; to prevent this, the members of all villages should therefore behave as if they were strong. Thus, the military threat creates a situation in which intervillage alliance is desirable, but at the same time spawns a military ideology that inhibits the formation of such alliances: allies need but cannot trust each other. They are obliged to behave aggressively in order to display their respective strengths.

Alliances between villages are the product of a developmental sequence that involves casual trading, mutual feasting, and finally the exchange of women. The most intimate allies are those who, in addition to trading and feasting, exchange women. Any developing alliance may stabilize at the trading or feasting stage without proceeding to the woman-exchange phase. These are weak alliances, but serve to limit the degree of war that might possibly obtain between the villages so related. The Yạnomamö tend to avoid attacking those villages with which they trade and feast, unless some specific incident, such as the abduction of a woman, provokes them. Allies that are linked by trade and feasting ties, for example, rarely accuse each other of practicing harmful magic. Allies bound to each other by "affinal" kinship ties, however, are more interdependent because they are under obligation to each other to continue to exchange women. It is, in fact, by the exchange of women that independent villages extend kinship ties to each other.

Members of allied villages are usually reluctant to take the final step in alliance formation and cede women to their partners, for they are always worried that the latter might not reciprocate as promised. This attitude is especially conspicuous in smaller villages, for their larger partners in defense pressure them into demonstrating their solidarity by ceding women; the strong can and do coerce the weak in Yạnomamö politics. The weak, therefore, are compelled to exaggerate their strength by bluff and intimidation and by attempting in general to appear to be stronger, militarily, than they really are, thereby hoping to convince their partners that they are equals, capable of an independent existence. By so doing, they also inform their partners that any attempt to coerce them out of women will be met with the appropriate reaction, such as a chest-pounding duel or a club fight. Nevertheless, each ally expects to gain women in the alliance and enters it with this in mind; and each hopes to gain more women than it cedes in return.

Hence, in order for an occasional nervous meeting of groups of men from different villages to evolve into a stable intervillage alliance based on the reciprocal exchange of women, the long and difficult road of feasting and trading usually must be traversed. Suspicion must give way to relative confidence, and this must develop into reciprocal feasting during the dry season. Only then has the intervillage relationship reached a point where the partners begin ceding women to each other; and even then, it is done cautiously, if not reluctantly.

This is, however, only the ideal pattern in the development of an alliance. Rarely does it develop far enough to reach the stage where women change hands, particularly if the two villages concerned are of approximately the same military strength. Fights and arguments over women, food, etiquette, generosity, and so on develop, and the principals withdraw temporarily on semihostile terms, perhaps attempting a rapprochement sometime in the future. Or, if the principals are of obviously different military potential, the stronger of the two will coerce its weaker partner into ceding women early in the alliance development, taking advantage of its own military strength, and thus altering the course of alliance development in the opposite direction.

Whatever the specific developmental sequence leading to the woman-exchange phase, the milieu within which these developments take place is not conducive to the establishment of warm ties of friendship. Each of the principals attempts to demonstrate his own sovereignty in order to convince the other that he does not really require political alliance to keep his enemies in check. This is accomplished by bragging about past military victories and fierceness in past club fights and chest-pounding duels, and by insinuating that one's group is always on the verge of exploding into a force so great that no combination of allies could overcome its terrible might. The smaller the village and more obvious its vulnerability, the greater is the pressure to insinuate or to demonstrate this potential.

Political maneuvering in this milieu is both a tricky and potentially hazardous undertaking. Each principal in the negotiation must establish the credibility of his own threats, while discovering the point at which his partner's bluff will dissolve abruptly into action; he must discover the point beyond which he must not goad his ally, unless he himself is prepared to suffer the possibly violent outcome. It is a politics of brinkmanship, a form of political behavior in which each negotiator is compelled to expose his opposite's threats as bluffs at the risk of inciting him to violence—a club fight, immediately and honorably, or, later and treacherously, a feast in which the hosts descend on their guests to kill their men and abduct their women.

Trading and Feasting in Alliance Formation

Because an ally is not beyond taking advantage of his weaker partner, especially when the alliance is just developing, there is very little in the way of natural attraction to encourage the two groups to visit each other. Considerations of pride and canons of ferocity preclude obvious attempts to develop stable and predictable alliances and military interdependency. The Yąnomamö cannot simply arrive at the village of a potential ally and declare that they need military assistance because of the raids of a superior enemy. Doing so would admit vulnerability and perhaps invite predation from the potential ally. Instead, they conceal and subsume the true motive for the alliance in the vehicles of *trading* and *feasting*, developing these institutions over months and even years. In this manner they retain an apparent modicum of sovereignty and pride, while simultaneously attaining the true objectives: intervillage solidarity and military interdependence.

Three distinct features of Yąnomamö trading practices are important in the context of alliance formation. First, each item must be repaid with a different kind of item: the recipient is under an *obligation* to repay his partner in a type of exchange called *no mraiha*. Secondly, the payment is delayed, a temporal factor in the trading techniques that is likewise implied by the *no mraiha*. The consequence of these two trading features is that one trade always calls forth another and gives the members of different villages both the excuse and the opportunity to visit each other; and once the trading starts, it tends to continue, for one village in an alliance always owes the other trade goods from their last confrontation. The third significant trade feature is the peculiar specialization in the production of trade items. Each village has one or more special products that it provides to its allies. These include such items as dogs, hallucinogenic drugs (both cultivated and collected), arrow points, arrow shafts, bows, cotton yarn, cotton and vine hammocks, baskets of several varieties, clay pots, and, in the case of the contacted villages, steel tools, fishhooks, fishline, and aluminum pots.

This specialization in production cannot be explained in terms of the distribution of natural resources. Each village is, economically speaking, capable of self-sufficiency. (The steel tools and other products from civilization constitute the major exceptions.) The explanation for the specialization must be sought, rather, in the sociological aspects of alliance formation. Trade functions as a social catalyst, the 'starting mechanism', through which mutually suspicious allies are repeatedly brought together in direct confrontation. Without these frequent contacts with neighbors, alliances would be much slower in formation and would be even more unstable once formed. A prerequisite to stable alliance is repetitive visiting and feasting, and the trading mechanism serves to bring about these visits.

Clay pots are a good example of the specialization in labor that characterizes Yąnomamö production and trade. The Mömariböwei-teri (see map, Fig. 5–1, below) are allied to both Kąobawä's group and the people of a distant Shamatari village, the latter being mortal enemies of Kąobawä. When I first began my fieldwork, I visited the Mǫmaribȯwei-teri, specifically asking them if they knew how to make clay pots. They all vigorously denied knowledge of pot making, explaining that they once knew how to make them but had long since forgotten. They explained that their allies, the Mȯwaraoba-teri (Sibarariwä's village), made them in quantities and provided all they needed, and therefore they did not have to make them any more. They also added that the clay in the area of their village was not of the proper type for making pots. Later in the year their alliance with the pot makers grew cool because of a war, and their source of pots was shut off. At the same time, Kạobawä's group began asking them for clay pots. The Mǫmaribȯwei-teri promptly responded by "remembering" how pots were made and "discovering" that the clay in their neighborhood was indeed suitable for pot manufacturing. They had merely created a local shortage of the item in order to have to rely on an ally for it, giving sufficient cause to visit them.

Often the specialization is less individualized than in the case of clay-pot manufacture. Kạobawä's group, for example, exports cotton yarn to one ally, but imports it from another. The exported cotton frequently is brought back in the form of manufactured hammocks, the importer merely contributing labor to the process. In some cases, the shortages are merely seasonal; Kạobawä's group may import cotton from a particular ally at one time of the year, but export it at another. Most of the trade, however, involves items that are readily manufactured or raised by any group, underscoring the fact that trade is the stimulus to visit. Food does not enter the trading system, although hospitality dictates that it must be given to friendly groups. Occasionally, a village will run short of plantains because of a particularly long hot spell, and its members may visit an ally to borrow food to last a week or so. This hospitality is usually reciprocated, but it is not properly a part of the trading network.

Alliances between villages may stabilize at any one of three points: sporadic reciprocal trading, mutual feasting, or reciprocal women exchange. These are cumulative levels in the sense that the third phase implies the first two: allies that exchange women also feast and trade with each other. Likewise, allies that merely feast together also trade, but do not exchange women. At the lower end of this scale of solidarity lie those villages with which one fights to kill, while at the upper end are those villages from whom one's group has recently separated. Frequently, the scale is circular rather than linear: a village's mortal enemy could be the group from which it has recently split. By way of example, Kạobawä's group trades sporadically with the Makorima-teri, Daiyari-teri, Widokaiya-teri, Mahekodo-teri, and Iyäwei-teri. These are fairly weak alliances and even permit limited fighting. Kạobawä's group has more intimate ties with the Reyabobȯwei-teri and Mǫmaribȯwei-teri, with whom it feasts regularly. The alliance with the Reyabobȯwei-teri has even reached the point at which they are exchanging women with each other. Finally, at the other end of the scale, Kạobawä's group is at war with the Iwähikoroba-teri, Mȯwaraoba-teri, and Patanowä-teri. The first two of these groups are historically unrelated to Kạobawä's group, although they have a common history with two of his staunchest allies, the Reyabobówei-teri and Mömaribówei-teri, from whom they separated in the past. The Patanowä-teri are related to Kạobawä and his followers, as was shown in Chapter 2 (Fig. 2–16). Nevertheless, they are bitter enemies and are at present raiding each other.

Although there is no rigid geographical correlation of the village settlement pattern to the degree of alliance solidarity, neighboring villages usually are at least on trading terms and are not actively conducting war on each other. Should war develop between neighbors, one of the two principals will abandon its site and move to a new location. Whether the ties between neighboring villages will be one of blood, marriage exchange, reciprocal feasting, or casual trading depends on a large number of factors, particularly on village size, current warfare situation with respect to more distant groups, and the precise historical ties between the neighboring villages. Whatever the nature of the ties between neighbors, each strives to maintain its sovereignty and independence from the others.

The Yạnomamö do not openly regard trade as a mechanism the ulterior function of which is to bring people repeatedly together, thus establishing an amicable basis from which more stable types of alliance can develop. Nor do they overtly acknowledge the relationships between trading and feasting cycles to village interdependency. In this regard they are like the Trobriand Islanders of Melanesia: they have a "functional ignorance" of the more significant adaptive aspects of their trading institutions (Malinowski, 1922). To both the Yạnomamö and the Trobrianders, the mechanisms by which peoples from different groups are compelled to visit each other are ends in themselves and are not conceived to be related to the establishment of either economic or political interdependency. For the Yạnomamö participant in a feast, the feast itself has its significance in the marvelous quantities of food, the excitement of the dance, and the satisfaction of having others admire and covet the fine decorations he wears. The enchantment of the dance issues from the dancer's awareness that, for a brief moment, he is a glorious peacock that commands the admiration of his fellows, and it is his responsibility and desire to present a spectacular display of his dance steps and gaudy accoutrements. In this brief, ego-building moment, each man has an opportunity to display himself, spinning and prancing about the village periphery, chest puffed out, while all watch, admire, and cheer wildly.

The hosts, too, have an opportunity to display themselves and strut before their guests. Moreover, the very fact that they have given the feast is in itself a display of affluence and surfeit apparently calculated to challenge the guests to reciprocate with an equally grandiose feast at a later date.[1] Each good feast deserves and calls forth another, and in this way allies become better acquainted with each other as they reciprocate feasts during the dry season and over the years.

[1] The competitive aspects of feasting in many primitive societies has been dealt with at length by Marcel Mauss, whose essay *The Gift* (1925) is now an anthropological classic.

Historical Background to a Particular Feast

One of the feasts I witnessed exhibited all the features of intervillage politics. Before describing this feast, I will give the historical antecedents to the event, recapitulating a number of points discussed in Chapter 2 in the context of the history of Kąobawä's village. The significance of these events will then become clear, for Kąobawä's group's prior relationships to the guests at the feast had a great deal to do with the outcome.

In 1950 Kąobawä's group, then living at Kreiböwei-teri, almost friendless, beleaguered by enemies, and somewhat isolated, began cultivating an alliance with the Iwähikoroba-teri (Fig. 5–1), a Shamatari village some two days' traveling distance south of their own village at Kreiböwei. The Iwähikoroba-teri were on friendly terms with another Shamatari group, the Möwaraoba-teri, from whom they had separated some years before. Kąobawä's group, on the other hand, was at war with this village because members of his own group murdered a friendly Möwaraoba-teri visitor in the 1940s, touching off a series of raids between them (see Prologue). Anxious to develop an alliance, Kąobawä's group accepted a feast invitation from the Iwähikoroba-teri and visited that village to participate in the feast. Up to that point they were only on trading terms with them.

The Iwähikoroba-teri, however, had made a prior arrangement with their friends, the Möwaraoba-teri, to help them massacre Kąobawä's men and abduct his group's women.[2] The Möwaraoba-teri were hidden in the jungle outside the village when Kąobawä's group arrived. The men of Kąobawä's group danced both singly and en masse, and were invited into the homes of their hosts. At this point their hosts fell upon them with axes and staves, killing about a dozen men before the visitors could break through the palisade and escape (see Prologue). Kąobawä's father was among the victims. Once outside, they were shot from ambush by the Möwaraoba-teri, who managed to kill a few more and wound many others with arrows. A number of women and girls were captured by the hosts, though some were later recaptured by Kąobawä's group in revenge raids. It was probably their hosts' greed for the women that permitted any survivors at all, as my informants asserted that the Iwähikoroba-teri began chasing the women while the men were still vulnerable. A few of the Iwähikoroba-teri refused to participate in the slaughter and even helped some of Kąobawä's group escape.

The survivors fled to Kobou, a site they had begun clearing for a new garden. Here they removed the arrow points and nursed their wounds before reluctantly returning to Kreiböwei, their only producing garden. Kobou was still too new to support the group, and hunger forced them to return to Kreiböwei. As this location was well known to their treacherous allies, they wished to abandon it as soon as possible, knowing that their enemies could easily kill the rest of the men and abduct the remaining women.

---

[2]It is very probable that a group of men from the village of Hasuböwä-teri participated as allies of the Iwähikoroba-teri in the treachery.

Within a week or so of the treacherous feast, the Mahekodo-teri, a visiting ally of Kąobawä's group, learned of the massacre and offered aid. The Mahekodo-teri headman himself visited Kąobawä's village and invited the entire group to his village to take refuge. They accepted the offer, and in January of 1951, after conducting one revenge raid on the enemies, moved to Mahekodo-teri.[3]

The Mahekodo-teri had been allied to Kąobawä's group a generation earlier, but after Kąobawä's group moved away from the Orinoco River, alliance activity had dwindled to just sporadic trading. True to Yąnomamö political behavior, the Mahekodo-teri, being in an obviously stronger bargaining position, offered their protection and aid with gain in mind: they demanded and received a number of their guests' women. Again, the members of Kąobawä's group suspected further treachery from their new protectors and assiduously worked at establishing a new garden. They were forced to stay with the Mahekodo-teri until their new garden could totally support them— about a year. Even during this time, however, they spent weeks on end away from their hosts' village, carrying their food with them and working on their new plantations. They would return to obtain new food supplies, rest for a few weeks, and leave again. When Mahekodo-teri later split into three factions, Kąobawä and his group learned from one of them the details of a plot in which the Mahekodo-teri were going to kill the men and abduct the women. The only thing that prevented them from doing so was the development of a new war between Mahekodo-teri and another village, one that required the assistance of Kąobawä and his group.

For a few years after the separation from Mahekodo-teri, Kąobawä's group was invited to feast there. Because they suspected that the Mahekodo-teri were plotting against them, however, usually the men alone would attend the feast, thereby reducing the probability of another massacre. The women and children were concealed in the jungle during the time the men were away at the feast. Gradually, the alliance cooled off again and the two groups remained relatively indifferent toward each other, but at peace.

By 1960, Kąobawä's group had regained some of its military strength and had begun cultivating an alliance with a third Shamatari group, one that was related to the two that conducted the massacre of 1950. The new Shamatari group, Paruritawä-teri (Fig. 5–1), was at war with the Iwähikoroba-teri, but on feasting terms with the Möwaraoba-teri. Kąobawä's group persuaded their new Shamatari allies to invite the Möwaraoba-teri to a feast and planned a massacre similar to that of 1950, but with the tables reversed: Kąobawä's group would lie in ambush while the Paruritawä-teri attacked the guests within the village. The Möwaraoba-teri were being ravished by a malaria epidemic at this time, and only a handful of them actually came to the feast: the others were too sick to travel. With the aid of their newly found allies, Kąobawä's group managed to kill three of the five men and abducted four of their women. The other two visitors escaped to tell of the treachery. This revenge feast was

---

[3]This date is accurately known, since James P. Barker, a Protestant missionary, began living with the Mahekodo-teri at that time and witnessed the influx of the refugees.

only considered to be partially successful, and Kạobawä's group was not satisfied with the outcome. Their Shamatari allies, Paruritawä-teri, were obliged to abandon their site to avoid the revenge raids, splitting into two groups in the process: Mömariböwei-teri and Reyaboböwei-teri, both continuing to remain friendly to Kạobawä's group.

In early 1965, just a few months after I began my fieldwork, Kạobawä and his supporters left to visit Reyaboböwei-teri, one of the two Shamatari allies, hoping to conduct another treacherous feast for the Möwaraoba-teri. They left a few men behind to protect the women and children. The men were gone almost two weeks. All during this time, those who remained behind flocked to my mud hut at dawn and remained in it the whole day, not permitting me to leave. Every hour or so they asked to see my shotgun. I soon discovered that they were frightened and suspected that the Widokaiya-teri (a village to the north, not on Figure 5–1) were going to raid them to abduct women, for they knew of the plot. My hut lay on the path most likely to be taken by Widokaiya-teri raiders, and the few remaining men stood guard next to my door, hoping to intercept the raiders should they attack at night.

I, unknowingly, guarded the women and children by day with my shotgun, while the men did the same at night with their own weapons. This incident indelibly underscores the almost complete lack of trust between allies; the members of Kạobawä's group expected a raid from their friends and allies rather than from their enemies!

About 10 days after the men had left, six visitors from another allied village passed through Upper Bisaasi-teri hoping to trade. It was obvious to them that the men were away and that the women were frightened. They carried word of the situation up the Orinoco River to their own allies, one of which was the Mahekodo-teri.

The evening before the men returned from the trip, one of the Salesian missionaries, Padre Luis Cocco, visited me, having traveled up the Orinoco River by dark—a dangerous undertaking at that time of the year. Padre Cocco had just received word by shortwave radio from the mission at Mahekodo-teri that a large party of men had left for Bisaasi-teri intent on capturing women. They had learned of the poorly guarded women from the six visitors and were determined to take advantage of the situation.

My house was full of women and children at dawn the following day, and the raiders were probably en route. I was in a difficult situation. On the one hand, if I told the Indians of the rumor, it would have been sufficient cause to start a war between Kạobawä's group and the Mahekodo-teri. This would have been most unfortunate if the story proved to be false. On the other hand, I dared not remain silent. If raiders were indeed coming, they would probably kill the defenders to capture the women. Fortunately, Kạobawä and the men returned

Fig. 5–1. Historical movements of the Bisaasi-teri (triangles) over approximately 125 years, beginning at the ancient site of Konata. Some neighboring villages of other population blocs are also shown to their north (hexagons) and south (circles). Contemporary villages are indicated in solid color.

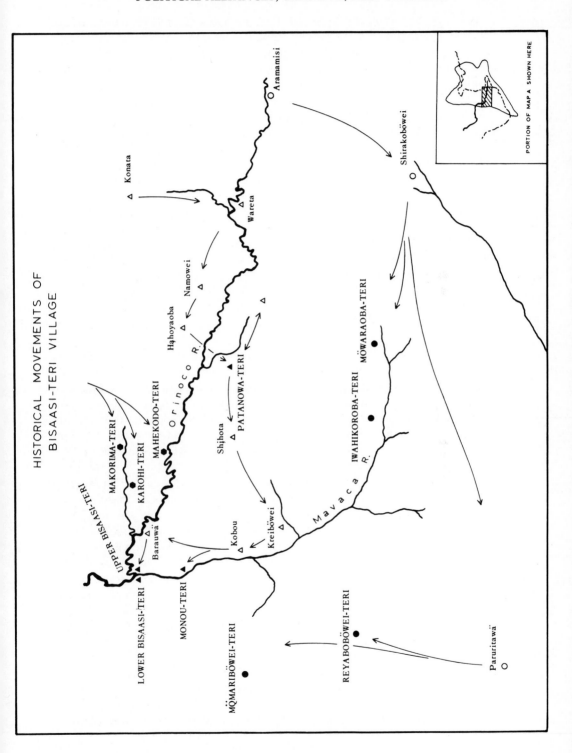

HISTORICAL MOVEMENTS OF
BISAASI-TERI VILLAGE

Aramamisi

Konata

Wareta

Shirakoböwei

Hąhoyaoba

Namowei

MAKORIMA-TERI

MÖWARAOBA-TERI

UPPER BISAASI-TERI

KAROHI-TERI

MAHEKODO-TERI

IWAHIKOROBA-TERI

Orinoco R.

PATANOWA-TERI

Shihota

Barauwä

Mavaca R.

Kobou

Kreiböwei

LOWER BISAASI-TERI

MONOU-TERI

MÖMARIBÖWEI-TERI

REYABOBÖWEI-TERI

Paruritawä

PORTION OF MAP A SHOWN HERE

early in the afternoon, and I was able to remain neutral. The treacherous feast for their Shamatari enemies proved to be unsuccessful. The intended victims had accepted the invitation, but were informed of the plot just before they arrived. One of the Reyaboböwei-teri who had close kinsmen among them had misgivings about the matter and warned them.

Late in the afternoon it was learned that the Mahekodo-teri were, in fact, in the vicinity of the village, allegedly on a "camping trip." Kaobawä, of course, suspected their story, but to demonstrate his friendship he invited them to be his guests at a feast. As he and his men had been away for nearly two weeks, there was an abundance of food in their gardens and they could easily afford to entertain the Mahekodo-teri and their traveling companions, the Boreta-teri. Together, the guests numbered about 100—after they fetched their women and children.

This sets the stage for the feast in the kind of context that makes it more intelligible: the specific historical relationships between the participants and the nature of their mutual mistrust. Now I will give the details of the events that followed.

The Feast

Perhaps because he suspected the Mahekodo-teri and Boreta-teri of intimidation, Kaobawä also invited the Karohi-teri to attend the feast. They are a small but dependable ally and had themselves separated from the Mahekodo-teri many years ago. This is the village from which Rerebawä comes. This established a balance of power at the projected feast should any trouble arise, for the combination of both Boreta-teri and Mahekodo-teri was of sufficient strength to worry any host. With the aid of the Karohi-teri, Kaobawä's group was more of a match for the visitors.

The feast started out on a sour note. It is the custom of the Yanomamö visitors to arrive only after an invitation from their hosts, sent by messenger on the day of the feast. The Mahekodo-teri and Boreta-teri, however, arrogantly arrived nearly a week before Kaobawä's group was prepared to receive them and set up a large, temporary camp a short distance from the village. They were guests and could legitimately demand to be fed. Because of this, Kaobawä and his covillagers were under obligation to feed them, some 100 or so people, and took them to the gardens to supply them with enough plantains to last a week. Kaobawä was a little disturbed that they would be so impolite as to arrive uninvited, but took the situation quite philosophically. After all, they had fed his group for the better part of a year.

He and several other men cut a large quantity of plantains, which were hung in his house and allowed to ripen for a week, to be boiled into *date*, a thick sweet soup, on the day of the feast. That afternoon Kaobawä and a few of the older men commissioned a hunting party composed of young men, several of whom were Kaobawä's brothers, whose responsibility would be to obtain a large quantity of fresh meat to give to the visitors on the day after the feast. Most of them were reluctant to go, as their feet were still sore from the trip to the Shamatari village. A few of them claimed to be sick and managed to escape recruitment into the hunting party in this way. This hunt, with the hanging of the plantains in the headman's house, initiated the feast. The excitement that usually attends a feast began at this time.

That evening the young men danced and sang in the village, an event called *amoamo*, thereby assuring themselves luck on the hunt. (The Yąnomamö also *amoamo* on other occasions, but invariably do so on the day the plantains are hung in the village in anticipation of a feast.) Every evening the men are away on their *heniomou*, the week-long hunt, the young women and girls sing and dance in the village to assure the men's success.

The hunters left at dawn the following morning, carrying a large supply of roasted and green plantains with them to eat while they hunted. They had picked a site some 25 miles up the Mavaca River for their hunt, as game was known to abound there. Their task was to obtain monkeys, armadillos, wild turkeys, wild pig, tapir, or paruri birds, the only meat deemed worthy to give to guests. They would not be permitted to eat any of this game, but could consume any other game they captured, such as deer, small birds, a small species of wild turkey, insects, or fish they happened to come upon. The feast meat, however, was earmarked for the guests and could not be eaten by the hunters. On this particular hunting trip the men miscalculated the amount of food they would need to sustain them during the hunt, and one of them returned after four days to fetch more plantains. He also gave Kąobawä a report on the hunt's success, creating a small sensation in the village: they had already killed a large number of *basho*, a particularly large and very desirable monkey. They had also come upon a quantity of turtle eggs at a sand bar and were eating as many as they could. When they returned later, they cached the remaining eggs in my house, so as not to have to share them with the visitors.

Meanwhile, the visitors were making gluttons of themselves, and the hosts started to grumble about the large number of plantains they had already eaten. The week's supply they originally provided had been consumed in half that time, and the guests had been given permission a second time to harvest more from their hosts' gardens. This was no way for guests to behave, and it soon became apparent that they were intimidating Kąobawä's group. Still, he and his followers continued to supply them with all the food they needed, keeping their complaints to themselves. They did not want it to be known that they were worried about running short of food. Instead, they planned to conduct the feast on a scale that would be difficult to reciprocate.

The hunters returned and presented their catch to Kąobawä. It was brought to his house and placed on the ground, wrapped up in leaves. Kąobawä ignored it for a while and then slowly began to unpack one package of it (Fig. 5–2) while everybody watched—especially the hunters, who were quite proud of the quantity of meat they had obtained: 17 *basho* monkeys, 7 wild turkeys, and 3 large armadillos.

Kạobawä and his group were anxious to conduct the feast for their visitors and present them with the food, because by so doing the visitors would be obliged to leave for home, thereby ending the drain on the gardens.[4]

The feast was scheduled for the day following the return of the hunters, even though the Karohi-teri allies had not yet arrived. Kạobawä and his group were so anxious to rid themselves of their ravenous guests by this time that they decided to hold a separate feast for the Karohi-teri on the day following the departure of the Mahekodo-teri. This would involve a considerable amount of extra work, but they were more than willing to undertake it if it meant getting rid of their first group of visitors, who, by this time, had spent nearly a week eating Kạobawä's produce.

On the morning of the feast three large pieces of bark from the *arapuri* tree were cut and brought to the village. These were made into troughs to contain the boiled, ripe plantain soup. All day long Kạobawä's younger brothers, who had returned from the hunt the day before, labored at cooking the enormous quantity of ripe plantains, pouring each boiling containerful into the trough as it was prepared.[5]

The plantains that Kạobawä had hung in his *shabono* roof a week before were now ripe. The young men who were preparing the soup would cut the bunches of plantains from the roof, split each fruit with a thumb, throw the two halves of the flesh into a cooking pot, and toss the skins onto a pile. They worked at this task from early morning until late afternoon, in addition to boiling a nearly equal quantity of green plantains, which provided the green vegetable food that customarily accompanies the presentation of meat. Yạnomamö etiquette dictates that meat must be accompanied by vegetable food and vice versa.[6] It is an insult, for example, to offer someone meat without simultaneously offering a vegetable food with it.

Peeling green plantains is a little more difficult than peeling ripe ones; they are very tough and brittle. The Yạnomamö solve this problem, as they solve so many others, by using their teeth. Each plantain is bitten along its length several times, cracking the peel, which in turn is removed with the fingernails and further application of the dentition. On this particular occasion, two young men peeled, with their thumbs, enough ripe plantains to make approximately

[4]I have seen several instances of Yạnomamö groups getting rid of visitors who have joined them semipermanently by holding a feast in their honor; when the ceremonial food is presented, the visitors are obliged to leave.

[5]Kạobawä's group has access to aluminum pots now and uses them extensively in food preparations. Most Yạnomamö groups used crude clay pots in 1965, although these were being rapidly replaced by aluminum ware that is traded inland to the remote villages.

[6]The three vegetable foods considered to be suitable accompaniments for the meat presentation are: boiled green plantains, boiled *rasha* fruit, and cassava bread. A number of missionaries and a few scientific observers have identified the Yạnomamö feast strongly with the *rasha* fruit (Zerries, 1955; de Barandiaran, 1966). If it is to be identified with any food, it should be called the "plantain feast," but to identify the feast with a food that sometimes (*rasha*) or invariably (plantains) accompanies it is to overlook the sociopolitical causes of the feast. *Rasha* is so unnecessary to the feast that it was served at only two of six feasts I attended between 1964 and 1966. In short, the Yạnomamö feast is a social and political event, not a harvest ceremony, and occurs independently of the abundance or availability of *rasha* fruit. *Rasha* fruit ripens in February, the peak of the dry season. It is only in the dry season that feasts can be held, because travel is difficult or impossible at other times of the year. The correlation of the ripening of *rasha* and feasting is rather more fortuitous than causal.

Fig. 5–2. Kąobawä unpacking a load of smoked meat which his hunters have brought home for the feast.

95 gallons of soup, and, with their teeth, a sufficiently large quantity of green plantains to fill a dozen large pack baskets.

In the morning on the day of the feast, Kąobawä went to the center of the village clearing where all could see him and proceeded to pull weeds. The clearing has to look presentable to visitors, as it functions as the dancing plaza. As noted before, since Yąnomamö headmen cannot directly order their followers to execute tasks such as these, they usually initiate them and hope that others will follow (see Asch and Chagnon, 1970). By and by, a number of older men joined him, as well as a few women, and when a sufficient number of workers were pulling weeds and hauling them out, Kąobawä quietly retired to his hammock, from which he oversaw the food preparations and calculated the distribution of meat.

Excitement in the village grew conspicuously as the hours passed, and by noon there was a constant din of laughter and chatter, punctuated now and then with a shrill scream from some young man overcome with the thrill of the feast. Occasionally, the visitors would reply to the shouts, setting off a brief contest of screaming between hosts and guests that gradually died off as each group busied itself in preparation for the dance.

Shortly after noon a rumor circulated through the village that the visitors had been raiding the gardens at night and stealing plantains. A number of people, particularly older men, were visibly upset by this new information, giving rise to another rumor that there would be a chest-pounding duel to set the matter straight. The guests had already worn their welcome thin by arriving uninvited a week in advance and by eating excessively. Their hosts were becoming angry with them, as it was all too obvious that they were deliberately taxing their hosts' patience: they were intimidating them.

The men of the host group had finished their preparations for the feast; they were all painted in red and black, bearing colorful feathers. They had cleaned the debris from their houses, had finished hauling out the weeds they had picked from the village clearing, and had brought in quantities of food to give their guests. Now, it was time for them to take *ebene*, their hallucinogenic drug. They separated into several groups and began blowing the brownish-green powder up each other's nostrils with 3-foot-long hollow tubes.

While the men were taking their drugs, the women were busy painting and decorating themselves with feathers and red pigment. The visitors, also, were busy at the same tasks, and the excitement of the feast reached fever proportions by midafternoon. A few women were still busy finishing trade baskets, while Kąobawä's younger brothers continued with the monotonous cooking of what seemed to them an endless number of plantains.

Finally, an old man from the visiting group entered the village and marched unceremoniously across the clearing while the members of Kąobawä's group cheered him. He was too old to join the dancing, but too respected to wait behind with the women and children while the younger men put on their display. This was evidence that the visitors were about to send in their delegate to accept the feast invitation at Kąobawä's house.

The members of Lower Bisaasi-teri had joined Kąobawä's group for the feast, as they, too, were on friendly terms with the Mahekodo-teri and had benefited from the latter's hospitality after the treacherous feast in 1950. Before Kąobawä's group had separated from the Lower Bisaasi-teri, there had been one headman over the entire composite village. This was a brother to Kąobawä's father; when the groups split, the older man led the faction of Lower Bisaasi-teri, leaving Kąobawä to lead the Upper group. On this particular day, when the two groups had temporarily coalesced for the feast, the older man was conceded the honor of chanting with the visitor's delegate, Asiawä, the son of the Mahekodo-teri headman.

Ten minutes after the old visitor entered the village, Asiawä entered the clearing, touching off an explosion of wild cheering that marked the opening of the dance. He was spectacular in his bright new loincloth, long red parrot feathers streaming from his armbands, and black monkey-tail headband covered with white buzzard down. He marched dramatically to the center of the village clearing, while all of Kąobawä's followers cheered, and struck the visitor's pose: motionless, head upward, and weapons held vertically next to his face. He stood there two or three minutes so his hosts could admire him. This gesture signified that he had come in peace and was announcing his benevolent intentions by standing where all could see him. If they bore him malice, they had to shoot him then or not at all.[7] He then marched to Kạobawä's house and was met by Kạobawä's father's brother, the temporary leader of the combined host group, and the two men immediately began to chant. This was the formal acceptance of the feast invitation by Asiawä on behalf of his entire group. They chanted for five minutes or so, bouncing up and down from the knees, now face to face, now side to side, but always lively and loud. Suddenly, they stopped, and Asiawä squatted, his back to the sun, while the hosts' representative retired to his hammock. The cheering died down. Asiawä squatted for several minutes before one of Kạobawä's younger brothers brought a half gourdful of plantain soup to him and set it on the ground. He ignored it politely for several minutes, staring into the distance, holding his weapons horizontally next to his mouth. Presently, he put his weapons down, picked up the container of soup, and drained it in one draft before setting it back down. As soon as he had set it down, one of Kạobawä's younger brothers brought him a large pack basket filled with boiled green plantains and smoked armadillo meat. Asiawä stood while the strap of the basket was placed over his head and adjusted across his shoulders so as not to crumple his headdress. Trying to look dramatic, he staggered rapidly out of the village under his burden of food, while the hosts again cheered wildly. This food was eaten by the visitors while they finished their decorating, each receiving a small portion.[8]

Within half an hour of Asiawä's departure the visitors had completed their decorating and had assembled just outside the entrance to the village. The men, all finely decorated, stood at the front of the gathering, while the women, girls, and young boys, also decorated, but each carrying a load of family possessions, brought up the rear. At the signal of Asiawä's father, the first two dancers burst into the village, separated, and danced around the periphery of the clearing in opposite directions, while Kạobawä's group welcomed them enthusiastically with shouts and shrill screams. Two at a time, the visiting dancers entered, pranced around the village periphery, wildly showing off their decorations and weapons and then returning to the group. Each dancer had unique decorations and a unique dance step, something personal that he could exhibit. He would burst into the village screaming a memorized phrase, wheel and spin, stop in his tracks, dance in place, throw his weapons down, pick them up again, aim them at the line of hosts with a wild expression on his face, prance ahead a few steps, repeat his performance, and continue on around the village in this manner, while the hosts cheered wildly. When everyone had had an individual turn, the entire group entered, danced single file around the periphery several times and gathered at the center of the clearing, where they formed a tightly knit group (Fig. 5–3). They stood

---

[7]I have a number of informants' accounts of visitors being shot down while standing in the clearing to announce their visit. Whenever I accompanied visitors to strange villages for the first time, I, too, was obliged to participate in this rite and always had an uneasy feeling about it.

[8]Our film *The Feast* (Asch and Chagnon, 1970) documents an alliance between the villages of Patanowä-teri and Mahekodo-teri and coincidentally has Asiawä performing the very same role there as he did in this feast.

Fig. 5–3. Visitors displaying themselves at the village center after they have each danced individually. They will now be invited to recline in particular hosts' houses.

motionless, except for the heaving of their chests, holding their weapons vertically. After they had stood there a few moments—in a final display of decorations—Kąobawä's followers emerged from their houses and approached the center of the village, each man inviting one or more of the visitors into his house, leading him away from the village center by the arm. As each visitor was led away, his family, watching from the village entrance, unceremoniously joined him at the host's house, bringing the family possessions along. Within a few minutes the dance plaza was deserted and the visitors were resting comfortably in their hosts' hammocks. Even in the hammocks, the Yąnomamö visitors are able to put on a silent display of their finery as they lie with their legs crossed, one arm behind their head, staring at the ceiling, waiting for their hosts to feed them ripe plantain soup from the bark troughs—it is almost as if they are strutting from a reclining position.

After the guests had been given their first round of soup, the men of Kąobawä's village assembled outside the entrance and came in to dance around the village for their guests. They, too, had an opportunity to put on a display of their own decorations, after which they retired to entertain their guests.

There were three troughs full of soup in the village. The first one was emptied in the process of bringing numerous gourdsful to the some 100 visitors (Fig. 5–4). After they had consumed this, the guests then assembled at

Fig. 5—4. After a polite period of reclining in their hosts' hammocks, the visitors go to the large troughs of plantain soup and begin drinking it. The soup trough can also be used as a crude canoe for crossing larger streams (Chapter 1).

the second trough and began eating there. Before this trough was finished, they moved as a group to the third trough and repeated their ceremonial consumption, before returning to their hammocks to rest and regain their appetites. Approximately two hours had passed from the time the first dancers entered the village until the guests retired from the third trough of soup. They had not yet eaten all of the contents—all in all, some 95 gallons of it—but managed to do so by morning.[9]

Shortly after dark the marathon chanting (*waiyamou*) began—it continued until dawn. At dawn the visitors conducted their trade and were given the baskets of going-home food: boiled green plantains with smoked meat. The visitors made requests through their headman, and Kạobawä would produce the item by enjoining one of the local men to give it. The item would be thrown at the feet of the man who wanted it. He would ignore it for a while and then give it a cursory examination, throwing it back on the ground. His peers would then examine it in greater detail and extol its virtues, while the giver would apologize for its defects. If it were a particularly poor item, just the opposite would occur; the giver would cite its not-so-obvious merits, while the recipient would draw attention to the conspicuous shortcomings. In every trade the hosts always feel as though they have been over generous, and the guests, after they depart, complain they have not received enough. The trade was conducted in an atmosphere of efficiency, but with considerable argumentation (see Asch and Chagnon, 1970). The hosts had concealed their choicest items and vigorously denied having some goods, and the guests had done likewise—sinking their prize bows in a river before arriving at the feast, for example, and bringing an inferior one along in case one of the hosts asked for

[9]During some feasts, the ashes of the dead are mixed with the boiled, ripe plantain soup and eaten by friends and relatives of the deceased. The feast also serves as a preliminary to a raid that involves two or more villages. The sponsor of the raid will entertain his allies in a feast the day before the raiding party departs. See Chapter 6 for a discussion of the raid.

it during the trading. As this was the first time in some years that the two groups feasted together, there was nothing for either one to repay. Instead, the visitors asked for items *no mraiha*—to be repaid later—and the guests did the same.

By 8:00 A.M. the going-home food had been presented to the visitors, and the trade had been conducted very early by feast standards. Had the visitors been polite, they would have left for home at that time. Instead, they decided to stay and witness the second, smaller, feast that Kaobawä was going to conduct for the Karohi-teri, who had not arrived in time for the major event. This capped the series of insults the visitors had heaped upon Kaobawä's group. The visitors were warned that if they should stay, they would be expected to fight in a chest-pounding duel.

It was obvious now that the visitors were looking for trouble, and Kaobawä's group was obliged to react or be subject to even further intimidation. Hence, the challenge to pound chests. At this point, the visitors broke camp and departed, much to the relief and joy of Kaobawä's group. In fact, they were pleased that they had been successful at intimidating their guests into leaving, and the men gloated over this accomplishment the rest of the day. They were convinced that their threats were credible enough to force their potential adversaries to withdraw, presumably because the Mahekodo-teri felt they were inferior in strength.

Kaobawä and his group held another feast for the Karohi-teri that same day, but without the assistance of the Lower Bisaasi-teri, who left shortly after the previous feast terminated.

The Chest-Pounding Duel

The feast for Karohi-teri was essentially the same as the one for the Mahekodo-teri and Boreta-teri. When the dancing was over and darkness fell, the men began to chant again. The first pair of chanters had not completed their rhythmic presentation when the jungle around the village erupted with hoots and screams, causing all of the people in the village to jump from their hammocks and arm themselves. When the men had found their arrows and were prepared, they began yelling back at the unseen guests, rattling the shafts of their arrows together or against their bows and/or pounding the heads of axes against pieces of firewood or on the ground to make noise. The Boreta-teri and Mahekodo-teri had returned to accept the chest-pounding challenge and entered the village, each man brandishing his ax, club, or bow and arrows. They circled the village once, feigning attack on particular men among the hosts, then grouped at the center of the village clearing. The hosts surrounded them excitedly, dancing with their weapons poised to strike, then entering into the mass of bodies. Heated arguments about food theft and gluttony developed, and the hosts and guests threateningly waved their weapons in each other's faces. Within minutes the large group had bifurcated and the chest pounding began. The Karohi-teri aided Kaobawä and his followers, whose joint numbers were even further swelled when the Lower Bisaasi-teri rushed to the village after hearing the commotion. There were about 60 adult men on each side in the fight, divided into two arenas, each comprised of hosts and guests. Two men, one from each side, would step into the center of the milling, belligerent crowd of weapon-wielding partisans, urged on by their comrades. One would step up, spread his legs apart, bare his chest, and hold his arms behind his back, daring the other to hit him (Fig. 5–5). The opponent would size him up, adjust the man's chest or arms so as to give himself the greatest advantage when he struck, and then step back to deliver his close-fisted blow. The striker would painstakingly adjust his own distance from his victim by measuring his arm length to the man's chest, taking several dry runs before delivering his blow. He would then wind up like a baseball pitcher, but keeping both feet on the ground, and deliver a tremendous wallop with his fist to the man's left pectoral muscle, putting all of his weight into the blow. The victim's knees would often buckle and he would stagger around for a few moments, shaking his head to clear the stars, but remain silent. The blow invariably raised a 'frog' on the recipient's pectoral muscle where the striker's knuckles bit into his flesh. After each blow, the comrades of the deliverer would cheer and bounce up and down from the knees, waving and clacking their weapons over their heads. The victim's supporters, meanwhile, would urge their champion on frantically, insisting that he take another blow. If the delivery were made with sufficient force to knock the recipient to the ground the man who delivered it would throw his arms above his head, roll his eyes back, and prance victoriously in a circle around his victim, growling and screaming, his feet almost a blur from his excited dance. The recipient would stand poised and take as many as four blows before demanding to hit his adversary. He would be permitted to strike his opponent as many times as the latter struck him, provided that the opponent could take it. If not, he would be forced to retire, much to the dismay of his comrades and the delirious joy of their opponents. No fighter could retire after delivering a blow. If he attempted to do so, his adversary would plunge into the crowd and roughly haul him back out, sometimes being aided by the man's own supporters. Only after having received his just dues could he retire. If he had delivered three blows, he had to receive three or else be proven a poor fighter. He could retire with less than three only if he were injured. Then, one of his comrades would replace him and demand to hit the victorious opponent. The injured man's two remaining blows would be canceled, and the man who delivered the victorious blow would have to receive more blows than he delivered. Thus, good fighters are at a disadvantage, since they receive disproportionately more punishment than they deliver. Their only reward is status: they earn the reputation of being *waiteri*: fierce.

Some of the younger men in Kąobawä's group were reluctant to participate in the fighting because they were afraid of being injured. This put more strain on the others, who were forced to take extra turns in order to preserve the group's reputation. At one point Kąobawä's men, sore from the punishment they had taken and worried that they would ultimately lose the fight, wanted to escalate the contest to an ax duel (Fig. 5–6). Kąobawä was vigorously

Fig. 5–5. Chest-pounding duel at the feast.

opposed to this, as he knew it would lead to bloodshed.[10] He therefore recruited the younger men into the fighting, as well as a few of the older ones who had done nothing but demand that the others step into the arena, thereby reducing the strain on those who wanted to escalate the level of violence. A few of the younger men retired after a single blow, privately admitting to me later that they pretended to be injured to avoid being forced to fight more. The fighting continued in this fashion for nearly three hours, tempers growing hotter and hotter. Kąobawä and the headman from the other group stood by with their weapons, attempting to keep the fighting innocuous, but not participating in it. Some of the fighters went through several turns of three or four blows each, their pectoral muscles swollen and red from the number of blows each had received. The fight had still not been decided, although Kąobawä's group seemed to be getting the worst of it. They then insisted on escalating the fighting to side slapping, partly because their chests were too sore to continue in that fashion, and partly because their opponents seemed to have an edge on them.

The side-slapping duel is nearly identical in form to chest pounding, except that the blow is delivered with an open hand across the flanks of the opponent, between his rib-cage and pelvis bone (Fig. 5–7). It is a little more severe than chest pounding because casualties are more frequent and tempers grow hotter

[10]See our film *The Ax Fight* for a dramatic example of this form of fighting (listed in Appendix A).

Fig. 5–6. The fight nearly escalated to clubs and axes; Kąobawä prevented this by compelling the reluctant men to take turns at chest pounding.

more rapidly when a group's champion falls to the ground, gasping for wind, and faints.[11] The side slapping only lasted 15 minutes or so; one of the more influential men of Kąobawä's group was knocked unconscious, enraging the others. The fighting continued for just a few minutes after this, but during these few minutes the men were rapidly changing the points of their arrows to war tips: curare and lanceolate bamboo. The women and children began to cry, knowing that the situation was getting serious, and they grouped into the farthest corners of their houses near the exits. One by one the men withdrew, returned to their houses, and drew their bows. The visitors pulled back and formed a protective circle around their own women and children, also fitting arrows into their bows and drawing them. The village grew almost silent. The leaders of the respective groups stepped into the no man's land separating the two groups of armed men and began arguing violently, waving axes and clubs at each other. Suddenly, the spokesmen from the visiting group surged toward Kąobawä and his supporters, swinging their axes and clubs wildly at them, forcing them back to the line of men whose bowstrings were drawn taut. Kąobawä and his followers regained their footing and repelled their adversaries at this point, while the women and children from both groups began fleeing from the village, screaming and wailing. It looked as if they were about to release their arrows point-blank at Kąobawä's attackers, but when he and his aides turned them back, the crisis was over. The leaders of the visiting group rejoined the other men, some of whom had picked up glowing brands of

[11]Shortly after this event, an argument developed between the Karohi-teri and some of their neighbors that precipitated a chest-pounding duel. The fight escalated to side slapping, then to side slapping with stones held in the fist. Two young men were killed, presumably with ruptured kidneys.

Fig. 5–7. *Chest pounding can be modified to a form in which men strike each other from a squatting position.*

firewood, and they backed out of the village, weapons still drawn, their way illuminated by those who were waving the brands.[12]

Kaobawä's group took no further action in this affair and was not invited to feast at Mahekodo-teri. Later in the year, their relationships worsened because of a club fight in yet another village, and for a while both groups threatened to shoot each other on sight. A temporary rapprochement developed after the club fight, when a group of raiders from Kaobawä's group met a group of hunters from the Mahekodo-teri while en route to attack the village of one of their enemies (described in Chapter 4). The men from both villages traded with each other and departed on friendly terms, the raiders abandoning their raid and returning to their village lest they be later ambushed on the way home by the Mahekodo-teri. They remained on trading terms with each other, but their relationship was somewhat strained and potentially hostile.

In general, feasts are exciting for both the hosts and the guests and contribute to their mutual solidarity. Under normal circumstances, allies who customarily feast with each other do not fight. Nevertheless, even the best allies occasionally agree beforehand to terminate their feast with a chest-pounding duel, thereby demonstrating to each other that they are friends, but capable of maintaining their sovereignty and willing to fight if necessary. Kąobawä's group had a chest-pounding duel with one of its staunchest allies in 1966, as each had heard that the other was spreading rumors that it was cowardly. Of the six feasts I witnessed during the first 19 months I spent with the Yąnomamö, two of them ended in fighting.

Any Yąnomamö feast can potentially end in violence because of the nature of the attitudes the participants hold regarding canons of behavior and obligations to display ferocity.

Still, the feast and its antecedent trade serve to reduce the possibility of neighbors fighting with each other at a more serious level of violence, and they contribute to intervillage solidarity and mutual interdependence.

[12]At this time, I was crouched in the house behind the line of bowmen, trembling in my sneakers.

6/Yąnomamö Warfare

Levels of Violence

The feast and alliance can and often do fail to establish stable, amicable relationships between sovereign villages. When this happens, the groups may coexist for a period of time without any overt expressions of hostility. This, however, is an unstable situation, and no two villages that are within comfortable walking distance from each other can maintain such a relationship indefinitely: they must become allies, or hostility is likely to develop between them. Indifference leads to ignorance or suspicion, and this soon gives way to accusations of sorcery. Once the relationship is of this sort, a death in one of the villages will be attributed to the malevolent *hekura* sent by shamans in the other village, and raids will eventually take place between them.

Yąnomamö warfare proper is the raid. That is, not all of their feuding and squabbles can be considered as war, although the values associated with war— bellicosity, ferocity, and violence—undoubtedly increase the amount of all kinds of fighting.

War is only one form of violence in a graded series of aggressive activities (Chagnon, 1967). Indeed, some of the other forms of fighting, such as the formal chest-pounding duel, may even be considered as the antithesis of war, for they provide an alternative to killing. Duels are formal and are regulated by stringent rules about proper ways to deliver and receive blows. Much of Yąnomamö fighting is kept innocuous by these rules so that the concerned parties do not have to resort to drastic means to resolve their grievances. The three most innocuous forms of violence, chest pounding, side slapping, and club fights, permit the contestants to express their hostilities in such a way that they can continue to remain on relatively peaceful terms with each other after the contest is settled. Thus, Yąnomamö culture calls forth aggressive behavior, but at the same time provides a regulated system in which the expressions of violence can be controlled.

The most innocuous form of fighting is the chest-pounding duel described in the last chapter (Fig. 5–5). These duels usually take place between the members of different villages and are precipitated by such minor affronts as malicious gossip, accusations of cowardice, stinginess with food, or niggardliness in trading.

If such a duel is escalated, it usually develops into a side-slapping contest (Fig. 5–7). Occasionally, the combatants will sue for the use of machetes and axes, but this is rare. If machetes are used, the object of the contest still remains the same: injure your opponent seriously enough so that he will withdraw from the contest, but try not to draw blood. Hence, opponents strike each other with only the flat of the blade when they resort to machetes. As you can imagine, this hurts.

In some areas the Yąnomamö modify the chest-pounding duel in another way: the opponents hold rocks in their clenched fists and strike their adversaries on the chest with an even more stunning blow. They try not to let the stone itself touch the flesh of the man they are fighting. Even without the use of stones, however, they are able to deliver their blows with such force that some of the participants cough up blood for days after having been in a duel.

Club fights represent the next level of violence (Fig. 6–1). These can take place both within and between villages. Most of the club fights result from arguments over women, but a few of them develop out of disputes associated with food theft. Dikawä, a young man about 20 years old, came home one day and discovered a bunch of eating bananas his father, about 55 years old, had hung up in his house, above his hearth, to ripen in the smoke. Dikawä, however, ate a number of them without his father's permission. When his father discovered the theft, he ripped a pole out of his house and began clubbing Dikawä. Dikawä armed himself with a similar club and attacked his father, precipitating a general melee that soon involved most of the men in the village, each taking the side of the father or son. In some brawls, individuals seem to join in the fighting just to keep the sides even. But kinship relationships play an important part in most fights (Chagnon and Bugos, 1979). If a group is badly outnumbered, they will be joined by remoter kin and friends whose sense of fairness stimulates them to take sides, no matter what the issue is. The net result of the above fight was a number of lacerated skulls, bashed fingers, and sore shoulders. The contestants try to hit each other on the top of the head, but when the fight gets out of hand, the participants swing wildly and rarely hit their opponents on the skull. More frequently, the blow lands on the shoulder or arm.

The clubs used in these fights are, ideally, 8 to 10 feet long. They are very flexible, quite heavy, and deliver a tremendous wallop. In general shape and dimensions, they resemble pool cues, but are nearly twice as long. The club is held at the thin end, which is frequently sharpened to a long point in case the fighting escalates to spear thrusting, in which case the club is inverted and used as a pike.

Most duels start between two men, usually after one of them has been accused of or caught *en flagrante* trysting with the other's wife. The enraged husband challenges his opponent to strike him on the head with a club. He holds his own club vertically, leans against it, and exposes his head for his opponent to strike. After he has sustained a blow on the head, he can then deliver one on the culprit's skull. But as soon as blood starts to flow, almost everybody rips a pole out of the house frame and joins in the fighting, supporting one or the other of the contestants (Fig. 6–1).

Needless to say, the tops of most men's heads are covered with long ugly scars of which their bearers are immensely proud. Some of them, in fact, keep

Fig. 6–1. A nocturnal club fight over infidelity. The man in the center has just been struck on the head and blood is streaming down his neck and back.

their heads cleanly shaved on top to display these scars, rubbing red pigment on their bare scalps to define them more precisely. Viewed from the top, the skull of an accomplished man of 40 years looks like a road map, for it is criss-crossed by as many as 20 large scars (Fig. 6–2). Others keep their heads shaved for decorative reasons only, irrespective of the number of scars they bear. Some do not shave their heads at all.

Club fighting is frequent in large villages, primarily because there are more opportunities for men to establish clandestine sexual liaisons without getting caught at it. Most affairs are, however, discovered. The larger the village, the more frequent the club fighting; and as fighting increases, so too does the probability that the village will fission and result in two separate groups. Most village fissioning I investigated resulted from a specific club fight over a woman, a fight that was merely one such incident in a whole series of similar squabbles. In addition to size, the lineage structure and kinship composition of villages affects the frequency of conflicts (Chapter 4).

The village of Patanowä-teri split during the last month of my first field trip. One of the young men took the wife of another because she was allegedly being mistreated by the husband. This resulted in a brutal club fight that involved almost every man in the village. The fight escalated to jabbing with

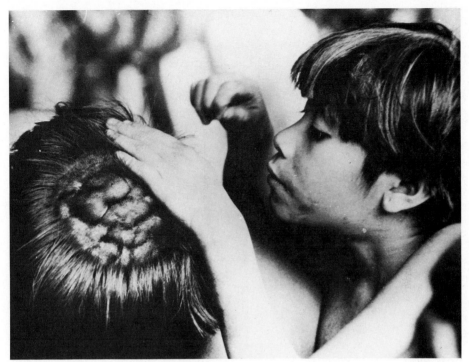

Fig. 6–2. Older men who have been in many club fights have enormous scars—of which they are very proud.

the sharpened ends of the clubs when the husband of the woman in question was speared by his rival and badly wounded. The headman of the village, a "brother" (parallel cousin) of Kąobawä, had been attempting to keep the fighting restricted to clubs. When the husband's rival speared his opponent, the headman went into a rage and speared him in turn, running his own sharpened club completely through the young man's body. He died when they tried to remove the weapon. The wife was then given back to her legitimate husband, who punished her by cutting both her ears off with his machete.

The kinsmen of the dead man were then ordered to leave the village before there was further bloodshed. The aggrieved faction joined the Monou-teri and the Bisaasi-teri because these two groups were at war with their natal village, and they knew that they would have an opportunity to raid their own village to get revenge. The Monou-teri and the two Bisaasi-teri groups acepted these new arrivals; they were kinsmen and would actively prosecute the war against the Patanowä-teri. The hosts, of course, took several women from the refugees, the price a vulnerable group must pay for protection.

Spears are not commonly used by the Yąnomamö. A rare form of fighting, however, does involve the use of these weapons. It is a formal contest in the sense that the fight is prearranged and the participants agree beforehand to refrain from using their bows and arrows. Fights such as these take place when the members of two villages are not angry enough with each other to shoot to kill, but are too furious to be able to satisfy their grudges with chest pounding or club fighting.

The spears themselves are about 6 feet long, lightweight, and frequently painted with red and black designs. They are merely peeled saplings sharpened to a long point at the heavy end. Each man makes several of them.

The single spear-throwing incident that took place during my fieldwork started over a woman. Her husband had been very cruel to her, so the woman's brother, the headman of one of the villages north of Kąobawä's area, took her away from him by force. This enraged his entire following, which was considerably smaller than that of the wife's brother. A club fight temporarily settled the dispute, but the smaller of the groups was thoroughly trounced by the followers of the wife's brother. They challenged their adversaries to a spear fight and notified them they were going to return with reinforcements.

The woman over which the dispute began then ran away from her brother and rejoined her husband. But the die was cast and the fight was now a matter of pride, the original cause being quite irrelevant. Each of the principals in the dispute busily recruited aid from its allies. Kąobawä's group sent a delegation of young men to the village that took the woman away from the cruel husband. When the cruel husband's incensed group and their allies arrived, about a week after the challenge, they entered their opponents' village and drove them out in a hail of spears. Many of them were wounded superficially, but one old man, not able to dodge missiles as well as he used to, suffered a bad wound and subsequently died. The victors stole all the hammocks, machetes, and cooking pots they could find and fled. This action, too, was rare. The losers regrouped and gave chase, this time intending to escalate the fight to shooting. Some of them tied pieces of steel (broken machete) to their spears to make them more effective.

They caught up to the victorious group and another spear fight took place. This time tempers grew hot because one man in each of the fighting groups had managed to borrow a shotgun from the missionaries associated with the respective villages; these were repeatedly discharged over the heads of the fighters. The Yąnomamö had deceived the missionaries into loaning them two guns on the pretext of getting fresh game for the mission personnel. One of the shotgun-wielding Yąnomamö, standing at the front of his group, was struck by two sharpened spears. At this, he discharged his shotgun into the face of the headman of the other group, terminating the fight. The wounded man nearly died from the blast, but after many months of nursing by the missionaries he managed to recover. He still carries several balls of lead in his face.[1] Thereafter, the two groups were at war and raided each other with the intention of killing.

---

[1]The members of two villages in contact with the missions occasionally borrow shotguns from the missionaries. The missionaries are usually very cautious about loaning the Yąnomamö firearms, knowing that they might be used in the wars. Since 1970, shotguns are becoming rather common in contacted Yąnomamö villages.

The Raid and Nomohoni

The raid is the next level in the scale of violence; this is warfare proper. The objective of the raid is to kill one or more of the enemy and flee without being discovered. If, however, the victims of the raid discover their assailants and manage to kill one of them, the campaign is not considered to be a success, no matter how many people the raiders may have killed before sustaining their single loss. Rerebawä told me of a raid he went on several years before I arrived. They managed to kill the headman of the village they raided, abduct his small son, and kill one more man as he fled to the village to recruit help. They were chased, but kept ahead of their pursuers for almost two days. Their pursuers caught up with them after dark on the second day and attacked them while they slept. They killed one man in his hammock, but in so doing, alarmed the others. A skirmish between the two groups developed, and the raiders managed to kill two more of their enemy in this struggle. Still, according to Rerebawä, the raid was not a good one because one of their own men was killed. The 10-year-old son of the slain headman was later shot by a man, who now lives in Monou-teri. The little boy was persecuted and tormented by the other children. Finally, the man got sick of seeing this, so he shot the little boy as he was bathing in the stream. The boy also reminded him of his enemies.

Although few raids are initiated solely with the intention of capturing women, this is always a desired side benefit. A few wars, however, are started with the intention of abducting women. I visited a village in Brazil in 1967 that had a critical shortage of women. A group of missionaries had moved into this village a few years earlier and later learned of the treachery by which the group managed to obtain a number of their women. One of the missionaries gave me this account. The headman of the group organized a raiding party to abduct women from a distant group. They went there and told these people that they had machetes and cooking pots from the foreigners, who prayed to a spirit that gave such items in answer to the prayers. They then volunteered to teach these people how to pray. When the men knelt down and bowed their heads, the raiders attacked them with their machetes and killed them. They captured their women and fled.

Treachery of this kind, the *nomohoni*, is the ultimate form of violence. Kąobawä's group suffered a massacre in 1950, as I have mentioned earlier (see Prologue), but the treachery in this case was in revenge for an earlier killing. Still, their assailants attempted to abduct women after the objectives of their treachery were accomplished. Had it not been for their greed to capture women, the massacre would have been even more complete. Many escaped because the assailants turned their attention to the women.

Generally, however, the desire to abduct women does not lead to the initiation of hostilities between groups that have had no history of mutual raiding in the past. New wars usually develop when charges of sorcery are leveled against the members of a different group. Once raiding has begun between two villages, however, the raiders all hope to acquire women if the circumstances are such that they can flee without being discovered. If they catch a man and his wife at some distance from the village, they will more than likely take the woman after they kill her husband. If, however, the raiders are near the village, they may flee without dragging a captured woman along, as the body of their victim will be discovered quickly and pursuit will be immediate. Hence, they do not take a chance on hindering their flight by dragging a reluctant captive with them. A captured woman is raped by all the men in the raiding party and, later, by the men in the village who wish to do so but did not participate in the raid. She is then given to one of the men as a wife. However, if the captured woman is related to her captors, she is usually not raped.

Most wars are merely a prolongation of earlier hostilities, stimulated by revenge motives. The first causes of hostilities are usually sorcery, murders, or club fights over women in which someone is badly injured or killed. Occasionally, food theft involving related villages also precipitates raiding. This was the cause of the first raids between Kąobawä's group and the Patanowä-teri; they split from each other after a series of club fights over women. Each group made a new garden and returned periodically to the old one to collect peach-palm fruit, a crop that continues to produce long after the garden itself has gone to weeds. Someone stole the peach-palm fruit belonging to a man in the other group, resulting in another food theft for revenge, a club fight, and then raiding, but it should be pointed out that the raiding came about only after a long history of disputes between the groups; food theft was merely the catalyst that finally initiated the hostilities. Food theft is often provoked by the intention of intimidating, not by hunger.

The Yąnomamö themselves regard fights over women as the primary causes of their wars. I was in one of the more remote villages in 1967, visiting with people I had met on my first field trip. The headman of the village, Säsäwä, coveted my British commando knife and kept begging me to give it to him. He wanted me to tell him all about the knife, its origin, history, and how often it had been exchanged in trades. When I told him that it was used by people of my 'group' when they went on raids against their enemies, his interest shifted to our military exploits.

"Who did you raid?" he asked.

"Germany-teri."

"Did you go on the raid?"

"No, but my father did."

"How many of the enemy did he kill?"

"None."

"Did any of your kinsmen get killed by the enemy?"

"No."

"You probably raided because of women theft, didn't you?"

"No."

At this answer he was visibly disturbed. He chatted for a moment with the others, seeming to doubt my answer.

"Was it because of witchcraft?" he then asked.

"No," I replied again.

"Ah! Someone stole cultivated food from the other!" he exclaimed, citing confidently the only other incident that is deemed serious enough to provoke man to wage war.

Perhaps the best way to illustrate Yąnomamö warfare, its causes, and the techniques of a raid is to give a history of the recent military activities of Monou-teri, a small village that split away from Kąobawä's group in the mid-1950s.

A Specific War

The headman of the village, whom I shall call Damowä (since he was recently killed by raiders), was a particularly aggressive man. According to Rerebawä and Kąobawä, Damowä was the only fierce man in the entire village, the true *waiteri* (fierce one) of the group.

Damowä had a habit of seducing the wives of other men, a factor that led to frequent feuding in the village and resulted in a number of club fights. Of the numerous affairs he had, two in particular illustrate the nature of possible consequences. His youngest brother was married to an abducted Shamatari girl. Damowä seduced her, thereby enraging his brother. The young man was afraid to vent his anger on the real culprit, his brother, so, instead, he shot the wife with an arrow. He intended only to wound her, but the arrow struck her in a vital spot and she died.

Manasinawä, a man of some 55 years at the present time, joined Damowä's group with his wife and young daughter. He fled from his own village in order to take refuge in a group that was raiding his own village, as he wanted to get revenge against them for a wrong they had committed. Damowä, who already had several wives, decided to take Manasinawä's wife from him and add her to his own family. This resulted in the final club fight that led to the separation of Kąobawä's group from the Monou-teri. Manasinawä's wife took the daughter and fled to yet another village. Kąobawä then organized a raid to recover the woman and child when their protectors refused to give them back. The two were taken by force from this group by Kąobawä's raiders. Nobody was killed in the incident. Manasinawä, his wife, and his daughter remained with Kąobawä's group, and he ultimately gave the daughter to Kąobawä for a second wife. Kąobawä still has her (Fig. 1–8).

At this time, the groups of Damowä and Kąobawä, respectively, were still at war with the Patanowä-teri, from whom they separated some 15 years earlier. Damowä's group, after separating from Kąobawä's, attempted to make peace with the Patanowä-teri, as they were now vulnerable and could ill afford to remain on hostile terms with them. Damowä's group also made an alliance with the two Shamatari villages, which had given them cooperation when they staged the revenging treacherous feast discussed in the last chapter. For about five years relationships between Damowä's group and the Patanowä-teri were relatively amicable, but as the former's alliances with the Shamatari grew in strength, their relationship to the Patanowä-teri grew cool once again.

The Patanowä-teri then became embroiled in new wars with several villages on the Orinoco River and turned to Kąobawä's group for aid, hoping to patch up their old grievances and remain at peace. The first day I began my fieldwork marked the initiation of complete peace between Kąobawä's group and the Patanowä-teri: they were having a feast together in Bisaasi-teri. Damowä's group, the Monou-teri, were not participating in the feast, but a number of men came anyway. They discovered a group of seven Patanowä-teri females outside the main village and could not resist the temptation: they forcefully took them back to Monou-teri. Later that day the Patanowä-teri men discovered that the women were missing, so they searched the neighborhood and found the tracks of the Monou-teri men at the site of the abduction, where signs of struggling abounded. The next morning they went to Monou-teri armed with clubs: they were bound to get their women back, but did not care to start another shooting war with the Monou-teri. They took five of the women away from the Monou-teri in a heated struggle, but had to pull back without the remaining two, unless they were willing to shoot to kill: the Monou-teri were determined to keep the other women at all costs.

The significance of this incident is that the headman of Monou-teri realized that the Patanowä-teri would not risk getting into a shooting war with them since they already had more enemies than they could comfortably handle. Hence, this provided an excellent opportunity for the Monou-teri to abduct women with relatively little chance of getting shot in retaliation.

Damowä, the headman of Monou-teri, was angry because the Patanowä-teri had recovered so many of their women. He then threatened to ambush the Patanowä-teri when they left for home after the feast at Bisaasi-teri was over. The Patanowä-teri, in view of this, cut their stay short and left for home before the feast was over, hoping to avoid trouble with the Monou-teri.

However, Damowä was not satisfied that he had forced the Patanowä-teri to capitulate, to leave for home, and not attempt to recover the two remaining women. He decided to raid them. In January of 1966 he and a party of men from Monou-teri raided the Patanowä-teri at the latter's village. They caught Bosibrei climbing a *rasha* tree, a prickly cultivated palm that must be climbed slowly and with the aid of a pair of moveable stick frames in order to avoid getting pierced by the needle-sharp thorns that protrude from the tree's trunk (Fig. 2–11). Bosibrei was almost at the top of the tree when the raiders caught him—he made an excellent target silhouetted against the sky. They shot him and killed him with one volley of arrows as he reached for the fruits of the palm. One of Damowä's "brothers"—who also participated in this raid—was married to one of the victim's daughters.

The Monou-teri had anticipated their raid by clearing a new garden site across the Mavaca River, where they hoped to take refuge after the inevitable revenge raids from Patanowä-teri began. They had hoped to complete their garden before the raids became intense, as the Mavaca River would have provided a natural obstacle to raiders. The Patanowä-teri, however, were infuriated by this killing and raided the Monou-teri immediately. Two of the raiders were Damowä's "brothers" (parallel cousins).

The raiders caught Damowä outside the new garden searching for honey. This was in the first week of February. He had two of his wives with him and one child. He was looking up a tree when the raiders shot a volley of arrows into his body, at least five of which struck him in the abdomen. He managed to nock one of his own arrows and shoot at the raiders, cursing them defiantly, although he was probably mortally wounded at the time. Then Bishewä, one of the raiders, shot a final arrow into Damowä, piercing his neck below his ear. He fell to the ground and died after being struck by this arrow.

The raiders did not attempt to abduct the women, as they were close to the Monou-teri campsite and they had to cross the Mavaca River to escape. The women ran back to the village to tell the others what happened. Instead of giving chase, as they ought to have done—according to Kąobawä and the others in Bisaasi-teri—the Monou-teri themselves fled into the jungle and hid until darkness, afraid that the raiders might return. Their fearsome leader, Damowä, was dead and they were now demoralized.

The man who fired the fatal arrow into Damowä's neck was a son of the man the Monou-teri shot in their raid. Two of the men who shot Damowä were his classificatory brothers (members of the same lineage), three were brothers-in-law (including the man who shot the fatal arrow), and one was a man who had been adopted into the Patanowä-teri village as a child, after he and his mother were abducted from a distant Shamatari village.

The Monou-teri burned the corpse of Damowä the next day. They held a mortuary ceremony that week and invited their allies, members of the two Shamatari villages and the two groups of Bisaasi-teri, to participate. Gourds of the dead man's ashes were given to specific men (who themselves could not drink them but would would be responsible for vengeance) in several of the allied villages, an act calculated to reaffirm solidarity and friendship. Damowä's widows were given to his two eldest surviving brothers.

Kąobawä, a classificatory brother to Damowä, then assumed the responsibility of organizing a revenge raid. Damowä's own brothers failed to step forward to assume this responsibility, and for a while there was no leadership whatsoever in Monou-teri. Finally, Orusiwä, the oldest and most competent member of the village, emerged as the de facto village leader, a position he acquired largely by default. He was related to the slain headman as brother-in-law, and their respective descent groups dominated village politics. Hence, leadership in Monou-teri shifted from one lineage to the other, equally large, lineage.

Kąobawä delayed the revenge raid until April, giving the Monou-teri time to expand their new garden. This date also coincided with the beginning of the rains, thus reducing the possibility of a retaliation until the next dry season and providing the Monou-teri even more time to expand their new garden and abandon the old one.

The Monou-teri were afraid to return to their producing garden, so they divided their time between their newly cleared site, where they worked at cutting timber and burning it, and Kąobawä's village, where they took occasional rests to regain their energy. (See "Macro" Movements, Figure 2–12, where these moves are graphically shown.) They returned to their old site only to collect plantains, which they carried to the new site. Kąobawä's group then built a new *shabono* and fortified it, anticipating the war they knew would be inevitable. Up to this point, Kąobawä's group, Upper Bisaasi-teri, maintained two small *shabonos* a few yards apart from each other, but they coalesced into a single larger group and moved into the new *shabono* when it was completed. The visiting Monou-teri also helped them work on the new structure.

Meanwhile, the Patanowä-teri, knowing that they would be raided by the Monou-teri and their allies, also began clearing a new garden (Fig. 2–12). They selected a site near one that was abandoned by Kąobawä's group many years ago, knowing that the peach-palm trees were still producing there. By this time the Patanowä-teri were in rather desperate straits. Their old enemies, the several groups on the Orinoco River, began raiding them with even greater frequency, as they had learned that the Monou-teri and Bisaasi-teri were again at war with the Patanowä-teri. A few additional villages began raiding the Patanowä-teri to settle old grudges, realizing that the Patanowä-teri had so many enemies that they could not possibly retaliate against all of them.

The Patanowä-teri then began moving from one location to another, hoping to avoid and confuse their enemies. They spent the dry season in turns at their main producing garden, with the Ashidowä-teri, their only ally, and at their new garden. Each group that raided them passed the word to other villages concerning the location of the Patanowä-teri. If they were not at one place, then they had to be at one of the other two. The raids were frequent and took a heavy toll. At least eight people were killed by raiders, and a number of others were wounded. Some of the dead were women and children, a consequence of the fact that the Patanowä-teri themselves sent a heavy volley of arrows into the village of one of their enemies and killed a woman. Females are normally not the target of raiders' arrows. The Patanowä-teri were raided at least 25 times while I conducted my initial fieldwork. They themselves retaliated as frequently as possible, but could not return tit for tat. They managed to drive their main enemies, the Hasuböwä-teri, away from their garden, forcing them to flee across the Orinoco. They concentrated on raiding this group until they had killed most of the *waiteri* (fierce ones). They were so successful at doing this that the Hasuböwä-teri ultimately withdrew from the war. Several of my informants claimed that they did so because their fierce ones were all dead, and nobody was interested in prosecuting the war any further.

When the Hasuböwä-teri withdrew from the raiding, the Patanowä-teri then concentrated on raiding the Monou-teri. Every time the Monou-teri returned to their main site they found the tracks of numerous men who had visited the village, tracks that always came from the direction of Patanowä-teri. Consequently, the Monou-teri moved into Kąobawä's group for protection, fearing to return to their old site until the jungle was inundated by the rains.

Kaobawä's group resented this somewhat and made no bones about reminding the Monou-teri that they were eating large quantities of food from their gardens. When complaining became intense, the Monou-teri moved into the village of the Lower Bisaasi-teri and lived off their produce until the latter also began to complain. Then they traveled to the Mömariböwei-teri and lived with them for a while, returning to Kaobawä's village when these allies wearied of the visitors. When the hosts, the Lower Bisaasi-teri, for example, wanted to get rid of the Monou-teri, they would hold a feast in their honor. When the going-home food was presented to them, they had no alternative but to leave. It would have been insulting to remain after the food was presented. In between their moves they returned to their own producing site to collect plantains and carry them to their new garden. They subsisted there off the food they carried with them.

The Monou-teri soon resented being treated like pariahs by their allies and began to regain their courage. Much of this treatment was due to the fact that they failed to chase the raiders when Damowä was slain, displaying cowardice instead of ferocity. Many of the men in the Bisaasi-teri groups resented the Monou-teri for this and were not timid about displaying their disgust. The Monou-teri were a burden, as they rarely helped at expanding Bisaasi-teri's gardens and ate a good deal of food.

The raid Kaobawä organized to avenge Damowä's death took place late in April. The Shamatari allies—Mömariböwei-teri and Reyabowei-teri—were invited to participate, but they failed to send a contingency. As allies never really trust each other, the raid was delayed because some of the Bisaasi-teri suspected that their allies were waiting for the raiders to leave so that they could descend on the poorly protected women and make off with captives. Finally, a few of them did arrive and the *wayu itou* (warrior line-up) got under way. Still, the Bisaasi-teri feared treachery on the part of their Shamatari friends, so the men of Lower Bisaasi-teri decided to stay home and protect the women left behind by the Monou-teri and Upper Bisaasi-teri raiders. A small feast was held to entertain the visiting Shamatari allies.

On the afternoon of the feast a grass dummy was set up in the village, and the men who were to participate in the raid conducted a mock attack on the dummy, which was supposed to represent the body of a Patanowä-teri man. They painted themselves black, crept slowly around the village with bows and arrows ready, searching for the tracks of the enemy. They converged at one point, spread out, crept toward the dummy, and, at Kaobawä's signal, let fly with a volley of arrows. The Yanomamö are good archers. None of the arrows missed its mark, and the dummy, looking like a pincushion, toppled ominously to the ground, a dozen or more bamboo-tipped arrows protruding from it. Then the raiders screamed and ran out of the village, simulating their retreat from the enemy. They drifted back into the village, one at a time or in small groups, and retired to their hammocks to wait for darkness.

The village became unusually quiet shortly after dark. Suddenly, the stillness was pierced by an animallike noise, half-scream and half-growl, as the first raider marched slowly out to the center of the village, clacking his arrows against his bow, growling his individualized fierce noise, usually a mimic of a carnivore: a wasp, or a buzzard. At this signal—not knowing fully what to expect and a little nervous—I crept from my own hammock and went to the center of the village with my tape recorder. The other raiders joined the first man, coming one at a time after short intervals, each clacking his arrows and growling some hideous noise. Kąobawä stood by and made sure the line was straight and faced the direction of the enemy; he would push or pull the individual warriors until they formed a perfectly straight line, joining them after the last one took his place.

The procession to the line-up took about 20 minutes, as about 50 or so men participated (Fig. 6–3). When the last one was in line, the murmurs among the children and women died down and all was quiet in the village once again. I squatted there, unable to see much of what was going on, growing more nervous by the moment, half suspecting that the warriors were sneaking up on me to murder me for tape recording a sacred rite. Then the silence was broken when a single man began singing in a deep baritone voice: "I am meat hungry! I am meat hungry! Like the carrion-eating buzzard I hunger for flesh!" When he completed the last line, the rest of the raiders repeated his song, ending in an ear-piercing, high-pitched scream that raised goose bumps all over my arms and scalp. A second chorus, led by the same man, followed the scream. This one referred to meat hunger of the kind characteristic of a particular species of carnivorous wasp. They screamed again, becoming distinctly more enraged. On the third chorus, they referred again to the buzzard's meat hunger, and a few men simultaneously interjected such descriptions of their ferocity as: "I'm so fierce that when I shoot the enemy my arrow will strike with such force that blood will splash all over the material possessions in his household!"

Then the line of warriors broke, and the men gathered into a tight formation, weapons held above their heads. They shouted three times, beginning modestly and increasing their volume until they reached a climax at the end of the third shout: "Whaaaa! Whaaaa! WHAAAA!" They listened as the jungle echoed back their last shout, identified by them as the spirit of the enemy. They noted the direction from which the echo came. On hearing it, they pranced about frantically, hissing and groaning, waving their weapons, until Kąobawä calmed them down, and the shouting was repeated two more times. At the end of the third shout of the third repetition, the formation broke, and the men ran back to the respective houses, each making a noise— "Bubububububububu"—as he ran. When they reached their hammocks, they all simulated vomiting, passing out of their mouths the rotten flesh of the enemy they had symbolically devoured in the line-up.

They retired for the night. Many of them wept and moaned, mourning the loss of their friend and kinsman, Damowä. At dawn the women went to the gardens and gathered large quantities of plantains. These were carried to the raiders, wrapped with their vine hammocks, and deposited outside the village for the men to collect as they marched in single file to war.

The men painted themselves black again (Fig. 6–3). Some even put on bright red loincloths which I had traded to them, as the warrior line-up is a spectacle in which the younger men can show off to the girls. The loincloths were left behind when the men departed. They tinkered with their bows and

Fig. 6–3. Raiders lining up at dawn prior to departing for the attack on their enemy. They paint their faces black with masticated charcoal, as well as their legs and chests.

checked to see if the bowstrings were weak at any spot, sharpened their best arrow points, and waited nervously for Kaobawä to signal for the line-up to begin again. The *wayu itou* was repeated, each man marching to the center of the village and taking his place in line. This time, however, they did not sing the war song. They merely shouted, as they had done the previous night, waited for the echo to return, and marched dramatically out of the village. Their mothers and sisters shouted last minute bits of advice as they left the village: "Don't get yourself shot up!" "You be careful now!" And then they wept.

The men picked up their supplies of food where the women had stacked them and left for Patanowä-teri. Kaobawä had been complaining all year of severe pains in his lower back, abdomen, and urinal tract, and was in considerable pain when he walked. Still, he insisted on going on the raid, suspecting that the others would turn back if he did not lead it. The raiders had not been gone five hours when the first one came back, a boastful young man, complaining that he had a sore foot and could not keep up with the others. The next day a few more young men returned, complaining that they had malaria and pains in the stomach. They enjoyed participating in the pomp of the *wayu itou*, for this impressed the women, but were, at heart, afraid.

The raiders travel slowly their first day away from the village. They have heavy burdens of food and try to pace themselves so as to arrive in the enemy's territory just as their food runs out. They also attempt to reach a point in the enemy's neighborhod that will permit them to reach his village at dawn: far enough away so that enemy hunters will not discover their presence, but close enough to the village that they can reach it in an hour or so from their last camp.

The men use fire only when they camp at a considerable distance from the enemy's territory. As they approach their destination, they exercise greater caution. Their final evening is spent shivering in the darkness, since they dare not make a fire to warm themselves. Most of the raiders emphasized this, as sleeping without fire is considered to be both dangerous and uncomfortable. The danger lies in the possibility of jaguar attacks, and in the fear that spirits will molest the unprotected raiders. On the last evening the raiding party's fierce ones have difficulties with the younger men; most of them are afraid, cold, and worried about every sort of hazard, and all of them complain of sore feet and belly aches.

The raiders always develop a strategy for attacking the unwary enemy. They usually split into two or more groups and agree to meet later at a predetermined location at some point between their own village and the enemy's. These smaller groups must contain at least four men, six, if possible. This is so because the raiders retreat in a pattern. While the others flee, two men will lie in ambush, shooting any pursuers that might follow. They, in turn, flee, while their comrades lie in ambush to shoot at their pursuers. If there are any novices in the raiding party, the older men will conduct mock raids, showing them how they are to participate. A grass dummy or soft log is frequently employed in this, as was the case in the *wayu itou* held in the village the day before the raiders left. Particularly young men will be positioned in the marching party somewhere in the middle of the single file of raiders so they will not be the first ones to be exposed to danger should the raiders themselves be ambushed. These young men will also be permitted to retreat first. Damowä had a 12-year-old son when he was killed. This boy, Matarawä, was recruited into the raiding party to give him an opportunity to avenge his father's death. The older men made sure he would be exposed to minimum danger, as this was his first raid.

The separated groups of raiders approach the village at dawn and conceal themselves near the commonly used paths to the source of drinking water. They wait for the enemy to come to them. A good many of the victims of raids are shot while fetching water or urinating outside the *shabono*.

Frequently, the enemy is wary and acts defensively at all times when there is an active war going on. Only large groups of people can leave the village, and these are well armed. Raiders will not attack a large group such as this. When the enemy is found to be this cautious, the raiders have no choice but to retreat or to shoot volleys of arrows blindly into the village, hoping to strike someone at a distance. They retreat after they release their arrows, depending on the gossip of other villages to learn if their arrows did find their marks. Rarely, one of the raiders will attempt to enter the village during the night and kill someone while he sleeps. Damowä's younger brother allegedly accomplished this on one raid, but few men are brave enough to try it. Most of the time the raiders manage to ambush a single individual, kill him, and retreat before they are discovered. This is considered to be the most desirable outcome of the raid.

The women were nervous, frightened, and irritable while the men were away, and they were constantly on the lookout for raiders from other villages. This is always a time to suspect raiders, since allies occasionally turn on their friends when the women are poorly guarded, abducting as many as possible while their husbands are away.

After several days the women were so frustrated and anxious that fights began to break out among them. One woman got angry because another one, her sister and cowife, left her to tend a small baby. When the mother returned, the angry one picked up a piece of firewood and bashed her on the side of the head with it, knocking her unconscious and causing her ear to bleed profusely.

The raiders had been gone almost a week when Kąobawä and his younger brother staggered into the village, nearly dead from exhaustion. Kąobawä's pains had gotten so bad that he decided to turn back just before they reached the Patanowä-teri village. He could barely walk by that time and would not have been able to elude pursuers should the enemy have given chase. Shararaiwä, his brother, decided to accompany him back lest he run into a group of Patanowä-teri hunters, or his condition grow even more severe. Shortly after they had dropped out of the raiding party, Shararaiwä stepped on a snake and was bitten. The rains had started, and the snakes were beginning to concentrate on the higher grounds, making walking a hazard. His leg began to swell immediately, and he could not walk. Hence, Kąobawä had to carry him on his back, despite the fact that he could barely walk himself. Carrying him for nearly two days, he managed to reach the Orinoco River. Here, he intended to make a bark canoe and float the rest of the way back down, but they located a dugout canoe someone had concealed, so they borrowed this and reached home about dark, three days after Shararaiwä had been bitten.[2] He survived the snake bite, but Kąobawä was very exhausted from the trip.

That night an advance party of the raiders returned, chanted briefly with Kąobawä, explaining that they had reached Patanowä-teri, shot and killed one man, and fled. The Patanowä-teri pursued them, got ahead of them at one point, and ambushed them when they passed. They wounded Konoreiwä of Monou-teri, shooting a bamboo-tipped arrow completely through his chest just above his heart.

The next morning the main body of raiders returned to the village, carrying Konoreiwä with them in a pole-and-vine litter. They had removed the arrow, but he was very weak and continuously coughed up mouthfuls of blood. They put him in a hammock and tended his fire for him. They asked me to treat his wound.

He lay in his hammock for a week, not eating or drinking all that time—the Yąnomamö have a taboo against taking water when wounded with a bamboo-tipped arrow, and Konoreiwä was slowly wasting away. Finally, I could stand it

[2]The canoe was hidden in the brush by Kąobawä's nephew, who lives in a village up the Orinoco. He had come to Bisaasi-teri that day to visit and hid his canoe so that the Bisaasi-teri would not borrow it.

no longer and made a batch of lemonade. I called for them to gather around, ceremoniously crushed an aspirin into the lemonade, and explained that this was very powerful medicine. So powerful that it had to be diluted with a large amount of water. I then demanded that he take some, which he gladly did, the others not interfering. By then he was so weak that he could not sit up, so I spoon-fed the liquid to him. A knowing glance passed between us as he gulped down the first spoonful of sweet liquid. He ultimately recovered.

The two men who shot the fatal arrows into the Patanowä-teri were both brothers of the slain Damowä. They were killers and had to purify themselves by going through the *unokaimou* ceremony.

They were given spaces in Kạobawä's *shabono* for their hammocks. The area each man occupied was sealed off from the adjoining houses by palm leaves, and the men had their food brought to them for the week they were confined to this small area. They each used a pair of sticks to scratch their bodies and did not touch the food with their fingers when they ate, again using sticks to transfer the food from the container to their mouths.

At the end of their confinement, the vine hammocks they used while they were on the raid, along with the scratching sticks, were taken out of the village and tied to a particular kind of tree. The hammocks were placed about 6 feet above the ground and separated from each other by about 1 foot. After this was done, the men resumed their normal activities, but began letting their hair grow.

Kạobawä felt that he had satisfied his obligation to avenge Damowä's death. The Monou-teri, however, wanted to prosecute the war further and continue raiding. It was at this point that Paruriwä of Kạobawä's group began to emerge as one of the more prominent men in the village. He stepped forward and actively prosecuted the war against the Patanowä-teri, encouraged by the esteem in which the Monou-teri held him. Still, he was not enthusiastic enough for the Monou-teri. On one raid he subsequently led, he elected to turn back and go home when the Patanowä-teri were not found at their main garden. The Monou-teri insisted that the party should continue on until they located the enemy, but Paruriwä refused to go any further. When he turned back, so did the entire party.

The Monou-teri and Bisaasi-teri raided against the Patanowä-teri six times while I lived with them, and each time the preparations for the raid closely followed the description given above. The Monou-teri returned to their producing site only when the jungle was inundated; only at that time could they exist without the support of their allies. The remainder of the year they had to take refuge with members of allied villages or expose themselves to the risk of being attacked by superior forces by remaining in their own producing garden.

The Monou-teri also raided the Patanowä-teri without aid from their allies. One of the raids was conducted near the end of the rainy season, and I was staying in their village at the time the raid was held.

A special ceremony took place the day before the raid. The gourds containing the ashes of the slain Damowä were put on the ground in front of his brother's house. Everyone in the village gathered around the ashes and wept aloud. The bamboo quiver of the dead man was brought to the gourds, smashed, the points taken out, and the quiver itself burned. While this was going on, the mourners were in a state of frenzy, pulling at their hair and striking themselves, screaming and wailing. One of his brothers took a snuff tube and blew some of the drug into the gourds containing the ashes (Fig. 6–4). The tube was then cut in half, one of the dead man's arrow points being used to measure the point at which the snuff tube was cut. I was never able to determine whether the arrow points taken from the quiver were possessions of the dead man or were, in fact, the points removed from his body. There were 10 of them, and my informants were too touchy about the matter to be questioned in detail: I received affirmative nods to both questions. In any event, the 10 bamboo points were distributed to the raiders, who fondled them and examined them carefully. Each man brought one with him on the raid that followed this ceremony. The severed snuff tube and the gourds of ashes were tenderly wrapped in leaves and put back in the thatch of the brother's house.

That night I think I became emotionally close to the Yąnomamö in a new way. I remained in my hammock and gave up collecting genealogies. As darkness fell Damowä's brothers began weeping in their hammocks. I lay there and listened, not bothering to tape record it or photograph it or write notes. One of the others asked me why I was not making a nuisance of myself as usual, and I told him that my innermost being (*buhii*) was cold—that is, I was sad. This was whispered around the village, and as each person heard it, he or she looked over at me. The children who inevitably gathered around my hammock were told by their elders to go home and not bother me anymore. I was *hushuo*, in a state of emotional disequilibrium, and had finally begun to act like a human being as far as they were concerned. Those whose hammocks were close to mine reached over and touched me tenderly.

The next day the raiders lined up, shouted in the direction of the Patanowä-teri, heard the echo come back, and left the village to collect their provisions and hammocks. I allowed them to talk me into taking the entire raiding party up the Mavaca River in my canoe. There, they could find high ground and reach the Patanowä-teri without having to cross the numerous swamps that lay between the two villages. There were only 10 men in the raiding party, the smallest the war party can get and still have maximum effectiveness. As we traveled up the river, the younger men began complaining. One had sore feet, and two or three others claimed to have malaria. They wanted to turn back because I had forgotten to bring my malaria pills with me as I had promised. Hukoshikuwä (Fig. 6–5), a brother of the slain headman, silenced their complaints with an angry lecture on cowardice. I let them all out at the mouth of a stream they intended to follow. They unloaded their seemingly enormous supply of plantains and politely waited for me to leave. I sat among them and chatted, thinking that they were doing essential tasks as they fiddled with arrows and retied their provisions. Finally, one of them hinted that I should be leaving because I had a long trip and might not get home before dark. It was then that I discovered they were dallying, trying to be polite to me. They all thanked me for taking them upstream in my canoe, one of the few times the

Fig. 6–4. Damowä's brothers assembled around his remains, blowing ebene *into the gourd containing his ashes.*

Yąnomamö ever expressed gratitude to me, and I got in my canoe to leave. Hukoshikuwä came down to untie my rope for me and shove me off the bank. He watched, silently, as my canoe got caught up in the current and drifted away. He looked frightened, reluctant, anxious, but determined. After I had gotten my motor started and was under way, I looked back to see him turn, pick up his plantains and weapons, and disappear into the jungle. Even he was not enthusiastic about going on the raid, despite the fact that he lectured the younger members of the raiding party about their overt reluctance and cowardice. He was older, however, and had to display the ferocity that adult men are supposed to show. In short, although Hukoshikuwä probably had very little desire as an individual to participate in the raiding, he was obliged to do so by the pressures of the entire system. He could ill afford to remain neutral, as his very own kinsmen—even Kąobawä—implied by word and action that it was disgusting for him not to avenge the death of his brother; and some of his kinsmen in other villages openly accused him of cowardice for not chasing the raiders when they shot Damowä. Again, his erstwhile allies, when they complained about having to feed him and his relatives, were blunt and discourteous. The Shamatari allies even managed to demand a number of women from Hukoshikuwä's group in payment for girls they had given them earlier, when the Monou-teri were superordinate in the alliance pecking order. In short, if Hukoshikuwä failed to put on a show of ferocity and vindictiveness, it would not be long before his friends in allied villages would be taking even greater liberties and demanding more women. Thus, the system worked against him and demanded that he be fierce. Since his own group was small, it had to protect its sovereignty even more rigorously, or be absorbed by a greedy ally whose protection would be tendered at the price of women.

Hukoshikuwä and his raiders did not locate the Patanowä-teri on this raid, although they searched for over a week. They knew it would be difficult to

find them in the rainy season, largely because they would have to make many detours around impassable swamps. It was with this in mind that they brought their larger than usual supply of plantains.

The war was still being conducted, but on a lesser scale, when I returned to the Monou-teri a year later. They had managed to kill two Patanowä-teri and abduct two women. The Patanowä-teri only killed one Monou-teri, the headman. Hence, the Monou-teri, at least for the time being, came out ahead. The Patanowä-teri will not cease raiding them until they kill at least one more Monou-teri, but then the Monou-teri will be obliged to avenge this death when it occurs.[3]

The Patanowä-teri group fissioned and subsequently lost a significant fraction of their size advantage. The Monou-teri completed their move to the new garden and lived there for several years, but eventually coalesced with the Bisaasi-teri, terminating their career as a separate sovereign entity. They 'fused' with the people whence they had originally fissioned (Fig. 2–16).

[3]The Bisaasi-teri were still trying to avenge Damowä's death 10 years later—and were actively raiding the Patanowä-teri—but had by then acquired shotguns and were using them in the raids. At least two Patanowä-teri were killed with shotguns, including Komaiewä, the headman, who is prominent in our film *The Feast*. He is the man who gave away his prized dog to the visitors.

7/The Beginning of Western Acculturation

Introduction

Those of us who live in industrialized societies look on change and progress as being "good" and "desirable." Our entire system of values and goals is constituted in such a way that we strive to make changes, improve and tinker with rules and technology, and reward those who are skillful at it. "Progress" for its own sake is beneficial by definition. The Yąnomamö are now entering a new and potentially hazardous time in their history, for our kind of culture is confronting them and urging, in the name of "progress," that they give up their way of life and adopt some rural form of ours. The agents of progress among the Yąnomamö are mostly missionaries—Salesian Catholics and several independent groups of Protestant Evangelists—whose presence among the Yąnomamö is permitted by Venezuelan and Brazilian law. Incorporation of the Yąnomamö into the national culture has been left almost entirely in the hands of the missionaries, who have been and continue to remain free to use whatever means or techniques they have to accomplish this objective. While the explicit goal of all the missionaries is the conversion of the Yąnomamö to Christianity and the salvation of their souls, a few far-sighted individuals in both groups have independently realized that they likewise have an obligation to prepare the Yąnomamö in other ways for their inevitable absorption into Western culture—teaching them to speak the Spanish or Portuguese language, reading, writing, and counting; introducing domesticated animals that can later serve as predictable sources of protein; explaining market principles, the use of money, scales of economic value, and so on. Other missionaries are more narrowly dedicated to saving souls at any cost, and are insensitive to the point of being inhumane in the techniques they use to bring salvation to the Yąnomamö.

It is inevitable that the Yąnomamö, and all tribal peoples, will be absorbed by the national cultures in whose territories they coincidentally reside. The process of acculturation is as old as culture itself: all dominant cultures impinge on and transform their less-dominant neighbors. There are, however, enlightened and humane ways of accomplishing this—and there are insensitive and inhumane ways. Knowing that acculturation is inevitable, I must conclude that it is essential that a rational and sympathetic policy of acculturation be developed for the Yąnomamö, for the process of change has already begun at a number of mission villages, and it is off to a poor start. Such a policy will

190

require the cooperation of missionaries, government officials, and field-experienced, informed anthropologists. It is yet to be developed.

This raises a dilemma for me. Anthropologists who have worked in "traditional" or "tribal" cultures are often frustrated and saddened by the vectors of change that transform the peoples they have grown to admire during their studies, especially when the changes diminish the freedom and dignity of those peoples. Many anthropologists are, in fact, alarmed by any change and would prefer to see native cultures persist indefinitely while the rest of the maddening world mires itself deeper into the technological, ecological, and political morass that is one certain artifact of cultural evolution and "progress." It is an open question whether particular anthropologists are attracted to primitive cultures because such cultures seemingly represent a more rational, more comprehensible means for coping with the external world—that is to say, a more human way. It is jokingly said that psychiatrists become what they are to better understand their own personal problems, and I suspect that some anthropologists, by analogy, are attracted to their craft for equally personal reasons. A few of my colleagues have even good-naturedly suggested to me that my own intensive involvement with the Yąnomamö is not without reason, for they suspect that I might fit as well in Yąnomamö culture as I do in my own!

But any similarity between an anthropologist and the people with whom he or she has spent a significant portion of his or her life is probably due more to association and learning than to initial equivalencies of personality. Anthropology as a science differs radically from, let us say, chemistry or genetics. Our subject matter is made essentially of the same kind of stuff as the observer—the "subject matter" itself has hopes, fears, desires, and emotions. It is easy to identify with people and become intimate with them; a chemist or geneticist cannot have much empathy for carbon or the genes that determine eye color.

My long association with the Yąnomamö, my intimate friendships among them, and my awareness of the values in their culture account for my sense of frustration and alarm when I reflect on the changes that are taking place in the mission posts and the means by which some of the changes have been effected. Some of them are wrong, in my estimation, perhaps even cruel. Others are ineffective and harmless. Still others are amusing and downright funny.

Acculturation is a subject that has all but become a major subdiscipline within anthropology. Perhaps the most appropriate way to end this case study would be to cast the process into academic terms and adopt a strictly formal, pedagogical stance as I discuss what is now happening to the Yąnomamö. I would like, however, to communicate something about the human dimension of the process, to relate a few incidents and anecdotes that reveal more than a neutral description can expose. What the Yąnomamö must now endure has happened to countless other tribesmen. Perhaps if more citizens of the twentieth century and industrialized culture knew, from the tribesman's point of view, what acculturation means, we might have more compassion and sympathy for the traumas they must endure as they are required to make, usually unwillingly, their transformation. Hopefully such knowledge will be used to a good end, and rational policies of directed change will be forged.

In addition, by looking at the means and methods of the changes that are being made in Yąnomamöland through their eyes, we can gain insights into the nature of our own culture. Very often the things that we ourselves take to be normal, progressive, and desirable look very different when viewed through a tribal lens. Sometimes they appear to be merely humorous. At other times they appear to be hideous.

Yąnomamö Glimpses of Us

Rerebawä looked frail and dwarfed in my trousers and shirt as we sat in the blistering sun on the savanna of Esmerelda waiting for the Venezuelan Air Force cargo plane to appear out of the cloudy north. The *piums*—tiny biting black gnats—were out in astronomical numbers; their annoying bites left miniscule blood clots that itched for a day and then turned black. The *piums* like the larger rivers and savanna areas, and I speculated about the distribution of the Yąnomamö villages—inland, on tiny streams, away from this annoying *plaga*. I pitied those groups that had started moving out to the Orinoco River to make contact with foreigners—to obtain the highly desirable steel tools that they brought with them. Life without clothing for them was unbearable in the dry season, and they would come to the mission stations to work for days at hard labor to earn a tattered garment that some charity had sent gratis into the missions. The Yąnomamö always looked so pathetic in European hand-me-downs, especially after wearing them for several months and not washing them. They would be crusted with filth and rancid, and their skins would begin to have boils and sores all over them.

I was in a gloomy mood, reflecting on the changes that I noticed were taking place among the Yąnomamö. Each year I returned to them there were more missionaries, new mission posts, and now alarming numbers of tourists were beginning to arrive. I did not like what I was seeing and it was no longer possible to ignore the problems that acculturation would bring the Yąno-mamö. My personal relationships with the Yąnomamö had deepened and grown more intimate every year. As I observed what some mission activities and the tourists were doing to the Yąnomamö, my attitude hardened.

Rerebawä had indicated to me several times in the past few years that he would like to see Caracas and how the Caraca-teri lived, especially the Caracateriyoma: "Perhaps I could abduct a few when nobody is looking and drag them back to Bisaasi-teri in the plane!" he would tease mischievously. "But they eat only cows and bread and sugar and would run away from you if you brought them only monkeys and *yei* fruits!" I teased back. "You have warts on your forehead!" he insulted me good-naturedly, and jabbed me in the ribs to make me laugh, for he knew I was ticklish. "You'd better be careful in

Caraca-teri," I warned. "Almost all the men run around with large guns like shotguns and they will ask you for your 'decorated leaves' they call 'papers' and if you don't have any, they will take you away—and me with you!" He puffed his chest out and said: "Huh! I'll just grab a large club and insult them and then we'll see who takes who away!" He adjusted the wad of chewing tobacco he always carried in his lip. "Will we bump into the upper layer when we fly to Caraca-teri?" he asked anxiously; I chuckled to myself. Rerebawä had spent many months with me during my annual returns to his people and he was quite cosmopolitan by Yąnomamö standards, but nevertheless a firm believer in the Yąnomamö notion of the cosmos—a series of rigid bowllike layers, one over the other, separated by only a few hundred feet or yards. "No, the *Hedu ka misi* layer is too high for the plane to reach," I responded, choosing to confirm his beliefs about the cosmic layers rather than arouse his anxiety further by denying their existence. This would be his first plane ride and his first glimpse of the civilization that lay beyind Yąnomamöland, and I wanted him to enjoy his experience.

It was always difficult for me to impress the Yąnomamö with the size of the world beyond their villages and tropical forest, including Rerebawä. I recall being teased by my companions on one of my inland trips as we sat around the campfire before retiring to our hammocks for the evening. They were bantering me about how numerous the Yąnomamö were and how few foreigners there were by comparison. Rerebawä was among them, and just as vociferous. I stood up to underscore my argument, pointing dramatically to the north, northeast, east, reciting names of cities as they came indiscriminately to my mind: "Over there lie the New York-teri, the Boston-teri, the Washington-teri, the Miami-teri; and over there are the London-teri, the Paris-teri, and the Madrid-teri, and Berlin-teri. . .," and on, around the globe. They chuckled confidently, and one of them rose to say, "Over there lie the Shibariwä-teri, the Yabroba-teri, the Wabutawä-teri, the Yeisi-teri, the Auwei-teri and over there the Niyaiyoba-teri, the Maiyo-teri, the Boreta-teri, the Ihirubö-teri. . .," and on around the cardinal points of the compass. I protested, arguing that ". . .Caraca-teri is huge! There are many people there and you are just a few by comparison!" Their response would be, inevitably, "But have you seen the new Patanowä-teri *shabono* or Mishimishimaböwei-teri *shabono*? They stretch in a great arc, like this. . ." and an arm would slowly describe the vast arc while the others listened intently, clicking their tongues to exaggerate the size. Caracas, to them, was just another large *shabono*, with a large thatched roof, and I knew that the only way to convince them otherwise was to take one of them there to see it with his own eyes.

Perhaps if Rerebawä saw the scope and magnitude of the culture that was moving inexorably to assimilate his own he would be more prepared to understand and deal with it when it eventually came. Would the same thing happen to Yąnomamö culture that happened to so many North American Indian societies? Would the Yąnomamö be reduced biologically and culturally to a mere shadow of the proud and free people I had grown to know and admire during 12 years of research among them? My personal dilemma was that I hoped that the Yąnomamö would be permitted to remain sovereign and unchanged, but my sense of history and understanding of culture contact told me that change was inevitable.

Storm clouds were piling up over Duida, the massive, abrupt cliff that rose 10,000 feet up from the small savanna at Esmerelda, and I hoped the plane would arrive soon, for in an hour the clouds would obscure the landing strip and it might be weeks or months before another flight would be scheduled to Esmerelda. A free lift out to Caracas with Rerebawä today would be very convenient, for I could spend five days with him working in comfort on myth translations and return with my bush pilot, who was coming in with my medical colleagues. There would be space for us in the plane.

"Avion! Avion!" shouted the Ye'kwana Indians who idly waited for the plane to arrive, for it always brought cargo for them. Rerebawä was on his feet in an instant, his hand over his brow, peering intently into the cloud-blackened northern sky. *"Kihamö kä a! A ösöwä he barohowä!"* he jabbered excitedly, and I agreed that indeed it was visible and very high. He raced over to his possessions, a small cluster of tightly bound cloth bags made from the remains of a shirt I had given him last year. "Hold on! It will not get here for a while yet. It has to circle the landing area and chase the cows off the savanna." He sat down, clutching his bags and grinning. I hadn't noticed his bags until now, and asked him what he had in them. "Just some 'things'," he responded nonchalantly. "What kind of 'things'?" I asked suspiciously. He untied the knot and opened the larger bag; it was full of grey wood ashes, about a quart of them. Before I could ask him why in the world he was bringing ashes to Caracas, he had opened the other bag: it was full of tightly bound cured tobacco leaves. I clicked my tongue approvingly and he wrapped them back up. The ashes were to mix with the chewing tobacco, and I recalled that he had asked me earlier if the Caraca-teri made fires on the floor of their houses to cook by. He was way ahead of me.

The gigantic transport plane—a C-123 designed for paratroop drops and hauling heavy cargo—lumbered to a dusty stop and the Ye'kwana descended on it to unload the cargo. The crew was in a hurry, for they had caught the edge of the storm and wanted to be airborne as soon as possible. They were reluctant to fly over Amazonas, a vast jungle with no radio communications or emergency landing strips, in a tropical storm.

Within an hour the plane was unloaded and the crew motioning for any passengers who wanted a lift to get aboard. We stepped into the giant, empty belly of the plane and I strapped Rerebawä into his safety harness. He had grown very quiet and was now obviously worried—if we weren't going to crash into the upper layer, why was it necessary to tie ourselves into the seats? The plane lumbered to the end of the savanna, turned, and screeched to a halt. The pilot tested the motors, and the roar was deafening: Rerebawä's knuckles were white as he clutched the edge of his seat. His breath smelled horrible. It was obviously traumatic for him. The plane lurched forward and gathered speed, bouncing unpredictably over the irregularities of the unimproved dirt landing strip. Then the nose tipped upward sharply and we were airborne.

It was one of the worst flights I ever had, for we hit the storm soon after we gained cruising altitude. The plane jerked and twisted violently, dipping first one wing and then, suddenly, the other. Gusts of wind bounced us around, and jarring losses of altitude would leave us breathless, pinning us against our safety harnesses and then, as the frail plane fought back upwards, forcing us into our canvas seats. We could hear the ominous beating of rain on the fuselage above the roar of the motors. In an hour we were over the llanos and the flight had become more calm, but the noise was still deafening as the two motors labored incessantly. I unsnapped my harness and walked around the plane, but I was unsuccessful in persuading Rerebawä to untie himself or look out one of the fogged-up portholes. He just sat there, staring blankly at the opposite side of the plane, his tobacco buried deeply between his lower lip and teeth, clutching his seat. He relaxed a bit when I told him that we were approaching our landing strip at Maracay, and whispered cautiously that he was very cold. I assured him that I, too, was cold but that it would be warm when we landed. He rolled his eyes back and nodded his understanding.

The tires squealed and gave off a puff of blue smoke as we touched the concrete runway, taxied in, and coasted to a stop in front of the gigantic hanger that Rerebawä immediately recognized as the "den" of the creature in which we were riding. The crew opened the tiny doors of the plane, and a blast of hot dry air burst in. Our ears continued to ring, even though the deafening engines had stopped. We climbed out and stood on the concrete pad that stretched as far as our eyes could see, disappearing in the shimmering heatwaves near the horizon. Rerebawä touched it carefully and asked me how we found so much flat stone to make such a huge trail. Before I could answer that question, a dozen more, equally startling, came from his dry lips. One of the crew asked me if I wanted a lift up to the headquarters, from which we could call a taxi to take us to Caracas, some 35 miles away. I accepted, and told Rerebawä that we were going to have a ride in a "car." "What is a 'car'?" he asked suspiciously, remembering his airplane trip. I pointed to the white Ford parked a short way off. "Why don't you get into it and wait for me there while I unload our things?" I suggested. He headed slowly for the car and I gathered our things from the plane. When I stepped out of the plane, he was standing by the car, examining it carefully, glancing periodically at me, then at the car. "Get into it!" I shouted, "I'll be right there!" I watched him walk slowly around the car, scratch his head, and look up at me with a puzzled expression. "Don't be afraid!" I shouted as I walked toward him. "Get in it!" He adjusted the tobacco in his mouth, took a half-step toward the car, and dived through the open window on the passenger's side, his feet and legs hanging curiously out the gaping hole in the side! I had forgotten to tell him about doors, and realized how much I had taken things for granted, and how incredibly bizarre much of our culture would be to the Yąnomamö.

The next week proved to be both sobering and outrageously funny at times as Rerebawä discovered what Caraca-teri and its customs and ways were like, and how much he would have to report to his co-villagers: the staggering size of the buildings reaching to the sky, built of stone laid upon stone; elevators;

people staying up all night; the bright lights of the automobiles coming at an incredible speed at you during night travel, looking like the piercing eyes of the *bore* spirits; the ridiculous shoes that women wore with high heels and how they would cause you to trip if you tried to walk through the jungle in them; and the marvels of flush toilets and running water. He was astounded at how clean the floors were in the houses, was afraid to climb suspended stairs for fear they would collapse, and could not drink enough orange soda pop, or get over the fact that a machine would dispense it when you put a coin in and pushed a button. "How could you invite these things to a feast?" He queried. "They certainly are generous and give their 'goods' away, but they expect to be reciprocated on the spot!"

He enjoyed himself in Caracas but was happy to return to the village, and spoke grandiloquently to his peers about the size of Caraca-teri. "Is it bigger than Patanowä-teri's *shabono*?" they asked him skeptically, and he looked at me, somewhat embarrassed, and knew that he could not explain it to them. We both knew that they would not be able to conceive of what Rerebawä had seen. His arm stretched out and he described a large arc, slowly, saying with the greatest of exaggeration his language permitted: "it stretches from here to—way over—there!" And they clicked their tongues, for it was bigger than they imagined.

In a few days Rerebawä had ceased discussing Caracas and his exciting trip there. He was busily and happily going about his normal Yąnomamö activities as if nothing extraordinary had happened. I marveled at his resiliency and was relieved that the experience in Caracas had not diminished his enthusiastic view of his own culture as being inherently superior to and dominant over the ways of the *nabä*—the rest of the world that fell short of full humanness, the non-Yąnomamö.

Rerebawä's almost nonchalant reaction to Caracas puzzled me, but it likewise reminded me of a similar reaction that Hioduwä, the headman of Iyäwei-teri, had after he had been taken to Rome to meet the Pope. Padre Luis Cocco, the Salesian priest at that village (Cocco, 1972), had spent 15 years attempting to introduce Western ideas and ways into Hioduwä's village. A kind and resourceful man, Padre Cocco went to ingenious lengths to expose the Yąnomamö to aspects of our culture that would impress them and, hopefully, encourage them to become more like us. Thus, when the opportunity arose to have an audience with the Pope in 1971, he arranged to bring Hioduwä with him. Hioduwä later told me that he treated the Pope very courteously, called him affectionately "Shoriwä," and presented him with a particularly beautiful Guacamaya parrot. What impressed him more than meeting the Pope, for he could not comprehend the awesomeness and pomp of the circumstances, was seeing the Roman ruins, which he perceptively described as the ". . .old abandoned villages of their ancestors." He thought that it was quite appropriate for the present Romans to hold the deeds and crumbling ruins of their "mythical" ancestors in awe, as a testimony perhaps that the past is connected to the present in an intimate, concrete way—as it is in Yąnomamö myth where present, past, and future are unchanging and indistinguishable.

Hioduwä, by comparison to Rerebawä and Kąobawä, was indeed a worldly, cosmopolitan man. If any Yąnomamö should be preadapted to coping with our kind of culture, it should be he. His group has been in constant contact with the outside world since 1955 or so, and, because of the mission there, has served as some sort of Amazonian center for visitors, tourists, scientists, government officials, and benefactors of the Salesian missionaries working in Yąnomamö territory.

Hioduwä had also been to Caracas on a number of occasions and had frequently accompanied the mission boat down to the Territorial capital, Puerto Ayacucho. Padre Cocco had hoped to teach Hioduwä enough about boatsmanship, outboard motors, and the ways of the Venezuelan settlers he would meet downstream so that he could eventually make the long trip himself—to sell plantains to the merchants of Puerto Ayacucho for a handsome profit. The Venezuelans who carried supplies upstream to the mission always bought plantains from the Yąnomamö for ridiculously low prices and sold them for up to 800% profit, and Padre Cocco thought it would be fair and reasonable if the Yąnomamö themselves made this profit. Thus, he sent Hioduwä up and down the Orinoco on the mission boat several times to familiarize him with the customs and procedures before he felt he was ready for his solo entrepreneurial venture.

Padre Cocco had arranged everything in advance to make sure that Hioduwä would be met by mission personnel at Puerto Ayacucho who would help him sell the plantains for a reasonable price. He loaned him the large mission launch, a giant dugout canoe that had been planked up on the gunwales to increase its carrying capacity. He also loaned him a large, new outboard motor and provided him with enough gasoline to make the voyage. Hioduwä cut and loaded the approximately 300 plantain *racimas* he and his kinsmen had produced for the venture and set out on his three-day trip to Puerto Ayacucho. If things had gone well, he would have earned a profit of about $500 for the load of plantains. However, things did not go well, for Yąnomamö trading customs dominated the trip. To make a long story short, Hioduwä visited a number of Venezuelan families on the lower Orinoco and they "asked" him for plantains as gifts. He also had motor trouble and a kind Venezuelan "traded" an old but still functioning tiny outboard motor to him for Padre Cocco's new, large but temporarily malfunctioning motor. As he passed by the National Guard post at San Fernando de Atabapo, he was a bit intimidated by the gun-toting soldiers, so he made them a handsome gift of more of his plantains to assure their friendship. By the time he reached Puerto Ayacucho, he had only 100 or so *racimas* of plantains left. His mission friends helped him sell these for a good price, but then he went shopping with the cash by himself—and the wily storekeepers quickly relieved him of that burden. He managed to acquire a few machetes, a dozen straw hats, a few trinkets, and several small transistor radios. He was happy as a lark, contented with his transaction. When he left Puerto Ayacucho for the five-day return trip, a clever settler correctly pointed out that his tiny motor was not able to push his very large boat very fast and that it would take him many days to reach his destination. Hioduwä agreed with him. The man, as it turned out, had a much smaller canoe and was willing to trade it for the clumsier boat. He would even throw in his dog as part of the bargain. Well, the boat *was* heavy and the dog *was* handsome, so the bargain was struck. Hioduwä returned triumphantly to the mission with his straw hats, transistor radios, trinkets, and dog—and matter of factly explained to a chagrined Padre Cocco what had happened to his new motor and mission launch.

While this might be an amusing anecdote, there are some very grave implications in it for the future of the Yąnomamö as they are placed under increasing pressure from the national culture to change their tribal ways and become incorporated into the nation state as civilized citizens. For if Hioduwä had such difficulty after years of sympathetic preparation by Padre Cocco, then it should be clear that premature exposure to national culture will be difficult for other Yąnomamö who have much less preparation. And while the pressures are now focused on only those few mission posts that currently exist in their land, the consequences of directed change will radically affect the entire tribe—even the most remote and as yet uncontacted villages.

The Beginning of Tourism and Change

Before discussing some of the implications of this emerging problem, let me briefly comment on my research since the publication of the first edition of this book, for the Yąnomamö are, in the 1980s, in a much different situation than they were in 1964, when I first visited them. On several of my many returns to the Yąnomamö since 1967 I had mentioned to Rerebawä and Kąobawä that the people in "my village" have heard of them and have grown very fond of them, indicating so through the "decorated leaves" (letters) they send to me. That always pleased them immensely, and they wanted to know if the females thought them attractive, why some people thought that Rerebawä should clear a garden in Kąobawä's area, or why my people thought they should stop raiding the Patanowä-teri ("But they don't know what a bunch of nasty critters they are!"). I also told them about our own wars and what some of my people think of theirs. They find us abominable for dropping napalm on women and children, or stupid for fighting over land—and that we should think more about the merits of wife stealing. Their perspective on war is both amusing and penetrating, and they clearly would enjoy reading Darwin on "sexual selection" rather than Marx on "means of production," and as academics would make some interesting observations about a number of theoretical debates in the contemporary anthropological literature—to a number of which their own behavior contributed (see Chapter 2)!

I have now spent more time among the Yąnomamö since I wrote the first edition of *Yąnomamö: The Fierce People* than I did initially to collect the information that went into that case study. My return trips each year made me increasingly aware of the gradual impact that our culture was having on the Yąnomamö, for each year saw the arrival of new missionaries and more visitors, the clearing of airstrips from the jungle, and the increased ease with which curious tourists or adventurers could visit Yąnomamöland. With these increased contacts came new dangers to the Yąnomamö, particularly health risks. In 1967, while participating with my medical colleagues in a biomedical study of selected Yąnomamö villages, we collected blood samples that clearly showed how vulnerable and isolated the Yąnomamö were: they had not yet been exposed to measles. Thus, in 1968, when we returned again to extend this study, we brought 3000 measles vaccines with us to initiate an innoculation program in the areas we visited. Unfortunately, the very week we arrived an epidemic of measles broke out at a number of mission posts and began spreading to the more remote villages as the frightened Yąnomamö tried to flee from the dreaded epidemic. We worked frantically for the next month trying to vaccinate a barrier around the epidemic, ultimately succeeding after visiting many villages and being reinforced, toward the end of our efforts, by additional amounts of vaccine flown into us by the Venezuelan government and through the efforts of a group of French researchers and the local missionaries. Still, a large number of Yąnomamö died in the epidemic in some regions—villages that were remote and difficult to reach (Neel et al., 1970).[1]

The health problems that are beginning to emerge among the Yąnomamö are far more serious in the remoter villages than they are at the mission stations, for at least at the missions there are radios with which assistance from Caracas can be solicited in emergencies, or stores of antibiotics and other medical supplies to treat the more common and more frequent illnesses. And most of the local missionaries are patient and good people who are sensitive to the medical problems that arise within their groups, working indefatigably at times to nurse the children and adults through a lingering malady that no shaman on earth could cure, but that no *hekura* from a distant village could have caused. Beyond the village help dwindles rapidly, for the Yąnomamö

---

[1]Many of my colleagues and students ask me what the Atomic Energy Commission had to do with some of my research support during my study of the Yąnomamö. The medical scientists with whom I collaborated at the University of Michigan's Department of Human Genetics had, after World War II, held positions in the Atomic Bomb Casualty Commission, a medical-genetics group whose responsibility it was to treat the survivors of the nuclear bombings at Hiroshima and Nagasaki. After they returned to their regular academic lives at various universities and medical schools across the United States, they continued some of their genetics studies, for the effects of radiation can show up generations after the initial exposure. When I joined Michigan's Department of Human Genetics in 1966 to participate in a multidisciplinary study of South American Indians, some of the studies of irradiated Japanese families were still in progress. By then, however, members of the department were turning to more academic projects, such as the study of non-Japanese populations and especially marriage and reproduction in those populations. The biomedical studies on the Yąnomamö Indians they made were, for a while, subsumed into their Atomic Energy Commission contract and justified in the sense that both the Japanese and the Yąnomamö reproduce according to cultural rules. As the Yąnomamö work became more conspicuous and expanded, it was difficult to continue that justification and, in time, we obtained National Science Foundation money to continue that work. (See Neel et al., 1971, for references to some of the results of that research.) As a result of this research, the Yąnomamö are biomedically one of the most thoroughly studied tribes in the world.

cannot communicate their problems in time, since the distances they must travel on foot to reach help are enormous.

The increased contact at mission posts has complicated the health problems dramatically. With airstrips, visitors can reach the area with tremendous ease and innocently carry with them the latest version of infections that our own population can live with relatively comfortably, for our biological systems have sustained similar abuses time and time again and we have, or can develop, ready cures for most of them. A Yąnomamö visitor to the same post, eagerly searching for a machete, just as innocently carries a new bug back inland to his fellow villagers, and by the time they realize they are sick, they are too weak or too isolated to get help. One remote village I had been studying for five years had never seen a foreigner other than me in their entire history. When I visited them in 1972, they numbered 179 people. I did not return to them for two years; in 1975 when I went inland to update my census on them, I found that they had suffered a 40% mortality the previous year and there were very few children below the age of 10 years. The only thing that had changed during my two-year absence was the initiation of contact with the foreigners downstream, whom they had begun visiting regularly to obtain machetes (Chagnon and Melancon, in press). Rerebawä, in reflecting on what was happening, commented introspectively: "When I was a boy we did not have epidemics like this. It did not begin until foreigners started coming here." I believe he was close to the truth.

There are only a dozen or so Yąnomamö villages in which missionaries have permanent posts in Brazil and Venezuela. This seems trifling in view of the fact that there are perhaps as many as 150 villages of Yąnomamö in total. However, the impact of mission contact is increasing every year. In 1964, when there were somewhat fewer posts, the missionaries generally concentrated their efforts in local areas and only sporadically visited the neighboring Yąnomamö groups. With time, and with increased competition between Catholic and Protestant missionaries, active and ambitious visiting programs have taken form and the missionaries aggressively try to visit more and more remote villages. There were vast areas of uncontacted Yąnomamö in 1964. In 1983 these areas had shrunk to just a few pockets of isolated villages, and their existence and location are enviously viewed by both mission groups as challenges—lest the competition get there first and establish a settlement. The Protestant groups have their own air support and have established posts in the very heartland of the uncontacted areas. They send their young men deep into the jungle on foot, with Yąnomamö guides from "saved" villages as evangelical helpers. Once near a remote village, they clear an airstrip with the help of the local and soon-to-be-saved Yąnomamö. Shortly thereafter, a family moves in and establishes a post. In time, the location of the airstrip becomes known to others, especially to wealthy Venezuelans who own their own private airplanes and who enjoy spending weekends or longer vacations in exotic places, observing naked Indians, collecting curios and mission anecdotes. Soon there are so many regular visitors to these remote posts that the missionaries have to build special houses to accommodate their regular but unpredictable guests, if for no other reason than to have some privacy for their family life. The few enterprising bush pilots who are skillful or daring enough to fly in this area soon find out about the strip and exploit the situation extensively, ever willing to take planeloads of prosperous tourists into the remote villages for a handsome fee. Such visiting begins innocently and often against the wishes of the local missionaries, but soon reaches grotesque proportions. Complaints, however, are averted by the substantial cash gifts that the tourists generally leave to "support" the mission work.

The Catholic missions likewise find themselves involved in catering to increasing numbers of visitors, sometimes unwillingly but sometimes by deliberate design and choice. One Salesian priest in particular actively promoted and cultivated tourism to his mission for several years. The mission had been established by others and lay dormant for a number of years, stagnating in the lethargy of its disinterested sequence of occupants until about 1970. When I visited it in 1969 there was only one official there—a lay brother, who was assisted by two Brazilian men. Shortly thereafter an ambitious Spanish priest was assigned to the post. In 1971 the Venezuelan government (CODESUR—Conquest of the South—project) cleared a large airstrip there, and the priest embarked on a vigorous campaign to promote tourism and civilization with a passion that would have embarrassed the Conquistadores (Fig. 7–1). A tour agent in Caracas soon had a fleet of sleek speedboats there and the priest kept him supplied with ample quantities of gasoline. He also built a number of guest houses to accommodate the visitors and soon the mission was a booming tourist center. Direct flights from Munich and other European cities were advertised in 1973, stopping briefly in Caracas for a changeover to a small twin-engine craft that would fly them directly to the Yąnomamö village of Mahekodo-teri on the Upper Orinoco, and into the Stone Age. This dimension of his scheme, however, was opposed by some of his ecclesiastical colleagues and superiors, and discouraged—with only partial success. Large numbers of tourists, many from Europe, visited there. In 1975 when I passed through his mission there were at least 40 Brazilians living there, engaged in some sort of support activity ranging from machine shop maintenance to lumbering and hunting. Their hunting techniques, I should add, are as devastating as they are illegal by Venezuelan law—hunting by night with large flashlights from motorized canoes, and fishing with seine nets. Apart from feeding themselves and their families, they kept the mission's kerosene-operated freezer full of fresh game and fish for the hordes of tourists that came every year. I might add that Yąnomamö hunting techniques do not lead to overexploitation of the fauna, but the use of shotguns, night hunting with torches and motorized canoes, and seining fish produces, in a short time, a severe impact on the balance of nature. I remember the incredible herds of capybara, wild pigs, flocks of ducks, and river otters that abounded in the upper Mavaca River from 1968 through 1971, when I was the only Westerner who ascended it. After the mission personnel and Venezuelan or Brazilian employees thereof began hunting it, it turned into a near desert. Now, not a single otter can be seen along its entire course, and many other species of

Fig. 7–1. Kṛhisiwä, headman of Patanowä-teri, peers inquisitively into the cockpit of a helicopter, a beast he had never seen before. The logo emblazoned on the side of the helicopter bodes ill for Yąnomamö culture: Conquest of the South.

common game animals are almost nonexistent. The impact of this intensity of hunting on the local game supply—and the Yąnomamö diet—could eventually be catastrophic.

The tourism-promoting priest justified his scheme by referring to the objectives of the Venezuelan Indian Commission—to acculturate the Indian populations as rapidly as possible, and his method, he argued, would accomplish that goal. The more the Indians were exposed to outsiders, the more rapidly they would learn Western ways and emulate them. The Yąnomamö, I might add, appeared to disagree with him: they abandoned their village and moved across the Orinoco to have some peace and respite from the tourists.

The introduction of shotguns by missionaries and those who work for them is also a major and serious issue. Several missionaries, both Catholic and Protestant, have told me that they like to give trade goods such as shotguns and flashlights, for it made the Indians dependent on them for batteries and ammunition—and the Indians would therefore be less likely to move away once they became accustomed to these items. The shotguns, however, are inevitably used in raids and they kill. The problem is more severe in Brazil than it is in Venezuela, for shotguns are very cheap there by comparison.

One missionary I met related, sadly, an incident in which several men from the village raided a distant group with their newly acquired shotguns and killed several people, including a few women and children. She was still giving shot and powder to the men "for hunting purposes," which I found incredible. When I asked her why she continued to dispense shot and powder, she explained, "Well, we only gave one shotgun to the men. A Brazilian trader came up and gave the other guns to them. We don't know for sure if the gun we gave them actually killed anyone on that raid and we are not going to ask, because we know we would have to take the guns away. If we do that, the Indians will probably move away from the mission and all our investment will be lost." Other missionaries I have spoken to about the known military use of shotguns by men in their villages likewise continue to give ammunition to the offenders, preferring to discount my information as "just another of those Yąnomamö 'rumors'." One Yąnomamö man I know has killed at least three people with his shotgun, and the missionaries continue to provide him with shot and powder. Komaiewä, the bearded man in the film *The Feast*, had his head blown off with a shotgun shortly after we completed the film (Asch and Chagnon, 1970). Some of the raids in which shotguns have been used were conducted only because the raiders had a new, superior weapon and wanted to try it out—the possession of the gun *caused* wars where none had previously existed. When I asked Rerebawä why a particular village, in possession of shotguns, raided an especially distant village with whom it had no previous contact, he replied: "The headman there is fierce. He now has a shotgun. When you give a fierce man a shotgun, he becomes even fiercer and wants to kill without cause."

There are many good and reasonable missionaries who are genuinely concerned about the Yąnomamö as human beings and who are patient enough to realize that conversion to Christianity is still a long way off and can only be effected through a gradual process of change. And there are many sympathetic Venezuelans who recognize the difficulties and dangers of abrupt and capricious acculturation practices that a minority of local missionaries occasionally practice. It would be both reasonable and humane if the civil authorities and missionaries established guidelines and policies based on sound information and developed an acculturation program that would at least attempt to preserve and enhance particular Yąnomamö beliefs and conceptions that might optimize their ability to cope with the larger national society. One particularly important step would be the "assignment" of family names according to Yąnomamö notions of descent and affinity. Patrilineal descent is an indigenous notion that could be used to bolster solidarity and a sense of oneness among the Yąnomamö. For example, all the descendants of a man acknowledge their agnatic relatedness irrespective of their village of residence. However, one must have detailed genealogical information to identify such lineal descent groups, and the work required to obtain this information is difficult, time-consuming, and at times unpleasant. At present the missionaries are arbitrarily inventing Christian family names for the Yąnomamö in such a way that members of the same sibship or agnatic group end up with completely different surnames. Eventually this will create artificial distinctions and promote dissension within culturally significant groups; it would be much more practical and beneficial to bestow the same family name on the entire agnatic group. Genealogical information of the kind discussed in this book could be used for a practical purpose, and it would be very desirable to have local missionaries follow Yąnomamö notions of descent when they create the names that become official.

A sound program of acculturation can only be developed with professional anthropological counsel and input. At present there are no Venezuelan anthropologists with first-hand experience among the Yąnomamö who could participate in the development of such a program. While many Venezuelan anthropologists are genuinely alarmed about the status of Venezuelan tribes and their future, and argue that something beneficial must be done for them, thus far none of their students has risen to the challenge of committing themselves to a long-term study of and involvement with Yąnomamö culture. This is an alarming situation, since it is imperative that a Venezuelan anthropologist represent these people to the national authorities and speak on their behalf with the authority that only long-term field knowledge can provide. It is all the more serious in view of the increased difficulty that foreign anthropologists have in obtaining research permits.[2]

As a foreigner, and especially as a North American foreigner, in Venezuela, I could not speak out publicly and criticize some of the harsher and questionable mission policies I witnessed—unless I was willing to risk the possibility that I would not be granted a research permit to continue my fieldwork. On the one occasion I took a public stand by signing my name to a relatively moderate document that expressed concern about what was happening to many of the native peoples of Venezuela, I was passionately accused by many Venezuelans of "meddling" in the internal affairs of their government. (Many of the signatories were Venezuelan anthropologists.) One of my graduate students, who was awaiting official word about his permission to initiate fieldwork in a newly contacted tribe of hitherto unknown Indians (Hoti, Yowana, Yuwana) just north of the Yąnomamö, was summarily denied a permit to work there—but a group of American Evangelists was simultaneously allowed to move in. One doesn't need a degree in logic to realize that the price of "concern" is the jeopardizing of research privileges.

While I could not freely express my opinion in the Venezuelan press or before my Venezuelan colleagues, things were different in the jungle where local policies and events took place before my eyes and where there were fewer official restraints to my reactions. In some cases I could speak to and reason with local missionaries about their particular methods and policies.

---

[2]In 1976 the Ministry of Justice of Venezuela, through which anthropological research permits then had to be obtained, announced that new permits for foreign anthropologists would be denied for an indefinite time. I went to Caracas to discuss the new policy with the representatives of this ministry and to request permits for myself and two of my advanced graduate students. At the same time, I discussed a collaborative project with several of my Venezuelan colleagues, a project in which two Venezuelan students would participate in a one-year field study among the Yąnomamö. The permits for myself and my students were contingent on the acceptability of my proposed collaboration with my Venezuelan colleagues. Unfortunately, they found the proposal unacceptable.

Some of them were willing to consider my views and at least listened politely. In rare cases the missionaries even asked my opinion and carried on a dialogue with me. I cherish the memory of these discussions and the people who initiated them, for enlightened reason and not dogma appeared to mean something to them. In most cases reason and dialogue were not possible, for the missionaries were incapable of viewing the differences between "good" and "bad" in anything other than narrow biblical or theological terms, and could not appreciate the argument that the wanton destruction of a culture, if not its human bearers, was morally "bad" by some standards. Evangelism was by definition "good" in their terms if only a single soul was saved, and any price was worth paying to accomplish that end and any method legitimate. I once put the hypothetical question to a Protestant missionary: "Would you risk exposing 200 Yąnomamö to some infectious disease if you thought you could save one of them from Hell—and the other 199 died from the disease?" His answer was unequivocal and firm: "Yes." A Catholic priest once comment-ed to me, "I believe the Yąnomamö are subhuman—they act like animals and lack the essential faculties of being human."

I had largely ignored the policies and motives of the missionaries during my first two years of field research, partly because they were not too obvious where I was working, partly because I wished to avoid confrontations with them, and partly because there were so many uncontacted Yąnomamö villages to study where these problems did not exist. There was a Salesian (Catholic) mission across the river from Kąobawä's village all during my initial research, but there were no Yąnomamö there. It was easy to ignore them at that time for they had no impact on the Yąnomamö. All of the Indians were on the south side of the Orinoco, where the Protestants had established two families to conduct their work among the Bisaasi-teri, who were then divided into two villages, "upper" and "lower." Indeed, during the first three months I lived among the Yąnomamö there were no missionaries whatsoever present, for one Protestant family was downstream recovering from malaria and the other was just returning from the United States after a year's absence from Venezuela. By the end of my fieldwork that year I was spending a good deal of my time in the more remote villages, which deflected my attention from local missionary activity in Bisaasi-teri.

When I left the field in 1966 that was what the missionary picture was like. In 1967 when I returned again to Bisaasi-teri, Kąobawä's village was only half the size it had been the year before. The Salesian priest across the river had taken advantage of the fact that a fission was developing in Kąobawä's village and that Paruriwä (Hontonawä), Kąobawä's brother-in-law, was emerging as a strong leader in the dissident faction: he lured Paruriwä and his group across the river with generous gifts of outboard motors, shotguns, and other desirable trade commodities. I saw Paruriwä in 1967 when I stopped to greet the priest; he was proudly bearing a presumptuous Spanish title, beating his chest with his fist, urging me to pay attention: "Me *Capitan*! Me *Capitan*! Me *Capitan*!" He swaggered off after I acknowledged that I understood that he was a leader now, carelessly shouldering a rusty 16-gauge shotgun, barking commands to his followers in the three or four Spanish words he had learned during the year, a shadow of the man I had last seen, dwarfed in the raggy and tattered pants that marked his new status and guaranteed in that status by *his* monopoly on the priest's trade goods.

I was depressed when I saw this and reflected on what lay behind the missionary attempts to make the Yąnomamö more worthy in God's eyes. I had returned to study the Shamatari groups south of Kąobawä's village and was glad that I had made that decision, for I knew that if I worked in Bisaasi-teri I would ultimately come into conflict with the missionaries and would, as they put it, "interfere in their work."

My Adventure with Ebene: A "Religious Experience"

On one of my annual return trips I became deeply involved with Kąobawä's relationship to the Protestant missionaries. A new missionary family had moved into his village to maintain the "field station" for a period of about a year while the resident local missionary returned to the United States on a "furlough." Missionaries, I might add, utilize a good many paramilitary phrases in their work—they regard themselves as "Commandos for Christ," "wage war on the Devil," and take "furloughs" from "active duty." I did not know this particular missionary very well, for he was usually living in Yąnomamö villages in a region that fell outside the area of my field study. However, I knew that "Pete," as I will call him here, was more prone to conduct his evangelical objectives through recourse to fire and brimstone techniques than most of the more patient, younger Protestant missionaries I had met, often flying into tirades whenever Yąnomamö would "revert" to chewing tobacco (". . .the work of the Devil. . ."), taking extra wives, or, most annoyingly, insufflating their hallucinogens and chanting to their *hekura* spirits. Pete particularly disliked the village shamans, and made extraordinary attempts to discredit them, for they constituted a serious threat to his attempts at convincing the others that there was only one true spirit and that a belief in many spirits was evil.

At first the Yąnomamö very diplomatically, but with considerable inconvenience to themselves, accommodated his peculiarities by moving off into the jungle a few miles to conduct their daily religious activities. This kept the trade goods flowing into the village. On the surface and verbally they behaved as though they had ". . .accepted Dios" and ". . .thrown their *hekura* away," for they were ". . .filthy spirits." The inconvenience, however, became too much, and eventually the shamanism and hallucinogens moved back into the village. The noisy chanting and curing ceremonies would bring an overheated Pete running into the village, screaming and yelling recriminations at the bewildered participants, embarrassing them and intimidating them. Most important, it frightened them, for Pete was not beyond showing them paintings of Yąnomamö-like people being driven off a cliff into a fiery chasm below as punishment by "Dios" for evil doings, such as shamanism. The Yąnomamö do not understand the difference between a painting and a photograph, and Pete knew this.

I tried to ignore this as much as possible, for it angered me; I knew that it would lead to bitter arguments with the missionaries and perhaps, ultimately, to trouble with the Venezuelan officials. In general, with most of the missionaries, the problem was not too serious, for most of them were relatively patient with the Yąnomamö and employed more inconspicuous and subtle methods, and a few of them were downright humane—given their ultimate goal of destroying Yąnomamö religion.

Kąobawä himself had recently taken up the use of hallucinogenic drugs and participated in the daily rituals—something he had not done during my first stay in his village. It puzzled me at first, but it ultimately made sense when I began to understand the extent to which the Protestant missionaries were intimidating and threatening his village's religious activities. It seems clear to me now that his use of hallucinogens was a calculated act to put his prestige as a leader behind the efforts of the village curers, giving them confidence and informing the missionaries that he, as the headman, approved of what they were doing.

It was a hot afternoon, threatening to rain, and the mugginess was almost unbearable. I was working on Shamatari genealogical notes in my hut when Kąobawä and Rerebawä appeared at the door, urgently demanding to speak to me about "God-teri." (The Protestant missionaries are all called "Diosi-urihi-teri"—those from the Village of God.) I let them in and could immediately see that they were very upset and were sincerely turning to me for help. For the first time I realized that I had ignored a moral question and I felt ashamed for having done so. They were beginning to question the relative potency of their spirits versus the one from God-teri. They were also very angry with the missionary, for he had just burst into the village and broke up their chanting, denouncing them violently, and "threatening" them. I asked Kąobawä what he meant when he said "threaten." He held up two fingers and explained: "He told us that if we didn't stop chanting to the *hekura*, Dios would destroy us all with fire in this many *rasha* seasons!" I was almost sick with anger and resentment. He and Rerebawä went on to explain that Pete did this regularly, and it was beginning to anger them. They asked me, quite sincerely, if I believed that Dios would destroy them with fire if they chanted to the *hekura* and I told them "No." I interfered in the "work" of the missionary thereby, but I felt, somehow, morally better for having done so. I did not stop there. I stripped down to my bathing trunks and said, "Let's all go chant to the *hekura*!"

We walked into the village and word soon spread that Shąki was going to chant to his *hekura*, and his *shoabe* and *oshe* were going to instruct him. I had lived among the Yąnomamö long enough by then to know quite a bit about the *hekura*, their particular songs and how to attract them into the great cosmos that resides in the breast of all shamans, where the *hekura* are given their intoxicating magical beverage, *braki aiamo uku*. Then they become as one with their human receptacle, flying through the air, visiting distant places, going to the edge of the universe where the layer becomes "rotten" and other *hekura* are suspended from trees, attacking enemies and devouring the *möamo* portion of their souls, inflicting sickness and death on them, or curing their loved ones.

We walked silently over to Kaobawä's house, for that is where the daily religious activities were to begin. "Let me decorate you, my dear brother!" said Rerebawä softly, and I knelt on the ground while all my friends generously made their special feathers and decorations available to me so that I might become more beautiful and therefore more worthy to the *hekura*. Rerebawä took his *nara* pigment out and began painting my face and, after that, my chest. Kaobawä gave me a *wisha* tail for my head; Koaseedema loaned me his turkey scalp armbands; Makuwä gave me his special *werehi* feathers; Wakewä gave me *ara* tail feathers. Other men began decorating me also. The village was quiet, but a happy excitement seemed to pervade the muggy air; everyone knew that some sort of confrontation between me and the missionary was inevitable, and they were looking forward to it.

Rerebawä took out his *ebene* tube and ran a stick through it to clean it out. His father-in-law, the most prominent shaman in the village, took out a package of *hisiomö* powder and made it available to us. We cleaned off an area in front of Kaobawä's hammock, for that is where we planned to parade and dance as we called to the *hekura*. "Bei!" said Rerebawä, and I knelt forward to receive the end of his filled ebene tube into my nostrils. I closed my eyes, knowing that it would be painful, and he filled his chest with air and blew the magical green powder deep into my head in a long, powerful breath (Fig. 7–2). I coughed and retched almost immediately, rubbing the back of my head violently to relieve the pain. "Bei!" he said again, and pushed the tube toward me. I took another blast, and felt the green mucus gush out of my other nostril as he blew. More pain, more retching, and still another blast, and another. The pain seemed to diminish each time, and I squatted on my haunches, waiting for the *hisiomö* to take effect. Others began to take the drug around me, and I gradually lost interest in them as my knees grew rubbery and my peripheral vision faded. "Ai!" I said, and Rerebawä gave me more. "Ai," I said again, and he smiled: "You've had enough for now," and pointed his tube toward someone else. I was beginning to feel light and felt as though I was filled with a strange power. Songs that I had heard the shamans from a dozen villages sing began to whirr through my mind and almost involuntarily my lips began to move, and I stood up and looked to Mavaca Mountain and began singing. Blips of light and spots flashed before me, and I began the methodical prancing that I had witnessed a thousand times. My arms seemed light and began moving almost of their own accord, rhythmically up and down at my sides, and I called to Ferefereriwä and Periboriwä, hot and meat hungry *hekura*, and asked them to come into my chest and dwell within me. I felt great power and confidence, and sang louder and louder, and pranced and danced in ever more complex patterns. I took up Makuwä's arrows, manipulating them as I had seen Dedeheiwä and other shamans manipulate them, striking out magical blows, searching the horizon for *hekura*, singing and singing and singing. Others joined me and still others hid the machetes and bows, for I announced that

Fig. 7–2. Rerebawä gave me several blasts of ebene *in each nostril and decided that I had enough. Soon my knees became rubbery and blips of light appeared.*

Rahakanariwä dwelled within my chest and directed my actions, and all know that he caused men to be violent. We pranced together and communed with the spirits and shared something between us that was as undefinable as it was fundamentally human, a freedom to create with our minds the mystical universe that began with the beginning of time, something that seemed to be lodged in the back of imagination, something hidden and remote from consciousness, and I knew intimately why the shamans went daily through the pain of taking their drugs, for the experience was exhilarating and stimulating. But the freedom to give complete reign to the imagination was the most startling and pleasurable part, to shed my cultural shackles and fetters, to cease being a North American animal up to a point and be Yąnomamö or the part of me that I and all others have in common with Yąnomamö. Wild things passed through my mind. I thought of Levi-Strauss' argument about the wisdom of looking for the nature of human logic and thought in primitive culture because it was not contaminated with layers of accumulated precepts and intellectual entanglements—and felt it was a marvelous idea. I could hear the initial strains of Richard Strauss' *Also Sprach Zarathustra.* I didn't care what the missionary, or the startled German visitor thought about me as he clicked off photos of the mad anthropologist going native. As my high reached ecstatic proportions, I remember Kąobawä and the others groaning as I broke the arrows over my head and pranced wildly with the shambles and splinters clutched tightly in my fists, striking the ground and enjoying the soft rain that had now begun to fall.

The village became suddenly silent, and through the haze I could see a stubby figure running into the village, screaming and shouting that the *hekura* were "filthy" and that Dios would "punish" us. And through the haze the stubby figure suddenly recognized the noisiest and most active sinner: it was the anthropologist. He gawked in astonishment at me and I grinned. My arm tropismatically described a smooth, effortless arc upward in his direction, and I noticed that it had the bird finger conspicuously and rigidly raised at him, and I felt the fire in my own eyes as I lined him up on it. Pious men do not curse—at least in their own language. He returned my signal with a Yąnomamö equivalent—a bared eyeball, exposed by pulling the eyelid down—and left in disgust. The others resumed their chanting, confident that if I didn't think Dios would destroy *me* in fire for chanting to the *hekura*, they shouldn't be too concerned either, for was I not myself a refugee from Dios-urihi-teri, and therefore knowledgeable about the machinations of Dios and the limitations on his power to destroy men with fire?

As the effect of the drug gradually wore off and the fatigue of my wild prancing began to be noticeable, I staggered over to Kąobawä's house and collapsed into one of the empty hammocks. Rerebawä's younger chidren happily surrounded me and looked at me with large, admiring eyes, gently stroking my arms and legs, inquiring whether I had seen the *hekura*, but not waiting for or expecting an answer. I wondered, in a shadowy daze, why Christian missionaries differed so strongly on simple issues, such as the putative "evil" or "innocence" of hallucinogenic snuff. Padre Cocco made no attempt to discourage it and felt that it was not only relatively harmless, but had some positive features—it gave the Yąnomamö hope when they concluded that they had been "bewitched" by enemies, a sickness that the nuns could not cure with penicillin or mercurochrome. Most of the Protestants, on the other hand, were passionately opposed to it and tried to abolish its use. I thought also about the expansion of our own culture and how politics and religion reinforced each other, as they had since the inception of the state; how the expansion of political authority often followed the proselytizing attempts of religious functionaries; how the destruction of cultures by dominant groups was expressed as moral or theological necessity; and how the sword accompanied or rapidly followed the Bible.

The Protestants, mostly American Evangelists, and the Catholics, mostly Italian or Spanish Salesians, differed radically. Indeed, the Protestants did not even regard the Catholics as Christians, for they "worshipped" idols and appeared not to oppose basic evils, such as drink, drugs, and polygamy. I recalled, with some amusement, an incident that Padre Cocco related to me. He had purchased a large quantity of manioc flour from a Ye'kwana Indian, within whose tribe both Catholic and Protestant missionaries had worked. He asked the man if he were a Protestant. The man answered: "No, Padre, I'm a Catholic. I smoke, I drink, and I have three wives."

Where the Protestants impatiently attack the whole culture and try to bring salvation to all, including adults, the Catholics are more patient and focus on the children, partially accounting for Pete's reaction to hallucinogens and shamanism and Padre Cocco's rather humane attitude about drug use. (See Asch and Chagnon, 1974; and Chagnon and Asch, 1974b for a comparison, through documentary films, of the different strategies and philosophies of Catholic and Protestant missionaries among the Yąnomamö Indians.) As early as 1967 I was aware that the Salesians had taken a few Yąnomamö youths downstream to their elementary school near Puerto Ayacucho, and that a few boys had been sent to Caracas to their trade school. I was disturbed when I learned about this, mainly because of the health hazards this raised, but in 1972/1973 I was alarmed to learn that the Salesians established a boarding school for Yąnomamö children as young as 6 or 7 years at La Esmerelda, and began taking children from many different villages away from their families and sending them to this school for months at a time. While the school was near the Yąnomamö tribal territory, it nevertheless was almost inaccessible to the parents in many villages whose children were taken away. The parents were "compensated" for their temporary losses by well-calculated gifts, but in time they wanted desperately to have their children returned to them—but were denied. This, I feel, is a terrible price to ask a Yąnomamö family to pay to insure incorporation into the nation, but an effective and ancient practice used by other dominant cultures to subdue, modify, and incorporate obdurate ethnic minorities who differ in custom and who remain independent of the nation at large:

> The Inca kings also disposed that the heirs of lords and vassals should be brought up at court and reside there until they inherited their estates so that they should be well indoctrinated and accustomed to the mentality and ways of the Incas, holding friendly converse with them so that later, on account of this familiar intercourse, they would love them and serve them with real affection. . . . The Inca kings sought thus to oblige their vassals to be loyal to them out of gratitude, or if they should prove so ungrateful that they did not appreciate what was done for them, at least their evil desires might be checked by the knowledge that their sons and heirs were at the capital as hostages and gages of their own fidelity (Garcilaso, 1966:404–405).

The Yąnomamö children will, of course, pass a significant and critical portion of their childhood in a foreign cultural environment and acquire a knowledge of its ways and expectations, and unknowingly forfeit a significant fraction of their own cultural heritage. I suspect that the emotional shock of living away from parents in such an exotic and insensitive environment will lead to serious developmental and emotional problems, crises of identity, and personality disturbances that could be avoided. As a parent and a human being, I would question the morality of a state organization that would remove or permit the removal of my children from me in order to indoctrinate them into beliefs that, by state definition, are superior to and more desirable than my own. I was sympathetic when Kąobawä told me, in 1975, that he would never again let the missionaries take his son, Ariwari, away from him and make him live at Esmerelda.

The adult Yąnomamö in villages where the Salesian missions are active, either because they have a mission post there or because they now visit regularly, are generally ignored insofar as intensive acculturation attempts are concerned. As one of the priests once mentioned, the effective incorporation and acculturation of the Yąnomamö is still a generation off—the children are the key. Thus, the adults are relatively free to do what they please, but encouraged to adopt some of the mechanical habits of Westerners, such as the use of clothing to cover up thought-provoking sex organs and standards of personal hygiene—where, when, and how to blow one's nose and what to do with the mucus when strangers from Caracas are around—and a system of etiquette that is congenial to visitors. Yąnomamö etiquette, I should add, is rather sophisticated in many respects and quite down to earth—and somewhat difficult to modify. A visitor to one mission awoke early one morning, stepped out of the house and ran into a Yąnomamö gentleman who was headed off to the jungle with his bow and arrows. The Western visitor was favorably impressed with the Yąnomamö man's decorum and politeness, for as the man passed by, he smiled at the visitor, and said cheerfully: "Ya shii!" The visitor, reciprocally, returned the greeting, whereupon the Yąnomamö again smiled and said, "Habo. Ya baröwo." When he reported his exchange of social amenities to the missionary, he was a bit distraught at the translation: "I'm on my way to defecate." Response: "I have to defecate (also)." Reply: "Come along, then; I'll lead the way."

Mission posts are, for both Catholic and Protestant missionaries alike, something of showpieces of what their efforts have yielded in civilizing the Indians. Clothing becomes an important concern, for missionaries are unhappy about obvious proclamations that nakedness reveals regarding the extent to which the Indians have not assumed a changed attitude about Western cultural amenities. Among the Yąnomamö, clothing serves two different functions. First, it serves a very important protective function—it effectively prevents the Yąnomamö from being pestered constantly by the biting gnats and mosquitoes, both of which are very noisome at certain times of the year along the major rivers. One must remember that the Yąnomamö traditionally avoid larger rivers and have only moved to them in the very recent past because of the allure of exotic trade goods, such as steel tools, fishhooks, fishline, matches, aluminum cooking pots, and other desirable items. No Yąnomamö would tolerate the discomfort of living near the bug-infested rivers unless there were powerful incentives, such as trade goods, to attract them there. The second function of clothing at the mission posts is essentially ideological from the missionaries' viewpoint: nakedness is assumed to be objectionable to Westerners. A sign of progress in the missions is the degree to which the "naked savages" visibly show their enlightenment by covering their private, and essentially sinful, parts. The Yąnomamö probably didn't realize that the naked body gives people sexy thoughts and evil ideas until Christianity covered it up on the argument that the nude body was sexy and thought-provoking. It conveniently crippled the patient and then provided the crutch. But nakedness to the Yąnomamö is a natural condition and many of the older people gladly accept the clothing given by the missionaries for the protective function it serves, but fail to see the "moral" dimension of the institution. I was amused one day as I passed through a mission village and stopped off to greet the priest and the nuns who lived there. As we were chatting, a Yąnomamö man and his wife strolled from the garden after their afternoon's work, he in a floppy hat and oversized khaki shirt and pants, she in her gingham smock. They came over to say hello, but their presence embarrassed the priest and nuns—he had cut the crotch out of his trousers because he apparently found the zipper cumbersome, and she had cut the bosom out of her smock so she could nurse her baby more conveniently. They stood there, grinning innocently and chatting happily—only their faces, their feet, and most of their sex organs visible. The baggy clothing seemed like a large frame around that which was not covered and to which the eye should be naturally attracted.

The younger people, especially young men, eagerly seek loincloths and rapidly acquire an attitude that a piece of cloth over the genitals is prestigious. More valuable than loincloths are bathing trunks or old underwear. These items are used as decorations at first, but later become almost "necessities," and any young man without either considers himself unfortunate and, the more accustomed he has become to them, embarrassed. I recall with some astonishment making first contact with the village of Mishimishimaböwei-teri (described in Chapter 1) and finding a young man in the village wearing a tattered pair of jockey undershorts! The villagers had never seen a non-Yąnomamö before my visit, but a pair of undies had managed to make it into the village via the trading network that also brought the broken and battered steel tools they acquired.

Balancing the Image of Fierceness

The Yąnomamö, largely through the extensive circulation of the first and second edition of this case study and a number of other publications by me, have become established in the anthropological literature as the prime example of a warlike, aggressive people. I would like to end this chapter with a few comments on their warfare and, hopefully, to correct some misunderstandings and false impressions that have crept into some of the literature that contains summaries of their culture based, allegedly, on my descriptions of it.

Warfare among the Yąnomamö—or any sovereign tribal people—is an expected form of political behavior and no more requires special explanations than do religion or economy. The quality of life that I witnessed when I lived among the Yąnomamö is not something that is readily found in our anthropological textbooks or journal articles. Yet it is a quality that should be documented and understood, for it can help us understand a large fraction of our own history and behavior. I decided, when I first went to live among the Yąnomamö in 1964, that their warfare was the most important single topic that demanded ethnological attention, for primitive warfare was a topic that had received very little attention from the profession, largely because the emergence of a mature anthropological discipline came long after most tribesmen had been pacified. The important fact is that very few anthropologists have had the opportunity to live with and study native peoples while warfare was a significant fact of life among them.

A meaningful description of Yąnomamö, or any other, warfare necessarily requires the presentation of facts and information that many of us would prefer not to consider. Personal ferocity, club fights, and raids are all part of the phenomenon and have to be described and explained, no matter how unpleasant they might appear to us. Viewed, however, against the violence and militancy found in other cultures—including, or perhaps *especially* our own, the Yąnomamö, to paraphrase Mark Twain, stand rather closer to the Angels than to the Devil. I have attempted, in part through the numerous ethnographic films I have made with my filmmaking colleague, Timothy Asch, to balance the "hyperfierce" image that is emerging as the exclusive characteristic of the Yąnomamö.[3] However, there is enough of an overall context in this case study or its earlier editions so that most of its readers have escaped with the correct impression that the Yąnomamö, as both individuals and as a population, exhibit a range of behavior that is found in other human societies, including humor, wit, happiness, and satisfaction with the good life.

The Yąnomamö are now threatened as a culture and as a population. I fervently hope that those who assume the responsibility for assimilating them into national culture treat them with the dignity they deserve and fully understand and appreciate what it is they are changing and the comparative value of what they provide in return. I also hope that my Brazilian and Venezuelan colleagues understand that there are still some very noble people in the remaining isolated and uncontacted Yąnomamö villages who are able to, as Dedeheiwä once proudly told me, teach foreigners something about being human. They are, as one of my anthropology teachers aptly phrased it, our contemporary ancestors.

---

[3]The large number of films presently available for purchase or rental are listed in a separate bibliography at the end of the book, along with information describing how to order the films.

Glossary

Affines: Relatives by marriage. These can also include blood relatives when, for example, a man marries his mother's brother's daughter. The word "cognate" is used to describe those blood relatives who are related by marriage. Cognates also include kinsmen who have a common ancestor.

Agnates: Persons who trace their relationships to each other through males. This is distinct from cognatic kinship, where the relationship may be traced through either males or females.

Banana, Wild: A distant relative to the common banana, but producing a fruit pod that is very different from the banana. The pod contains seeds that taste like maize. It is the only American member of the Musaceae family. Plantains and bananas now cultivated by the Yąnomamö were probably introduced to the Americas after Columbus.

Bifurcating Merging: A term used to describe the widespread type of kinship system in which an individual's paternal relatives are distinguished (bifurcated) from maternal relatives in the terminology. Furthermore, a single term is used in reference to, for example, father and father's brother; that is, they are merged terminologically into the same kinship category. The Yąnomamö have the most commonly found variant of this type, the Iroquois system. *See* Iroquois kinship terms.

Bilateral Cross-cousins: In practical terms, an individual's mother's brother's children *together* with his father's sister's children. Unilateral cross-cousins are mother's brother's children *or* father's sister's children, but not both. These two terms are frequently used in discussions of types of marriage rules found in primitive societies. Mother's brother's daughter is a *uni*lateral cross-cousin; properly speaking, she is a *matri*lateral cross-cousin. In Yąnomamö (Iroquois) kinship this person is simultaneously father's sister's daughter. Some societies have rules forbidding marriage with the latter type of cousin, that is, they have a *uni*lateral cross-cousin marriage rule. *See* Cross-cousins.

Cognates: Individuals who are related to each other through either males or females. *See* Affines, Agnates.

Corporation: A group of people sharing some estate, having definite rights with respect to each other and to the estate, and able to demonstrate their membership to that group by citing a recognized rule concerning recruitment.

Cross-cousins: The children of a man and his sister are cross-cousins to each other. The children of a man and his brother are *parallel* cousins to each other. Similarly, the children of a woman and her sister are parallel cousins.

Demography: The study of populations with the intention of gathering certain kinds of vital statistics, such as birth rate, death rate, and family size.

Demonstrated Kinship: Tracing relationships to kinsmen by citing the putative biological links. *See* Lineage.

215

Iroquois Kinship Terms: Classifying both kinds of cross-cousins (matrilateral and patrilateral) into the same kinship category and distinguishing them from brothers and sisters and parallel cousins. In most Iroquois systems the parallel cousins are called by the same terms that are used for brothers and sisters.

Levirate: A rule enjoining a man to marry the widow of his dead brother.

Lineage: A kinship group comprising people who trace relationships to each other through either males or females, but not both. If the relationship is traced through males, as among the Yąnomamö, the group so defined is a *patri*lineage. The distinctive feature of the lineage is that the relationships are demonstrated by citing genealogical links. In a clan, relationships are merely *stipulated* by citing the fact that the two individuals in question belong to the same named kinship group. In short, a clan is a *named lineage*, the members of which do not remember or do not care how they are related to each other biologically. *See* Demonstrated kinship.

Local Descent Group: Among the Yąnomamö, a group of people who are related to each other patrilineally, who live in the same village, and one of whose major functions is to arrange marriages for the younger members of the group. It is usually the older males of the group who arrange the marriages.

Machete: A broad-bladed, long knife commonly used throughout South America for cutting brush. The closest English equivalent is the cutlass.

Matrilateral: Tracing relationships on the mother's side.

Parallel Cousins: Cousins who are descended from two brothers or from two sisters.

Patrilateral: Tracing relationships on the father's side.

Plantain: A member of the banana family. The fruit looks like the common banana, but is considerably larger. When ripe, the fruit resembles the common banana in taste, but differs in that its texture is crude and stringy. Plantains are usually eaten cooked. Green plantains resemble raw potatoes in taste, even after cooking. Plantains appears to have been introduced to the Americas after the arrival of Europeans, but they spread with such rapidity that many travelers described them as being native crops. (*See* References, Reynolds, 1927).

Siblings: One's brothers and sisters.

Sororal Polygyny: A type of marriage in which a man marries two or more women who are related to each other as sisters.

Teknonymy: The practice of addressing an individual by the name of one of his children rather than by his own personal name. A kinship term is used in combination with the child's name, such as *father* of so-and-so.

References Cited

Arvelo-Jimenez, Nelly, 1971, *Political Relations in a Tribal Society: A Study of the Ye'cuana Indians of Venezuela.* Latin American Studies Program, Dissertation Series, No. 31. Ithaca, N.Y. Cornell University Press.

Asch, Timothy, and Napoleon A. Chagnon 1970, *The Feast* (16mm film). Documentary Educational Resources, Watertown, Mass.

———, and ———, 1974, *New Tribes Mission* (16mm film). Documentary Educational Resources, Watertown, Mass.

———, and ———, 1975, *The Ax Fight* (16mm film). Documentary Educational Resources, Watertown, Mass.

Aspelin, L., 1975, *External Articulation and Domestic Production: The Artifact Trade of the Mamainde of Northwestern Mato Grosso, Brazil.* Latin American Studies Program, Dissertation Series, No. 58. Ithaca, N.Y.: Cornell University Press.

Barandiaran, Daniel de, 1966, "La fiesta del Pijiguao entre los Indios Waikas," *El Farol,* 219:8–15. Caracas.

Bates, Daniel, and Susan Lees, 1979, "The Myth of Population Regulation." In N. Chagnon and W. Irons, Eds., *Evolutionary Biology and Human Social Behavior: An Anthropological Perspective.* North Scituate, Mass. Duxbury Press, pp. 273–289.

Becher, Hans, 1960, *Die Surára und Pakidái: Zwei Yanonámi-Stämme in Nordwest-Brasilien,* vol. 26. Hamburg: Mitteilungen aus dem Museum für Völkerkunde.

Beckerman, Stephen S., 1978, "Reply to Ross," *Current Anthropology,* 19(1):17–19.

Berlin, Elois A., and Edward Markell, 1977, "An Assessment of the Nutritional and Health Status of an Aguaruna Jivaro Community, Amazonas, Peru", *Ecology of Food and Nutrition,* 6:69–81.

Biocca, Ettore, 1970, *Yanomama: The Narrative of a White Girl Kidnapped by Amazonian Indians.* New York: E. P. Dutton & Co.

Briggs, Asa, 1983, "The Environment of the City" In Donald Ortner, Ed., *How Humans Adapt: A Biocultural Odyssey.* Washington, D.C.: Symposia and Seminar Series, Smithsonian Institution, pp. 371–394.

Carneiro, Robert L., 1960 "Slash and Burn Agriculture: A Closer Look at Its Implications for Settlement Patterns." In Anthony Wallace, Ed., *Men and Cultures. Selected Papers of the Fifth International Congress of Anthropological and Ethnological Sciences,* pp. 229–34. Philadelphia.

———, 1961, "Slash and Burn Cultivation Among the Kuikuru and Its Implications for Cultural Development in the Amazon Basin." In Johannes Wilbert, Ed., *The Evolution of Horticultural Systems in Native South America, Causes and Consequences: A Symposium.* Anthropologica, Supplement Publication No. 2, pp. 47–67. Caracas.

———, 1970, "A Theory of the Origin of the State." *Science,* 169:733–738.

Chagnon, Napoleon A., 1967, "Yąnomamö—The Fierce People," *Natural History,* 76:22–31.

———, 1968a, *Yąnomamö: The Fierce People,* first edition. Case Studies in Cultural Anthropology. New York: Holt, Rinehart and Winston.

———, 1968b, "The Culture-Ecology of Shifting (Pioneering) Cultivation Among the Yąnomamö Indians," *Proceedings VIII International Congress of Anthropological and Ethnological Sciences,* Tokyo. 3:249–255.

———, 1972, "Social Causes for Population Fissioning: Tribal Social Organization and Genetic Microdifferentiation." In G. A. Harrison and A. J. Boyce, Eds., *The Structure of Human Populations.* Oxford: Clarendon Press. pp. 252–282.

———, 1973, *Magical Death,* (16mm film). Documentary Educational Resources, Watertown, Mass.

———, 1974, *Studying the Yąnomamö.* Studies in Anthropological Method. New York: Holt, Rinehart and Winston.

———, 1975a, Response to Marvin Harris' "Protein Theory of Warfare," *Psychology Today,* 8(12):6–7.

———, 1975b, "Genealogy, Solidarity and Relatedness: Limits to Local Group Size and Patterns of Fissioning in an Expanding Population." *Yearbook of Physical Anthropology,* 19:95–110. American Anthropological Association. Washington, D.C.

———, 1979a, "Mate Competition, Favoring Close Kin and Village Fissioning among the Yąnomamö Indians." In N. A. Chagnon and W. Irons, Eds. *Evolutionary Biology and Human Social Behavior: An Anthropological Perspective.* North Scituate, Mass.: Duxberry Press. pp. 86–131.

———, 1979b, "Is Reproductive Success Equal in Egalitarian Societies?" In N. A. Chagnon and W. Irons, Eds., *Evolutionary Biology and Human Social Behavior: An Anthropological Perspective.* North Scituate, Mass.: Duxbury Press. pp. 374–401.

———, 1981, "Terminological Kinship, Genealogical Relatedness and Village Fissioning Among the Yąnomamö Indians." In R. D. Alexander and D. W. Tinkle, Eds., *Natural Selection and Social Behavior: Recent Research and New Theory.* New York: Chiron Press. pp. 490–508.

———, 1982, "Sociodemographic Attributes of Nepotism in Tribal Populations: Man the Rule Breaker." In King's College Sociobiology Group, Ed., *Current Problems in Sociobiology.* Cambridge: Cambridge University Press. pp. 291–318.

———, and Timothy Asch, 1974a, *A Man Called Bee: Studying the Yąnomamö* (16mm film). Documentary Educational Resources, Watertown, Mass.

———, and ———, 1974b, *Ocamo Is My Town* (16mm film). Documentary Educational Resources, Watertown, Mass.

———, and ———, 1975, *Moonblood: A Yąnomamö Creation Myth as Told by Dedeheiwä* (16mm film). Documentary Educational Resources, Watertown, Mass.

———, and ———, n.d., *Young Shaman.* (16mm film; pre-publication copy). Available for rental through Documentary Educational Resources, Watertown, Mass.

———, and Paul Bugos, 1979, "Kin Selection and Conflict: An Analysis of a Yąnomamö Ax Fight." In N. A. Chagnon and W. Irons, Eds., *Evolutionary Biology and Human Social Behavior: An Anthropological Perspective.* North Scituate, Mass.: Duxberry Press. pp. 213–238.

———, and Raymond Hames, 1979, "Protein Deficiency and Tribal Warfare in Amazonia: New Data," *Science* 203:10–15.

———, and ———, 1980, "La 'hipotesis proteica' y la adaptacion indigena a la cuenca del Amazonas: una revision critica de los datos y de la teoria", *Interciencia,* 5(6):346–58. Caracas.

———, and William Irons, Eds. 1979, *Evolutionary Biology and Human Social Behavior: An Anthropological Perspective.* North Scituate, Mass.: Duxberry Press.

———, P. LeQuesne, and J. Cook, 1971, "Yąnomamö Hallucinogens: Anthropological, Botanical, and Chemical Findings," *Current Anthropology,* 12:72–74.

———, and T. Melancon *in press.* "Reproduction, Numbers of Kin and Epidemics in Tribal Populations: A Case Study", Paper presented at the International Union for the Scientific Study of Populations, Center for Population Studies, Harvard University, February 1981. To be published in *Working Papers on South American Indians,* K. Kensinger, Ed. Bennington, VT.: Bennington College.

Cocco, Luis, 1972, *Iyëwei-teri: Quince años entre los Yąnomamös.* Caracas: Libreria Editorial Salesiana.

Cock, J. H., 1982, "Cassava: A Basic Energy Source in the Tropics," *Science,* 218(4574):755–762.

Conklin, Harold C. 1961, "The Study of Shifting Cultivation", *Current Anthropology,* 2(1):27–61.

Darwin, Charles, 1859, *On the Origin of Species by Means of Natural Selection, or the Preservation of Favored Races in the Struggle for Life.* London: John Murray.

———, 1871, *The Descent of Man, and Selection in Relation to Sex.* Two Vols. London: John Murray.

Divale, William T., and M. Harris 1976, "Population, Warfare, and the Male Supremecist Complex", *American Anthropologist,* 78:521–538.

Durkheim, Emile, 1958 [1895], *The Rules of the Sociological Method.* George E. Catlin, Ed. John H. Mueller and Sarah A. Solovay, translators. Glencoe, Ill.: The Free Press.

———, 1933 [1893], *The Division of Labor in Society.* George Simpson, translator. Glencoe, Ill.: The Free Press.

Fortes, Meyer, 1959, "Descent, Filiation and Affinity: A Rejoinder to Dr. Leach," *Man,* 59(309):193–197 and (331):206–212.

———, 1969, *Kinship and the Social Order: The Legacy of Lewis Henry Morgan.* Chicago: Aldine.

Fredlund, Eric V., 1982, *Shitari Yąnomamö Incestuous Marriage: A Study of the Use of Structural, Lineal, and Biological Criteria When Classifying Marriages* Ph.D. Dissertation. The Pennsylvania State University. University Park.

Garcilaso de la Vega, 1966, *Royal Commentaries of the Inca, Part One.* Austin: University of Texas Press. (Originally published in 1609 and 1616/7.)

Gross, Daniel, 1975, "Protein Capture and Cultural Development in the Amazon", *American Anthropologist,* 77(3):526–49.

Hames, Raymond, 1978, *A Behavioral Account of the Division of Labor Among the Ye'kwana Indians of Southern Venezuela.* Ph.D. Dissertation. University of California, Santa Barbara.

———, *in press,* "Time, Efficiency, and Utility in the Amazonin Protein Quest." In Emilio Moran, Ed., *Neither Hell nor Paradise.* New York: Academic Press.

Harner, Michael, 1977, "The Ecological Basis for Aztec Sacrifice," *American Ethnologist,* 4:117–135.

218

Harris, Marvin, 1974, *Cows, Pigs, Wars, and Witches: The Riddles of Culture*. New York: Random House.

———, 1975, *Culture, People, Nature: An Introduction to General Anthropology*. Second Ed. New York: Thomas Y. Crowell.

———, 1977, *Cannibals and Kings: The Origins of Cultures*. New York: Random House.

———, 1979, "The Yąnomamö and the Causes of War in Band and Village Societies". In M. Margolies and W. Carter, Eds., *Brazil: an Anthropological Perspective, Essays in Honor of Charles Wagley*. New York: Columbia University Press. pp. 121–32.

Hurault, J., 1972, *Francais et Indiens en Guyane*. Paris: Union Generale d'Edition.

Holmberg, Allan, 1969 [1950], *Nomads of the Long Bow*. American Museum of Natural History. Garden City, N.Y.: Natural History Press.

Irons, William, 1979a, "Investment and Primary Social Dyads." In N. A. Chagnon and W. Irons, Eds., *Evolutionary Biology and Human Social Behavior: An Anthropological Perspective*. North Scituate, Mass.: Duxbury Press. pp. 181–213.

———, 1979b, "Cultural and Biological Success" In N. A. Chagnon and W. Irons, Eds. *Evolutionary Biology and Human Social Behavior: an Anthropological Perspective*. North Scituate, Mass.: Duxbury Press. pp. 257–272.

———, 1980, "Is Yomut Social Behavior Adaptive?" In J. Silverberg and G. Barlow, Eds., *Sociobiology: Beyond Nature/Nurture?* Selected Symposium, American Association for the Advancement of Science, No. 35. Boulder, Co.: Westview Press. pp. 417–463.

Keesing, Roger M., 1975, *Kin Groups and Social Structure*. New York: Holt, Rinehart and Winston.

Leach, Edmund, 1957, "Aspects of Bridewealth and Marriage Stability Among the Kachin and Lakher," *Man*, 57(59):50–55.

———, 1970, *Claude Levi-Strauss*. Modern Masters Series. New York: Viking Press.

Lee, Richard, 1968, "What Hunters Do for a Living, or How to Make Out on Scarce Resources." In R. B. Lee and I. DeVore, Eds., *Man the Hunter*. Chicago: Aldine. pp. 30–43.

———, 1979, *The !Kung San: Men, Women, and Work in a Foraging Society*. Cambridge: Cambridge University Press.

———, and Irven DeVore, Eds. 1968, *Man the Hunter*. Chicago: Aldine.

Levi-Strauss, Claude, 1949, *The Elementary Structures of Kinship*, 1969 English translation. Boston: Beacon Press.

Lizot, Jacques, 1971a, "Aspects économiques et sociaux du changement culturel chez les Yanomami" *L'Homme*, 11(1):32–51.

———, 1971b, "Remarques sur le vocabulaire de parente Yanomami" *L'Homme*, 11(2):25–38.

———, 1971c, "Société ou économie? Quelques thèmes à propos d'une communauté d'Amerindiens" *Journal de la Société des Américanistes*, 60:136–75.

———, 1972, "Poisons yanomami de chasse, de guerre et de pêche," *Antropológica*, 31:3–20.

———, 1973, "Onomastique yanomami", *L'Homme*, 13(3):60–71.

———, 1975, *El Hombre de la Pantorrilla Preñada*. Monografia No. 21, Fundacion La Salle de Ciencias Naturales. Caracas.

———, 1976, *Le Cercle de Feux*. Paris: Editions du Sueil.

———, 1977, "Population, Resources, et Guerre chez les yanomami". *Libre*, 2:111–145.

———, 1978, "L'Economie Primitive". *Libre*, 4:69–113.

Malinowski, Bronislaw, 1922, *Argonauts of the Western Pacific*. London. Routledge and Kegan Paul, Ltd.

Mauss, Marcel, 1925, *The Gift*, 1954 English translation. New York: The Free Press.

Murphy, Robert L., 1960, *Headhunter's Heritage*. Berkeley: University of California Press.

National Academy of Sciences, 1980, *Firewood Crops*. Washington, D.C.

Neel, James V., 1970, "Lessons from a 'Primitive' People," *Science*, 170:815–22.

———, W. R. Centerwall, N. A. Chagnon, and H. L. Casey, 1970, "Notes on the Effect of Measles and Measles Vaccine in a Virgin-Soil Population of South American Indians," *American Journal of Epidemiology*, 91:418–429.

———, T. Arends, C. Brewer, N. Chagnon, H. Gershowitz, M. Layrisse, Z. Layrisse, J. McCluer, E. Migliazza, W. Oliver, F. Salzano, R. Spielman, R. Ward and L. Weitkamp 1971, "Studies on the Yanomama Indians", *Proceedings of the Fourth International Congress of Human Genetics*. *Human Genetics*. September, 1971:96–111.

Neitschmann, Bernard, 1980, "The Limits to Protein." In R. Hames, Ed., *Studies in Hunting and Fishing in the Neotropics*. *Working Papers on South American Indians*, K. Kensinger, General Editor. Bennington, VT.: Bennington College. pp. 131–35.

Ortiz de Montellano, Bernard R. 1978 "Aztec Cannibalism: An Ecological Necessity?", *Science*, 200:611–17.

Reynolds, Philip Keep, 1927, *The Banana: Its History, Cultivation and Place Among Staple Foods.* Boston: Houghton Mifflin Company.

Rice, A. Hamilton, 1921, "The Rio Negro, The Casiquiare Canal, and the Upper Orinoco, September 1919–April 1920", *The Geographical Journal,* 58:321–43.

Ross, Eric B., 1978, "Food Taboos, Diet, and Hunting Strategy: The Adaptation to Animals in Amazon Cultural Ecology," *Current Anthropology,* 19(1):1–36.

Sahlins, Marshall D., 1968a, "Notes on the Original Affluent Society." In R. Lee and I. DeVore, Eds., *Man The Hunter.* Chicago: Aldine. pp. 85–89.

———, 1968b, *Tribesmen* Englewood Cliffs, N.J.: Prentice-Hall.

Secoy, Frank R., 1953, *Changing Military Patterns on the Great Plains.* Monographs of the American Ethnological Society, E. Goldfrank, Ed. Locust Valley, N.Y.: J. J. Augustin.

Service, Elman R., 1969, "Models for the Methodology of Mouthtalk." *Southwestern Journal of Anthropology,* 25:68–80.

Spindler, George, D., Ed., 1970, *Being an Anthropologist: Fieldwork in Eleven Cultures.* New York: Holt, Rinehart and Winston, Inc.

Taylor, Kenneth, 1974, *Sanuma Fauna: Prohibitions and Classification.* Monografia No. 18, Fundacion La Salle de Ciencias Naturales. Caracas.

Turnbull, Colin, 1965, *Wayward Servants: The Two Worlds of the African Pygmies.* Garden City, N.Y.: Natural History Press.

———, 1983, *The Mbuti Pygmies: Change and Adaptation,* Case Studies in Cultural Anthropology. New York. Holt, Rinehart and Winston.

———, 1972, *The Mountain People.* New York: Simon and Schuster.

Wilbert, Johannes, 1972, *Survivors of El Dorado.* New York: Praeger.

Vickers, William T., 1978, "Reply to Ross," *Current Anthropology,* 19(1):27.

Williams, George C., 1966, *Adaptation and Natural Selection: A Critique of Some Current Evolutionary Thought.* Princeton, N.J.: Princeton University Press.

———, 1971, Ed. *Group Selection.* New York: Aldine-Atherton.

Wright, Sewall, 1922, "Coefficients of Inbreeding and Relationship," *American Naturalist,* 56:330–338.

Zerries, Otto, 1955, "Das Lashafest der Waika Indianer," *Die Umschau in Wissenschaft und Technik,* 55:662–65.

———, 1964, *Waika: Die Kulturgeschichtliche Stellung der Waika-Indianer des Oberen Orinoco im Rahmen der Völkerkunde Südamerikas.* Munich: Klauss Renner Verlag.

Ethnographic Films on the Yąnomamö

During the several years of my field research among the Yąnomamö I filmed selected activities that, I felt, could not be adequately documented by the more traditional means of note-taking and written descriptions. It became apparent that a more thorough filming effort would be necessary to document Yąnomamö culture and behavior than what I could accomplish by myself. Thus in 1968 I invited an anthropological filmmaker, Timothy Asch, to join me in the field and participate in this aspect of my field research. The collaborative effort during that season resulted in two films: *The Feast* and *Yanomama: A Multidisciplinary Study,* the latter film incorporating some of the footage that I had taken in previous years. In 1971 Asch and I received a grant from the National Science Foundation to extend our film study. A sound man, Craig Johnson, joined us in the project. We shot approximately 80,000 feet of synchronous-sound film in 1971 in the village of Mishimishimaböwei-teri, a remote Shamatari village that had become the focus of my more recent field investigations (see Chagnon 1974). We have thus far completed approximately 20 documentary films out of that material. They are listed below. Current catalogs of Yąnomamö, Bushmen, and other films can be obtained directly from D.E.R. In addition to D.E.R., the Psychological Cinema Register (P.C.R.) of the Pennsylvania State University distributes the Yąnomamö films. Catalogs of their listings can be obtained by writing to P.C.R. The addresses and telephone numbers of both distibutors are:

(1) Documentary Educational Resources
5 Bridge St.
Watertown, Mass. 02172
Telephone: [617] 926–0491

(2) Psychological Cinema Register
Audio-Visual Services
Special Services Building
University Park, Pa. 16802
Telephone: [814] 865–6314

All films are 16mm, in color and with optical sound track.

The Feast,[1] 1970, 29 min. This film focuses on the alliance practices of the Yąnomamö and documents the emergence of a specific alliance during the context of a feast held in the village of Patanowä-teri in 1968.

Yanomama: A Multidisciplinary Study,[1] 1971, 43 min. This film describes the nature of multidisciplinary field research by a team of human biologists, geneticists, serologists, dentists, and anthropologists. It includes an ethnographic vignette of Yąnomamö culture and is very useful in showing how many scientific disciplines can collaborate in the study of human populations and culture.

Magical Death, 1973, 28 min. This film depicts the interrelationship of religion, politics, and the use of hallucinogenic snuff in shamanism. It focuses on a specific two-day incident in the village of Mishimishimaböwei-teri during which all the prominent shamans of the group collectively demonstrated their good will toward visitors from Bisaasi-teri by practicing harmful magic against enemies of the latter.

A Man Called Bee: Studying the Yąnomamö, 1974, 40 min. This film illustrates the methods of field research used by Chagnon during 42 months of fieldwork among the Yąnomamö, emphasizing investigations of genealogy, settlement pattern, politics, demography and mythology.

Ocamo Is My Town, 1974, 23 min. This film describes the attitudes, accomplishments and objectives of a Salesian missionary who has spent fourteen years in a Yąnomamö village. Skeptical about the possibility of immediate success in Christianizing the Yąnomamö, the priest emphasizes the importance of his attempts to introduce practical measures that will help soften the impact of civilization when it eventually comes to this village.

Arrow Game, 1974, 7 min. This film depicts Yąnomamö boys learning to shoot accurately under duress and to dodge arrows shot in return. Man-sized arrows with the points removed are

---

[1]Available for rental and purchase through D.E.R.; available for rental only through PCR.

used in this somewhat hazardous game, which terminates when one of the boys is hit in the face with an arrow—damaging his ego more than his face.

Weeding the Garden, 1974, 14 min. Even the most prestigious members of the village must engage in all the economic activities. Dedeheiwä, the most respected shaman in the village, weeds his garden, interrupted periodically by his wife and children, who groom him while he rests.

A Father Washes His Children, 1974, 13 min. Dedeheiwä, respected shaman and political leader, takes his younger children to the river and bathes them. His wife remains in the village and recovers from a minor sickness.

Firewood, 1974, 10 min. Yąnomamö women spend several hours each day collecting firewood and maintaining the family fire. The irksomeness of chopping and carrying firewood is shown as a woman strenuously brings home the daily kindling. Her older son quietly babysits for his infant son while the mother works.

A Man and His Wife Make a Hammock, 1974, 9 min. Yąnomamö hammocks are manufactured on a pole frame consisting of two upright poles between which the spun cotton threads are plaited. A strong headman, Möawä, quietly works on the hammock while one of his wives and infant daughter rest in their hammock and quietly chat with him.

Children's Magical Death, 1974, 8 min. A group of young boys between the ages of 4 and 10 years imitate the shamans as they blow wood ashes into each other's nostrils through hollow reeds. Their amusing pantomime clearly reveals how socialized they have become by observing the elders. This film should be used in conjunction with *Magical Death.*

Climbing the Peach Palm, 1974, 9 min. Fruits from the cultivated peach palm tree can only be harvested by climbing the spiny trunk. The Yąnomamö have invented an ingeneous device— a climbing frame—for this purpose. Young men carefully ascend the thorny tree with this vine-and-pole frame, lowering the bunches of fruit with long vines.

New Tribes Mission, 1974, 12 min. Dedicated members of the New Tribes Mission, an Evangelical Protestant missionary group, explain their reasons for attempting to bring Christianity to the Yąnomamö and why the Yąnomamö must stop worshipping their "false demons."

The Ax Fight, 1975, 30 min. A fight erupts in Mishimishimaböwei-teri, involving clubs, machetes, and axes. The structure of kinship and marriage ties is revealed by the participants as they take particular sides in the fighting. Slow-motion replay and freeze-frame editing make this film useful as a methodological tool in both ethnographic and ethno-cinematographic studies.

Tapir Distribution, 1975, 12 min. The distribution of meat, particularly large game animals, reveals within-group alliance patterns based on kinship and marriage ties. The village headman presents his kill to his brothers-in-law, who ceremoniously redistribute the meat and cooked vegetables to household heads within the village. After the ceremonial distribution the women move in to distribute the scant remains, followed by the village dogs.

Tug of War, 1975, 9 min. The more playful and amicable aspects of daily life are illustrated by this film, which portrays a group of women and children in a tug-of-war during a rainstorm.

Bride Service, 1975, 10 min. A young man returns from hunting and collecting with a large wild turkey and a heavy basket of wild fruits. Through his father, he presents the food to his father-in-law. A 10-year-old girl is sent to fetch the food. She is embarassed and self-conscious, complicating her own situation by collapsing under the weight of the load amidst the laughter of village onlookers.

The Yąnomamö Myth of Naro as Told by Kąobawä, 1975, 22 min. The intimate relationships among Man, Spirit, and Animal are revealed in the amusing and complicated myth of Opossum (Naro), who invents harmful magic to treacherously slay his brother and acquire the latter's two beautiful wives. Kąobawä's dramatic and intimate presentation of the story brings out his acting and narrative skills. English voice-over narration.

The Yąnomamö Myth of Naro as Told by Dedeheiwä, 1975, 22 min. The same myth that is described above is told by Dedeheiwä, an accomplished and reknown shaman who lives in a remote village far to the south of Kąobawä's village. This film provides an excellent contrast for students interested in comparative mythology. English voice-over narration.

Moonblood: A Yąnomamö Creation Myth as told by Dedeheiwä, 1975, 14 min. The origin of Man (Yąnomamö) is revealed in the myth of Peribo (Moon), who, in Ancestral times, descended to earth and ate the ashes of the deceased Ancestors. Moon is shot in the belly by one of her Ancestors, his blood spilling to earth and transforming into fierce people. English voice-over narration.

Jaguar: A Yąnomamö Twin-Cycle Myth, 1976, 22 Min. The Ancestor, Jaguar, nearly devours all of humanity. All that remains is Curare-Woman, who is too "bitter" to eat, and her pregnant daughter, hidden in the roof. Jaguar discovers the daughter and eats her, but Curare-Woman saves the unborn Twins, Omawä and Yoasiwä, who miraculously grow to adulthood and exact their revenge on Jaguar. English subtitles.

Index